National Institute of
Economic and Social Research
Economic Policy Papers 2

# De-industrialisation

National Institute of
Economic and Social Research
Conferences on Economic Policy

## STEERING COMMITTEE

7

National Institute of
Economic and Social Research
Economic Policy Papers 2

# De-industrialisation

Edited by
FRANK BLACKABY

Heinemann Educational Books · London

Heinemann Educational Books Ltd

LONDON EDINBURGH MELBOURNE AUCKLAND TORONTO
HONG KONG SINGAPORE KUALA LUMPUR NEW DEHLI
NAIROBI JOHANNESBURG LUSAKA IBADAN
KINGSTON


**British Library Cataloguing in Publication Data**

---

De-industrialisation. – (Economic policy papers).
  1. Great Britain – Industries – Congresses
I. Blackaby, Frank Thomas  II. National
Institute of Economic and Social Research
III. Series
338′.0941      HC256.6

ISBN 0–435–84076–2
ISBN 0–435–84077–0  Pbk

Published by Heinemann Educational Books Ltd
48 Charles Street, London W1X 8AH
Printed by Richard Clay (The Chaucer Press) Ltd
Bungay, Suffolk

# Foreword

This book contains the papers, and a report of the discussion, at a conference on 'De-industrialisation' organised by the National Institute of Economic and Social Research. This conference was the second in a series on Economic Policy assisted by a grant from the Nuffield Foundation. A third conference, on International Financial and Economic Policy for the UK, is in course of being organised (and the Foundation has generously agreed to finance further conferences jointly organised by the NIESR with the Policy Studies Institute and the Royal Institute of International Affairs).

There is no difficulty in devising a definition of 'de-industrialisation' by which it is an established statistical trend in Britain and in some other countries. It does not follow that it is a trend to be deplored. As can be seen from Frank Blackaby's summary, however, it was the general view of the conference that, in the circumstances of the United Kingdom, de-industrialisation is associated with a general economic sickness which urgently calls for a cure. But the doctors were not agreed on the causes of the sickness, nor in proposing means by which rival formulations of the cause can be tested and the wrong answers eliminated. (It is of course possible, and indeed likely, that several of the causes mentioned are simultaneously operative.) Disagreeing on cause, opinions were unconvincing about the cure; there is evidently a long way to go before economists are able to propose policy changes which are effective but also consistent with political and administrative realities. So the conference must be regarded as a start down a long and difficult path of enquiry, not a completed work. Nevertheless, it was a brave and lively start, and our thanks are due to all the contributors of papers and participants in the discussion who helped to make it so.

Charles Carter
*Lancaster, July 1978*

# Contents

# Notes on Contributors

| | |
|---|---|
| Lord Balogh | Economic Adviser, British National Oil Corporation. |
| Professor C. A. van den Beld | Director of the Central Planning Bureau, The Netherlands. |
| C. J. F. Brown | Research Officer, National Institute of Economic and Social Research. |
| Sir Alec Cairncross | Master, St Peter's College, Oxford. |
| T. F. Cripps | Senior Research Officer, Department of Applied Economics, Cambridge. |
| W. A. Eltis | Fellow of Exeter College, Lecturer in Economics, Oxford. |
| Professor C. Freeman | Director, Science Policy Research Unit, University of Sussex. |
| S. Holland | Department of Economics, University of Sussex. |
| P. M. Jackson | Director, Public Sector Economics Research Centre, University of Leicester. |
| Lord Kaldor | Fellow of King's College, Cambridge. |
| Mrs A. D. Morgan | Senior Research Officer, National Institute of Economic and Social Research. |
| M. V. Posner | Fellow of Pembroke College, Reader in Economics, Cambridge. |
| G. F. Ray | Senior Research Fellow, National Institute of Economic and Social Research. |
| T. M. Rybczynski | Economic Adviser, Lazard Bros & Co. Ltd. |
| J. R. Sargent | Chief Economic Adviser, Midland Bank Ltd. |
| T. D. Sheriff | Research Officer, National Institute of Economic and Social Research. |
| A. Singh | Fellow of Queen's College, Lecturer in Economics, Cambridge. |
| D. K. Stout | Economic Director, National Economic Development Office. |

A. R. Thatcher          Registrar General, Office of Population
                        Censuses and Surveys.

*Editor:*

F. T. Blackaby          Deputy Director, National Institute of
                        Economic and Social Research.

# Introduction

by Frank Blackaby

In choosing 'de-industrialisation' as the subject for the second of the NIESR series of Economic Policy Conferences, the Steering Committee was well aware that it was an expression whose significance was not clear: that it had gatecrashed the literature, thereby avoiding the entrance fee of a definition, and also avoiding critical scrutiny at the door. The purpose of the conference was to subject the phrase to that critical scrutiny: in the words of the outline, it was 'to consider whether, and if so in what sense, there was a trend to de-industrialisation in the UK; if so, whether it mattered; and if it mattered, what should be done about it'.

Given the nature of the subject, a number of exploratory papers were commissioned. Brown and Sheriff prepared a general background paper.* Although there are plenty of arguments concerning the meaning of the concept, there is a general agreement about statistical material which is relevant – material on manufacturing output and employment in the UK and other countries, and about the share of UK manufacturing in world output and trade. The background paper discusses the various views in the light of the figures. Thatcher, also, presents in his paper an extensive survey of the relevant employment figures, which are brought together from a wide variety of sources. The statistical background was comprehensively covered.

Cairncross was asked to write a definitional paper on 'What is de-industrialisation?' His conclusion – which was supported in a number

---

* Chapter 10 in this book contains summaries of Brown and Sheriff's tables; the full Statistical Appendix which they prepared is too big to be included. It is available as a Discussion Paper from the National Institute of Economic and Social Research. 2 Dean Trench Street, Smith Square, London SW1 (£1.50 including postage).

of the other papers – was that 'De-industrialisation becomes meaningful not in terms of a trend as such but in relation to an explanation
of the trend.' Cairncross considers two explanations: that offered by
Bacon and Eltis, pointing to rising government expenditure as the
source of manufacturing industry's contraction, and that offered by
various Cambridge economists in terms of a loss of competitive power
in British industry. Cairncross comes down in favour of the Cambridge
view, that 'a contraction of industrial employment is a matter for
concern if it jeopardises our eventual power to pay for the imports we
need'. Kaldor, in commenting on this paper, puts great stress on the
extent to which the rise in UK output has been constrained by inadequate competitive performance, calculating that if imports of
manufactures had risen in line with output and no more, on a conservative estimate manufacturing output in 1974 would have been
24 per cent higher than in fact it was.

A second set of papers covers some of the explanations which have
been put forward; most of these had implications for the discussion
of policy as well. Posner and Steer show clearly that price competitiveness cannot explain the UK's falling share in world manufacturing
output; the fall must be explained by non-price factors. Thatcher –
together with other authors – cannot accept that British manufacturing industry was actually starved of labour; however – together
with other authors – he is less unsympathetic to the proposition that
rising public expenditure led to rising personal taxation, and this has
increased wage pressure, which has reduced profits and so has had
an effect on investment and growth.

Freeman considers the weakness of technical innovation and the
management of technical change. First, he presents evidence to suggest
that in the capital goods industries 'the relative scale of inventive and
innovative activities' is related to export performance. That raises a
further question, since in the 1950s the UK ranked fairly high in the
R and D league table. Freeman argues that there was 'a completely
inappropriate allocation of government and industrial R and D
resources', with a very high concentration on the aircraft industry
and military technology – where the UK was up against American
competition supported by much greater R and D resources – and a
low and declining proportion of expenditure directed to R and D in
machinery. There was a demand as well as a supply problem here –
'perhaps the biggest single long-term contrast between British and
German industry has been in the number and quality of engineers
employed in all managerial functions in manufacturing'.

Sargent considers Britain's performance in services. He supports the view that the UK has developed a comparative advantage in services, since, although the UK share of world exports has fallen, so also has its share of world imports. In the past, world trade in services has risen a little more slowly than world trade in manufactured goods – though the movement has been more stable. In the future it is possible that trade in services may benefit more than trade in goods from further liberalisation; further, trade in services should remain relatively immune to the challenge from newly industrialising countries. However, there is a scale problem: the UK's share in world trade in services would have to rise by a third to offset a single percentage fall in the share in world trade in manufactures. Rybczynski argues that the UK has been particularly successful in the category of 'fully-freely tradeable' services, and that consequently greater freedom of movement for services would be of particular benefit to the UK.

Mrs Morgan was asked to consider foreign manufacturing by British firms. Her assessment is unequivocal: British firms do manufacture abroad more than German firms and much more than Japanese. However, there is no reason to believe that British firms' overseas manufacturing activities have unfortunate effects on the balance of payments or on unemployment – rather the reverse. Holland is more doubtful about the operation of multinational companies. He argues that firms which manufacture abroad will place less emphasis on exports and export teams than on foreign production, and will not tend to follow through devaluation with lower export prices, since this would undercut their own overseas manufacturing activity. He considers that governments should be much more fully informed than they are at present about multinationals' activities, and should be prepared to exert leverage on their operations.

Stout is doubtful about many explanations of industrial decline, because while they account for a low *level* of productivity or trade performance they do not make it clear why that low level should not make rapid growth thereafter easier rather than more difficult.

The last two papers – and the comments of a number of other authors – are concerned with policy. Posner and Steer can raise only one and a half cheers for the use of the exchange rate. They are concerned both about the rapidity with which a price advantage can be eroded and about the possibility that devaluation would encourage the production of 'down-market' goods which compete on price and not on design or technological excellence. Stout also has the same fear of a possible move down-market; Cripps doubts it. Stout defends the ideas behind the industrial strategy: neither demand-led national planning 'from the top down' nor the reliance solely on a benign macroeconomic environment are likely to suffice; although regeneration is the responsibility of government, it cannot be realised by imposed solutions – 'the detail of existing industrial deficiencies is intricate and the necessity of cooperative solutions paramount, so that policies have to be discovered and agreed upon by those actively engaged in each industry'.

Balogh is doubtful whether such a policy is powerful enough. Singh uses the two models available at Cambridge – the Cambridge Economic Policy Group model and the Cambridge Growth Project model – to show how difficult it will be, if present import and export trends continue, to combine full employment and an adequate balance of payments. He is afraid that, during the period when the North Sea oil contribution to the balance of payments is rising, nothing will be done to strengthen the competitive power of British manufacturing industry. Van den Beld's paper on recent economic developments in the Netherlands supports this position; Dutch manufacturing industry, which was competitive in world markets before natural gas came on stream, is much less competitive now. Singh comes down in favour of a policy of import controls, 'used in conjunction with an active industrial policy of the Japanese (or the French) type'. Eltis is critical of the Cambridge arithmetic on three counts: an exaggerated expectation of import penetration, exaggerated export pessimism and an exaggerated expectation of productivity growth in manufacturing. Stout is unhappy about import controls: 'such a policy would reduce the competitive pressure to increase both productivity and non-price competitiveness, so that one has to rest more faith than I think is justified in the scope to realise economies of scale that would flow from increased self-sufficiency'.

There is a brief report on the discussion at the conference on page 263. To keep to the timetable of rapid production of the book, and to keep the size of the book within reasonable bounds, it proved necessary to make some cuts in the original papers. I am grateful to the authors for accepting this necessity, and very grateful to Gillian Little for working so hard and so expertly to prepare the papers for the printer.

# 1 What is De-industrialisation?

by Alec Cairncross

## Introduction

De-industrialisation is an ambiguous term and is used by different writers in different senses or at least with different overtones. Sometimes it is used without reference to a country's international trading position while at other times it relates to a structural maladjustment that 'cannot properly be considered in terms of the characteristics of the domestic economy alone' (Singh [2]). It may be useful to begin, therefore, by looking at a number of possible uses and implications of the term.

First of all, it may be taken to mean a straightforward decline in employment in manufacturing. On this definition the United Kingdom is undoubtedly experiencing de-industrialisation, since employment in manufacturing has been declining since the mid-1960s and at the end of 1977 was some 15 per cent lower than the peak reached twelve years earlier at the end of 1965.

This usage is not, however, very satisfactory. For how long must the decline continue in order to qualify as 'de-industrialisation'? A prolonged industrial depression might give rise to the appearance of a steady downward trend, when in fact industrial employment was merely taking the brunt of a cyclical fall in demand. In other industrial countries taken together, there was a negligible increase in manufacturing employment between 1969 and 1973, and in the next three years manufacturing employment fell at about the same rate as in the United Kingdom. But this would hardly justify the conclusion that there has been a continuing downward trend in the industrial countries as a group. The most one could reasonably argue is that there has been a general slowing-down in the expansion of manufacturing in developed countries, intensified by the world depression.

It is also not clear why employment rather than output should be treated as the significant variable. There could well be an upward trend in manufacturing output at the same time as a downward trend in employment. In fact, UK manufacturing output rose by 16 per cent between the end of 1965 and the end of 1977, while manufacturing employment fell by 15 per cent. One can go further: the share of manufacturing in GDP at constant prices was on a fairly steady upward trend from the late 1950s right up to 1973, although at current prices the trend was downwards (page 239). In other industrial countries taken together, manufacturing output was maintained, even over the three years 1973–6 when employment was falling. The fact that manufacturing *employment* is falling need not be of any special significance if output is increasing satisfactorily.

The same conclusion follows if we take account of the trend in the working population. If this trend is downward, as it was in the United Kingdom in the years after 1966, it is not necessarily disturbing if there is a similar downward trend in manufacturing employment. It is true that the fall in the working population was small and of short duration, so that by 1977 it had been more than made good. But the point remains that one has to look at manufacturing employment in relation to the total labour market.

When one does this it becomes clear that there has been a downward trend in manufacturing employment in relation to other employment for at least the past twenty years. Manufacturing employment showed a relative expansion in the first decade after the war and an accelerating *relative* contraction thereafter (Table 1.1).

*Table 1.1   Trend growth rates of manufacturing and total employment, Great Britain, 1948–76 (annual percentage rates of change)*

|  | 1948–56 | 1956–66 | 1966–74 | 1974–6 |
|---|---|---|---|---|
| Manufacturing employment | + 1.6 | + 0.5 | − 1.1 | − 3.8 |
| Total employment | + 1.0 | + 1.0 | − 0.3 | − 0.7 |
| Difference in rates | + 0.6 | − 0.5 | − 0.8 | − 3.1 |

Source: M. F. G. Scott, 'Can we get back to full employment?' (unpublished).

One factor in those trends lay in the development of Britain's foreign trade. The years between 1948 and 1956 saw a rapid growth of exports produced by manufacturing industry, while the parallel growth in imports was largely in foodstuffs and raw materials, not finished manufactures. The shift in resources over those years can therefore be interpreted as shift into net exports of manufactures. In the same way, the later period, in which imports of manufactures grew at a much faster rate than exports, can be interpreted as one in which there was shift of resources out of manufacturing associated with a fall in net exports.

As will be shown later, these shifts were not sufficiently large to account for the whole of the relative decline in manufacturing employment after the mid-1950s. Other forces operating in the same direction were at work in the structure of domestic demand and in the movement of labour productivity in different sectors of the economy.

Moreover, manufacturing was not the only sector in which employment contracted sharply. Distribution showed very much the same trends over the postwar period as manufacturing, with a shift first in its favour, then against it. The construction industry, although reaching its peak rate of expansion rather later than both manufacturing and distribution, experienced an even sharper decline in employment from the mid-1960s.

Although employment in manufacturing has contracted relatively to total employment for over twenty years, the change was relatively small until after 1970. At that time the proportion of manufacturing to total employment was exactly the same as in 1950 and only slightly less than in 1960. In the fifteen years to 1970 the proportion fell from a peak of 35.9 to 34.7 per cent; in the next five years it fell to 30.9 per cent. Even after this fall, the proportion was higher in Britain than in most other industrial countries, Germany and Italy being the most important exceptions.

If the decline in the share of manufacturing in total employment were balanced by a shift of consumer demand towards services, or if less spending on manufactures were offset by a higher rate of saving for investment either at home or abroad, there would be no obvious reason for concern. The change in employment would merely reflect this shift in consumer preferences. That there *has* been some shift seems evident from the increase in the share of services from 52.0 per cent of total employment in 1970 to 56.4 per cent in 1975. But this reflects the behaviour of government spending rather than that of private consumers and has coincided with a conspicuous failure to absorb all the labour released by manufacturing.

The declining share of manufacturing in total employment continues to be attributed partly to external and partly to domestic factors. There have been shifts in demand away from manufactures, and from British manufactures in particular. It is when we come to examine the reasons given for these shifts that controversy begins. On the one hand, there is the explanation associated with the work of Bacon and Eltis [1] that points to rising government expenditure as the source of manufacturing industry's contraction; on the other, there is the explanation advanced by various Cambridge economists in terms of a loss of competitive power in British industry. The first explanation would hold even in a closed economy, while the second would cease to apply in a closed economy and refers only to a single country in an open world economy.

## The Bacon and Eltis Argument

Let us take these two arguments in turn. In its crude form, the hypothesis that manufacturing industry is being forced to contract because of the pre-emption of resources through a rapid increase in government spending is not very convincing on general grounds. It is hard to believe that over the last ten years British industry has had to face shortages of manpower of the kind that were chronic in the days when manufacturing was out-pacing the rest of the economy. This consideration acquires added strength from the circumstances that the employment provided by higher government spending has been very largely female employment and that about 750,000 more women have entered the labour market, so that additional government demands have been largely offset by a higher female participation rate. Men, on the other hand, have suffered higher unemployment rates than were experienced earlier, in spite of a rundown in the supply of male workers by one million. It might indeed be argued that, so far from squeezing manpower from manufacturing industry, the expansion in government spending was designed to maintain full employment in the absence of sufficient demand for labour.

The more sophisticated version of the argument put forward by Bacon and Eltis turns largely on the pressure exerted by government spending on various surpluses necessary for steady growth: the supply of savings for productive investment; the balance of payments required to maintain adequate foreign exchange reserves; the rate of profit necessary to encourage industrial expansion. Central to their argument is the contention that efforts to finance government spending out of higher taxation will both drain away profits and savings and produce demands for higher money wages, as capitalists on the one hand and workers on the other resist the fall in consumption standards required of them.

The argument starts from the proposition that the increasing claims of government have left an inadequate output of marketed goods and services for the community to purchase. 'The claims on marketed output from outside the market sector', they argue, 'increased from 41.4 per cent of marketed output in 1961 to 60.3 per cent in 1974, thus apparently reducing the proportion of output that market-sector producers could themselves invest and consume by nearly one-third' (Bacon and Eltis, [1], page 93).

The squeeze on the purchasing power of wage-earners in relation to marketed output set off higher wage claims that were either offset by faster inflation or increased the compression of other incomes, notably profits. The compression of profits, in turn, reacted back on investment and the rate of growth, so intensifying the squeeze. At the same time a higher proportion of marketed output had to be retained at home because of the resistance of wage-earners to a diminution of their share of marketed output and this cut into net exports of manufactures and threw the balance of payments into deficit.

There are many aspects of this thesis that one might develop and many that are open to criticism. For present purposes it is sufficient to note that the argument is in terms of competing domestic claims on resources and, although it overflows on to the balance of payments, this aspect of the matter is secondary and could be immediately put right by a reduction in claims on marketed output. There is no suggestion that the key to de-industrialisation lies in a weakening of competitive power, except in so far as any compression of profits might be expected to react on competitive power through low investment. The argument also appears to fly in the face of the quite substantial *increase* in the volume of manufacturing investment throughout the 1960s.

An alternative view of the period, concentrating in the same way on structural changes within the economy, would be that the government sought to maintain demand and employment under conditions of falling net exports of manufactures and a rising female activity rate, and found a convenient way to square the circle by expanding the public sector, so helping to absorb the growing female labour force. The expansion in public spending also helped to reduce the propensity to import and to avoid the increase in import requirements that would have attended an equally large expansion in the private sector. On this view, de-industrialisation would be a temporary expedient involving a warping of the economy in the interests of full employment and in the hope that by other methods the fall in net exports of manufactures could in course of time be reversed. This view, although not without some relevance, is not easily squared with the comparatively small increase in the *volume* of government spending on goods and services, and fails to take account of the much bigger increase in transfer expenditure to which Bacon and Eltis rightly give more prominence.

## The 'Cambridge' View

Let us turn next to the 'Cambridge' view of de-industrialisation. This explicitly rejects as the criterion of de-industrialisation the *domestic* trend in manufacturing, whether in employment or output, and whether in absolute terms or as a proportion of total employment or activity. It would be quite consistent with Singh's analysis, for example, to speak of de-industrialisation when manufacturing output was actually growing in proportion to GDP (as on one measure it did up to 1973), or even when manufacturing employment was growing in proportion to total employment. For in his view de-industrialisation is to be interpreted as a progressive failure to achieve a sufficient surplus of exports over imports of manufactures to keep the economy in external balance.

'Given the normal levels of the other components of the balance of payments', he writes, 'we may define an efficient manufacturing sector as one which, currently as well as potentially, not only satisfies the demands of consumers at home, but is also able to sell enough of its products abroad to pay for the nation's important requirements' (Singh [2], page 128). He goes on to add 'the import restriction' that these objectives must be achieved 'at socially acceptable levels of output, employment and the exchange rate', on the grounds that without these qualifications almost any manufacturing sector might be able to meet the criteria of efficiency.

De-industrialisation can then be defined as involving the absence of an efficient manufacturing sector in this sense. This puts the emphasis on the failure of British industry to maintain its share of world trade in manufactures, on the one hand, and on increasing import penetration of the domestic British market, on the other.

This might seem no more than a balance-of-payments constraint in a new guise, and one for which devaluation would provide an obvious remedy. But it is argued that the forces at work are such that they cannot be arrested by a once-and-for-all devaluation. On the side of demand the conditions for an expansion on British exports in response to devaluation are unpropitious, while on the side of supply there is a vicious circle of declining market share, declining profits and investment, and declining competitive power, which must aggravate the weakness of British industry in the absence of resolute government action. In some versions great emphasis is laid on dynamic economies of scale and the advantages enjoyed by other countries supplying expanding markets, able to invest more and innovate more rapidly, reinforcing their competitive position and so establishing themselves in an ever-widening range of markets. A picture is painted of a relentless cumulative process working in favour of the strong and against the weak. De-industrialisation on this showing is the lot of the weak unless they assert themselves against the strong.

There is much in this picture that tallies with recent experience. In particular there is no doubt about the falling share of British industry in foreign and domestic markets. In the 1960s the emphasis was on the loss of share in world trade in manufactures – a share that fell from 16.5 per cent in 1960 to only 10.8 per cent in 1970. In the 1970s the emphasis has switched to the loss of share in the domestic market. On world markets the slide has become much less pronounced – from 10.8 per cent in 1970 to 9.3 per cent in 1977 – but in the domestic market import penetration has increased sharply in the 1970s. On a rough calculation imported manufactures took 8 per cent of the home market in 1961 and 13 per cent ten years later. But in the next three years the proportion rose to 19 per cent and by 1976 it was 21 per cent (page 244, and sources there quoted). For imported manufactures sold to final buyers the rise was even steeper: from 4 per cent in 1961 to 8 per cent in 1971 and 20 per cent by 1974 (Bacon and Eltis, [1], pages 176–7). More to the point, the surplus of exports of manufactures over imports has been whittled away. The excess of exports in 1970 (measuring exports f.o.b. and imports c.i.f.) was roughly £6000 million at 1977 prices, but in 1977 it was not much over £1000 million. Moreover, this was at a comparatively low level of economic activity in 1977; at a less depressed level the surplus would cease to exist *now*, quite apart from any underlying trend making for its early disappearance.

This might not matter if there were other trends offsetting the deterioration in the balance of trade in manufactures. But, it is argued, there is either no such trend, or it is not powerful enough to counterbalance the large absolute deterioration from year to year in the balance of trade in manufactures. This applies in particular to services, where there has been little, if any, improvement over the past decade, and where in any event the base is too small to allow of fully compensating changes. There is, however, a large, if temporary, exception in the form of North Sea oil. But it is part of the 'Cambridge' argument that, precisely because North Sea oil helps to close the gap in the balance of payments, de-industrialisation will be allowed to continue for longer without check. When the oil runs out the competitive power of British industry will have been still more enfeebled and will be still harder to revive, while its role in balancing the current account of the balance of payments will have become even more important and harder to fulfil.

If the contraction of employment in manufacturing is to be explained in terms of the decline in the export surplus of manufactures, we ought to begin by looking at the magnitudes involved. Let us compare 1961 and 1974 on the basis of the figures given by Bacon and Eltis [1]. Net exports of manufactures (SITC categories 5–8) rose from £1680 million to £1757 million at current prices, but if we adjust for the change in prices the excess in 1961 comes to about £3860 million at 1974 prices and the loss of markets to £2100 million. This compares with sales of industrial products to final buyers of British manufactures of £41,000 million, so that the actual shift in the trade balance would not account for more than a contraction of about 5 per cent.

The rise of manufacturing output over the period was 44 per cent and employment fell by 8 per cent. Had demand and output increased by 5 per cent more, so maintaining the excess of exports unchanged, this might have been expected to cut the loss in employment by about 3 per cent. On this calculation rather less than half the contraction in employment would be accounted for by the loss of markets to foreign competitors.

It might, however, be argued that one ought to start not from the actual loss of markets but from the loss in relation to the rate of expansion of the economy and the consequent expansion in import requirements. Suppose, for example, that imports and exports had both kept pace with output. This would certainly have been a very satisfactory outcome. What difference would it have made to the market for UK manufactures? The answer is that, roughly speaking, the surplus of exports over imports of manufactures in 1974 would have been £3800 million greater than the recorded surplus. This is equal to about 9 per cent of output in 1974 and would account for perhaps 6 per cent of the drop in employment. This calculation may go a little too far in its assessment of what would have been required on Singh's criteria to pay for 'necessary' imports [2]. But it is probably fair to regard the loss of markets to foreign competitors, measured in

relation to a stable balance of payments, as accounting for a contraction of 5 per cent or so in manufacturing employment by 1974,
while the rest originated in other shifts in the structure of demand away
from manufacturing. Since the number of employees in employment
increased slightly – by about 2.3 per cent – these other shifts were
larger than the difference between 8 per cent and 5 per cent, and may
have been comparable in importance to the loss of markets to foreign
suppliers.

If we ask what underlies the loss of markets, we are referred to
estimates of elasticities on the side of demand and to various non-price
factors on the side of supply. The UK's income elasticity of demand
for imports is well above unity, while the rest of the world's income
elasticity of demand for UK exports is well below unity, so that there
is a persistent tendency towards deficit as world income rises through
time. On the other hand, the UK's price elasticity of demand for
imports is comparatively low and so also is the world's price elasticity
of demand for British manufactures. The responsiveness of the trade
balance to a change in the terms of trade is very low. On top of this, the
power of the authorities to bring about a change in the terms of trade
through devaluation is also low, largely because devaluation cannot
be effected without repercussions on wage settlements that tend to
bring export prices back into line with import prices.

On the demand side, therefore, there is a chronic tendency for the
British balance of payments to deteriorate and for price adjustments
sufficient to offset this tendency to be very difficult. On the supply side
there are other weaknesses which, on the 'Cambridge' view, spring
from, or are at the very least much aggravated by, the weakness of
demand. This weakness deprives British industry of the dynamic
economies of scale enjoyed by its competitors and results in products
of poor quality, design and performance. This in turn causes the British
consumer to turn to imports and so accounts for the high income
elasticity of demand for imports.

This view of British de-industrialisation has considerable intellec-
tual appeal because of the way in which the different components fit
together so neatly. The forces at work are represented as interacting
so powerfully and ineluctably to bring about the downfall of British
industry that one almost hesitates to ask whether its position and
prospects can be quite so bad. It seems a little inconsistent with the
general picture, however, that the proportion of manufacturing output sold abroad has continued to increase over the past ten years. It
was 15 per cent in 1966, 19 per cent in 1971 and 22 per cent in 1974

(page 244, and sources quoted there). This is not easily reconciled with diminishing competitive power. It also seems a little odd to reach such devastating conclusions without investigation in more detail of the trends in imports and exports of manufactures. Some of the more interesting changes are shown in Table 1.2.

*Table 1.2   United Kingdom exports and imports of manufactures by category, 1970–7 (£ millions)[a]*

| | Exports | | Imports | | Excess exports | |
|---|---|---|---|---|---|---|
| | 1970 | 1977 | 1970 | 1977 | 1970 | 1977 |
| Chemicals | 196 | 967 | 136 | 591 | 60 | 376 |
| Textiles | 99 | 287 | 64 | 283 | 35 | 4 |
| Iron and steel | } 240 | } 717 | { 56 | 246 } | } 32 | } 189 |
| Non-ferrous metals | | | { 152 | 282 } | | |
| Machinery | } 825 | } 3084 | { 300 | 1325 } | } 450 | } 888 |
| Transport equipment | | | { 75 | 871 } | | |
| (Total of above items) | (1360) | (5055) | (783) | (3598) | (577) | (1457) |
| Other semi-manufactures | } 342 | } 645 | { 217 | 1067 } | } −18 | } −1177 |
| Other finished manufactures | | | { 143 | 755 } | | |
| *Total* | 1702 | 5700 | 1143 | 5420 | 559 | 280 |

Source: *National Institute Economic Review*, February 1978.
[a] Quarterly rates at current prices.

Although it is difficult to interpret Table 1.2 without price adjustments and without further detail, it brings out some neglected aspects of the situation. First of all, over a quarter of the imports in 1970 and nearly a quarter in 1977 took the form of machinery. Exports of machinery appear to have out-paced imports over the seven years. The same is true of chemicals and metals, but not, of course, of textiles. The main deterioration is in transport equipment (motor cars), in semi-manufactures and in miscellaneous finished goods. Of these we need spend no time on motor cars, and the position on the miscellaneous group of finished manufactures is clear enough, but the big increase in semi-manufactures calls for comment. It is largely accidental that these are included under manufactures rather than under raw materials. One of the main trends over the postwar period has been towards the manufacture of materials as substitutes for raw materials in the more usual sense. This is reflected in the fall in the importance of basic materials in the total import bill; the rise in imports of semi-manufactures should be seen in this light rather than simply as a reflection of a decline in competitive power. Between 1970 and 1977, for example, imports of basic materials fell by 12 per cent in volume and imports of fuel by 26 per cent, while imports of all semi-manufactures increased by 57 per cent. If comparisons are drawn between the growth of imports and of industrial production it is necessary to look at the whole picture, not just at manufactured imports. This is all the more necessary because imports of manufactured goods for final sale represent only about half total imports of manufactures.

But let us accept that there is a stronger trend towards rising imports of manufactures than towards rising exports and that this bodes ill for the current balance. What follows? Is the situation any different from what it must have looked like in the 1870s, when rising imports of foodstuffs threatened the balance of payments and it was doubtful whether exports in the face of increasing competition from industrialising countries could pay the bill? At that time the adjustments were made first through the capital balance, which moved towards deficit, and later through increased emigration and improving terms of trade until world expansion pulled up exports again in the 1890s. Now the problem could in some ways be a more formidable one because of entrenched social attitudes. If, for whatever reason, the United Kingdom has become a comparatively unpromising location for carrying on manufacturing, the adjustments required are not likely to be easy or agreeable or socially cohesive. They can of course be made to *appear* easy if all that is the matter is excessive government spending or unwillingness to limit the growth of imports. But what if the weaknesses on the side of supply are not within the control of the government, do not respond to protection of the domestic market, have little to do with the dynamics of market expansion, and have their origin in ingrained attitudes or long-standing aptitudes?

This brings us back to look more closely at Singh's definition of de-industrialisation and particularly at the requirement that industry should do its part in maintaining external balance 'at socially acceptable levels of output, employment and the exchange rate' [2]. If it is true that without these qualifications the problem might never arise, it seems equally true that with these qualifications it might well prove insoluble. The external pressures on an economy may make it virtually impossible to maintain full employment or to hold the exchange rate within prescribed limits. In the last resort, if a country's competitive position is enfeebled it may have to allow one or other of various 'unacceptable' options to take its course. In Ricardian economics the going-rate of wages was the pivot on which external balance turned and, even if Ricardian economics have had their day, it is reasonable to doubt whether adjustment to a deteriorating competitive position can ever be achieved without acceptance of the implied change in living standards and real wages. If we had not ceased to put our faith in devaluation because we doubt its power to react on real wages, however temporarily, we would be much less concerned about de-industrialisation.

One last general reflection on the 'Cambridge' view. It is natural to ask whether, on the same definition, the United States is also experiencing de-industrialisation and for similar reasons. Her share of world trade in manufactures has fallen from 20 per cent in 1968 to 16 per cent in 1977, faster than the falling-off in the UK's share. Import penetration of the US domestic market in manufactures has been at least as pronounced as of the British market and the trend seems just as firmly upwards. The balance between exports and imports is set in the same direction as in Britain and there is a similar failure on the part of US manufacturing industry to achieve a sufficient surplus of exports over imports. US manufacturing productivity has increased at a rate not very different from Britain's. So does the same diagnosis apply? Does the international tail wag the domestic dog just as strongly when the tail is as short and stubby as the American?

## Other Possible Meanings

There are other possible meanings that might be attached to de-industrialisation. Suppose, for example, that industry is becoming increasingly capital-intensive and that this leads simultaneously to higher output and a displacement of labour. Such a situation might be brought about by rising real wages, combined with subsidies to investment in manufacturing, and falling real rates of return on capital throughout the economy. If capital was available on very cheap terms, jobs might be extinguished in manufacturing faster than they were created by the expansion of the economy, and this could then be represented as a form of de-industrialisation. If investment increasingly took a labour-saving form – as it well might if markets failed to expand – this would intensify the rate of destruction of jobs and make the process look even more alarming.

Explanations of the contraction of industry along those lines have been put forward by a number of economists including Maurice Scott. They are not, however, very convincing. There is not much evidence that the capital stock in manufacturing in the UK has changed appreciably in relation to output. The process by which the capital stock grows along with output, while employment grows more slowly or actually declines, is quite normal in industrial countries and does not by itself explain why there should be an accelerating relative contraction in manufacturing employment. While it is conceivable that there may be some recent change in the kind of industrial investment undertaken and that a higher proportion of it is now job-destroying rather than job-creating, the change would have to be a very striking one to eliminate 15 per cent of all jobs in manufacturing. Similarly, while there might in principle be extensive changes disturbing the balance between skilled and unskilled employment, so that new industrial growth was held back by lack of a sufficient number of key workers with the skills necessary to form a nucleus round which unskilled workers might be organised, there is not much evidence that this accounts for the contraction of British manufacturing industry. Some lack of balance in relation to demand is a normal feature of industrial life and, although it is quite possibly worse in conditions of industrial depression, it does not usually serve to *explain* the depression.

## Conclusion

Where does all this leave us? Of all the meanings that can be attached to de-industrialisation the one that makes most sense is what I have called the 'Cambridge' view. A contraction of industrial employment is a matter for concern if it jeopardises our eventual power to pay for the imports we need. A loss of reserves or confiscation of overseas assets would have a similar effect. It is the loss of economic potential that is the crux of the matter. But whether that loss arises for the reasons given in Cambridge, whether it can be made good in the way propounded there, and whether it might yield to other, more familiar, but less agreeable treatment are matters on which there is not likely to be general agreement.

*References*

[1] Bacon, R. and Eltis, W. A., *Britain's Economic Problem: too few producers*, London, Macmillan, 1976.
[2] Singh, A., 'UK industry and the world economy: a case of de-industrialisation?', *Cambridge Journal of Economics*, June 1977.

# Comment

## by Nicholas Kaldor

After discussing several alternatives, Sir Alec expresses a preference for the Cambridge definition of 'de-industrialisation' as a state of affairs in which there is a continued decline in a country's share of world trade in manufactures and/or a continued increase in the share of imported manufactures in domestic expenditure, in consequence of which it becomes progressively more difficult to achieve a sufficient surplus of exports over imports of manufactures to keep the economy in external balance.

Sir Alec admits that 'there is much in this picture that tallies with recent experience' both on the side of the loss of export share (particularly in the period up to 1970) and on the side of increasing import penetration (which has 'sharply increased' in the 1970s).

However, he is inclined to play down the practical importance of de-industrialisation for the following reasons:

(1) The reduction in effective demand for manufactures due to the deterioration in the trade balance in manufactures has been relatively small – it accounts for only 5 per cent of the total demand for manufactures in 1974 as compared to what it would have been if the trade balance had remained at its 1961 level in real terms.

(2) Even if exports and imports had 'both kept pace with output' ('this would certainly have been a very satisfactory outcome') output would only have been 9 per cent greater in 1974 and this would not have prevented a substantial loss of employment in manufacturing. The latter must thus have been due to 'shifts in the structure of demand from manufacturing ... [which] may have been comparable in importance to the loss of markets to foreign suppliers'.

(3) The Cambridge view is difficult to reconcile with the fact that the proportion of manufacturing output sold abroad rose from 15 per cent in 1966 to 19 per cent in 1971 and 22 per cent in 1974.

(4) Moreover, in the period 1970 to 1977 the record was particularly satisfactory, since the excess of exports diminished by very little – only £319 million at current prices, or 5 per cent of 1977 exports. The value of exports of machinery actually increased more than the value of imports (Table 1.2).

All these conclusions are vitiated in my view by a single major error – he measures the importance of these factors *ex-post* and not *ex-ante*.

It is the same error as if the Treasury (or the National Institute) measured the importance of a fall in investment expenditure on the economy in terms of the resulting *ex-post* change in the share of investment in output and, finding that the share had not fallen, or had fallen only very little, declared that the primary reduction in expenditure was causally unimportant, whereas in fact the failure of the share of investment to deteriorate was an indication of the strength of the deflationary force and not its weakness.

For a country like Britain which mainly exports manufactures to pay for imports of food and raw materials, the export of manufactures represents the exogeneous component of demand which plays the role of autonomous investment in a Keynesian closed-economy model. The propensity to import has the same importance as exports, since this determines the size of the multiplier or the super-multiplier (Hicks, [2]) (which embraces induced investment as well as induced consumption). Thus, if the (average and marginal) propensity to import remained constant over time, and one assumed that business investment was predominantly financed out of retained profits and neglected other autonomous components of demand such as public loan expenditure in excess of personal savings, the level of output would be determined by Harrod's foreign trade multiplier, which in its simplest form can be written

$$Y = \frac{1}{m} \cdot X$$

where $m$ is the proportion of consumption and investment expenditure spent on imports, while $Y$ and $X$ represent output and exports respectively. The growth rate of $Y$ (as Hicks has demonstrated) will then be determined by the growth rate of $X$, provided that the resulting growth rate is a feasible one in terms of resources.

It follows that, in an economy which is not constrained by labour shortages (either because of the existence of open or disguised unemployment, or because of the absence of restrictions on immigration), the (trend) rate of growth of manufacturing output will be determined by the (trend) rate of growth of exports provided that the propensity to import (average and marginal) remains constant over time – or, in Cairncross's terminology, 'imports rise in line with output'. In such an economy, the rate of growth of GDP as a whole would also be determined in accordance with the well-known stylised formula:

$$\dot{GDP} = I + o.6\dot{M}_y$$

where the dots indicate compound growth rates of GDP and $M_y$ (manufacturing output) respectively.

Taking the period chosen by Sir Alec, 1961–74, the growth of exports of manufactures at constant prices was 80 per cent or 4.5 per cent a year. The Harrod formula suggests that with a constant $m$ manufacturing output would also have risen by 80 per cent. The actual recorded rise in manufacturing output however was only 45 per cent or 2.9 per cent a year. The difference must then be explained by the rise in the propensity to import; that such a rise had taken place is shown by the fact that imports of finished manufactures increased by 420 per cent over the same period, or by 12.8 per cent a year. If instead imports had only risen in line with output, output would have risen in line with exports, and all three would have risen by 80 per cent or 4.5 per cent a year. The higher rate of growth of output (by 1.6 per cent a year) would have added 180/145 or 24 per cent to actual output in 1974, which would have required (according to another stylised formula, invented by Verdoorn) a 12 per cent increase in employment accompanied by a 12 per cent increase in productivity. (This should be compared with Sir Alec's estimate of a 9 per cent increase in output and a 6 per cent addition to employment.)

The above estimate is, however, an extremely conservative one, mainly because it assumes that there is no feedback from the higher rate of growth of output and productivity to competitiveness and export performance. World demand for manufactured goods increased over the period 1961–74 by 9.1 per cent a year and there were numerous individual countries (such as France) which maintained a constant share of world trade over that period. We could not, of course, succeed in doing this and keep a unity elasticity of imports at the same time, since this would have involved an unattainably fast growth of output. But it might have been possible to maintain a constant share of world trade, combined with a rate of growth of manufacturing output of, say, 5 per cent a year, which would have been associated with unchanged net exports (as a percentage of exports), if the income elasticity of demand for finished manufactures with respect to manufacturing output had been held at 1.8, instead of the recorded estimate of 4.4 (12.8/2.9), thus limiting the growth of manufactured imports to 9 per cent a year. This would have meant that manufacturing output would have risen by 92 per cent, or 32 per cent more, and real GDP would have risen by 4 per cent a year (instead of the recorded 2.5 per cent), making it 22 per cent higher in 1974 than it actually was. The benefits to be derived from aligning the growth of imports to the growth of exports would therefore have been much greater than Sir Alec's calculations suggest. (During the period 1932–55, when manufactured imports were discouraged first by high tariffs and later by import licensing, the growth of manufacturing output averaged 5.7 per cent and of real GDP 3.9 per cent a year, if the war years 1939–45, during which output was unchanged, are excluded.)

It will also be seen how misleading figures can be concerning the rise in the export ratio (page 244) or the small reduction in net exports (as shown in Table 1.2). Our exports over the period 1966–74 have in fact increased by only two thirds of the rate of growth of world demand; if they nevertheless increased so much faster than manufacturing output, this was simply a reflection of the fact that the depressing effect of increasing import penetration was more powerful than the stimulus afforded by the higher rate of growth of exports. The true lesson to be derived from Table 1.2 is not that import penetration was quantitatively unimportant, but that the fall in the 'Harrod multiplier' due to the rise in import propensities succeeded in reducing output and incomes sufficiently to keep the deterioration of the trade balance within modest dimensions. In fact, if the Harrod formula had been 100 per cent efficient there would have been no deterioration in the trade balance at all! The output of manufacturing was in fact virtually stagnant – the annual increase between 1970 and 1977 was only 0.5 per cent a year – whereas in other industrial countries, despite the recession, it was four to six times as large. The share of imported manufactures in home sales rose, on Sir Alec's figures, from 13 per cent in 1971 to well over 21 per cent in 1977.

In the final section of his paper Sir Alec introduces two further thoughts to allay our anxieties. One is that the whole story of import penetration and slow growth is *déjà-vu*: it had appeared already in the last quarter of the nineteenth century, when equally gloomy prognostications could have been made (and actually *were* made) as now. The second is that everything that can be said about increasing import penetration and a deteriorating trade balance in manufactures is equally true of the United States, and surely nobody would suggest that America is going to the dogs, so why should we?

These are interesting points. An unpublished study by Sir Arthur Lewis does indeed show that in the period 1873–1913 industrial production rose in Britain by only 2.1 per cent a year as against 4.2 per cent a year for Germany and 5 per cent a year for the US, and a 'climacteric' rate of 3.3 per cent a year for Britain in the period 1866–73.

The reasons also appear very similar. Britain's share in world trade of manufactures declined from 37.1 per cent in 1883 to 25.4 per cent in 1913. The growth of imports in manufactures exceeded the growth of exports of manufactures and the difference showed an acceleration; in 1873–83 the growth of imports exceeded exports by 1.1 per cent a year; in 1883–9 it was by 2.6 per cent a year. *Net* exports of manufactures, which grew at 5.7 per cent a year in the period 1836–53, grew at only 1.5 per cent a year in the period 1873–1913. The share of manufactures in total imports increased from 5 per cent in 1860 to 25 per cent in 1899 (Lewis [3], page 579), whilst the share of imports in total domestic supplies of manufactures rose to 17 per cent by 1913 (Maizels, [4], page 136).

Throughout that period the economy was demand-constrained, not supply-constrained. There was considerable unemployment and under-employment as shown by the heavy net emigration, estimated at six million from Great Britain alone in the period 1880–1910. The extent of unemployment is not shown by the rates of unemployment among members of trade unions, since these relate only to that part of the working population who had regular employment in particular trades and became unemployed only for temporary periods. Capital accumulation in industry was limited by lack of opportunities due to low demand, not by lack of savings, as is shown by the heavy capital exports throughout the period.

There can be little doubt that Joseph Chamberlain was right (though rather late) in his tariff reform campaign of 1903 and, if we had adopted a policy of protection simultaneously with Germany and France in the early 1880s, our rate of economic growth could have been very much faster; even our export record might have been better, since we would have had a much faster development of the new industries such as chemicals, optics and electricity.

Indeed without the first world war our situation would have deteriorated much more (Barnett, [1]). During that war all kinds of new industries were created and some of them remained afterwards under the umbrella of a protective tariff. In 1932 a general *ad valorem* duty of 20 per cent was introduced on all manufactures, with 30 per cent in sensitive sectors like steel and chemicals. Despite the recession after 1929, the growth rate throughout the period 1921–38 was much higher than in the forty years preceding world war I. Manufacturing production in 1937 exceeded its previous peak in 1929 by 38 per cent – a growth rate, straddling the biggest world recession in history, of nearly 3.6 per cent a year.

Relatively high growth continued in the period since world war II, until manufactured imports began to rise in earnest in the early 1960s and our share in world trade (which for a brief period regained its 1913 level in 1950) began to fall at a precipitous rate. However the free trade ideology became triumphant again and the entry into the Common Market rendered the continuance and the acceleration of our industrial decay well nigh inevitable. The growth rate of our manufacturing output was only half as high in the decade 1967–77 as in the decade 1957–67; in the period 1973–7 it was actually negative. This was in spite of the considerable improvement in our export performance after 1967, both absolutely and relatively to world trade (Table 1.3).

*Table 1.3   UK output, exports and imports of manufactures, pre-1967 and post-1967 (average percentage growth rates, constant prices)*

| | Pre-devaluation | Post-devaluation | | Ten-year comparison | |
|---|---|---|---|---|---|
| | 1961–7 | 1967–73 | 1973–7 | 1957–67 | 1967–77 |
| Total manufactures | | | | | |
| (1) Output | 2.6 | 3.5 | −1.6 | 2.8 | 1.4 |
| (2) Imports | 8.6 | 12.3 | 4.2 | 9.4 | 9.0 |
| (3) Exports | 2.8 | 8.6 | 4.3 | 2.7 | 6.7 |
| (4) World trade | 8.8 | 10.5 | 5.1 | 7.7 | 8.3 |
| Ratios | | | | | |
| (2):(1) | 3.31 | 3.51 | a | 3.35 | 6.43 |
| (3):(1) | 1.06 | 2.45 | a | 0.96 | 4.78 |
| (2):(4) | 0.98 | 1.17 | 0.82 | 1.22 | 1.08 |
| (3):(4) | 0.31 | 0.82 | 0.84 | 0.35 | 0.81 |

Source: *National Institute Economic Review.*
[a] Meaningless, due to negative sign in (1).

With regard to the United States, Sir Alec is right in thinking that she faces the same kind of problem as Britain did in 1870–1913, and has done from around 1960 onwards. But that is not much consolation to us. Moreover, in at least two important respects the United States is better placed to deal with the problem. The first is that, despite the periodic homage rendered to free trade by leading officials, the American administration (and Congress) are in fact far more ready and able to impose protectionist measures than we are. (She is not a member of the Common Market.) If they have not done so yet (or not on an adequate scale), it is not because the US is in any less need of it (from a long-term point of view) than Britain; it is because American economists, though far more numerous, are no more able to analyse the causes of the 'American disease' than their British counterparts are to analyse the causes of the 'British disease'.

The second is that the world is on a dollar standard and is likely to remain so for a considerable time. While this lasts, America is able to generate sufficient internal purchasing power through budgetary deficits to maintain reasonable growth rates at reasonable levels of unemployment, without regard to the balance-of-payments consequences.

There is one passage in Sir Alec's paper which, though brief, is strikingly out of tune with the reassuring tone of the rest. This is where he says that if we wish not only to maintain external balance but to do so 'at socially acceptable levels of output, employment and the exchange rate ... the problem ... might well prove insoluble'. This is the statement on which attention should be focused. What are the conditions in which this would be so? Would it be true of every country or only just Britain? And would it remain true if we were free to set a ceiling on the rate of growth of manufactured imports of $x$ per cent a year?

In one passage Sir Alec emphasises the importance of income elasticities in determining divergences in the trends of imports and exports, the UK's income elasticity for foreign manufactures being rather high, whereas the world's income elasticity for British goods is relatively low. 'On the other hand the UK's price elasticity of demand for imports is *comparatively* low and so also is the world's price elasticity of demand for British manufactures' (italics mine). On page 16 on the other hand he argues that 'in Ricardian economics the going-rate of wages was the pivot on which external balance turned ... If we had not ceased to put our faith in devaluation because we doubt its power to react on real wages, however temporarily, we would be much less concerned about de-industrialisation.'

There is, I think, some inconsistency between these two statements. If we live in a world where income elasticities not price elasticities 'rule the roost', the adjustment mechanism of the balance of payments is not the Ricardian but the Harrodian one: in the short run imports tend to adjust to exports through variations in the level of domestic production and incomes; in the longer run (or in dynamic terms) the adjustment will take the form of generating appropriate differences in growth rates. (Of course the Harrod mechanism can be rendered partially inoperative by attempts to maintain employment through fiscal policies which in turn generate excess imports; in this context the government's loan expenditure takes the place of missing exports.) If we divide the world into two areas, A and B, and assume that A's income elasticity for B's goods is 2, whereas B's income elasticity for A's goods is 1, A will tend to grow at half the rate of B as a result of the automatic operation of the Harrod multiplier, because it is at that particular difference in growth rates that the rise in imports will keep in balance with the rise in exports, and hence production will grow at the same rate as effective demand for the area's products. A change in real wages is not capable of altering this result – however permanently, let alone however temporarily! – unless it succeeds in changing the relationship of *income* elasticities. It could not hope to do this unless the import propensities themselves are highly pliable or highly sensitive to changes in relative costs and prices. If they are, we are back in a Ricardian world and not a Harrodian–Keynesian one; we believe with Ricardo that it is the changing distribution of the world's gold stock and the consequential change in relative price levels which determine the movement of imports relative to exports. On the other hand, all *non* neo-classical theories which rely on the factors determining the level and the rate of growth of effective demand, and not on changes in 'resource-endowment' for explaining the growth of production and employment are, in *ultima ratio*, asserting the superiority of income elasticities as against price elasticities; they believe that forces making for balance operate mainly through income variations, not through relative price variations.

## References

[1] Barnett, C., *The Collapse of British Power*, London, Cassells, 1972.
[2] Hicks, J., *The Trade Cycle*, Oxford, Clarendon Press, 1950.
[3] Lewis, W. A., 'International competition in manufactures', *American Economic Association Proceedings*, May 1957.
[4] Maizels, A., *Industrial Growth and World Trade*, Cambridge University Press, 1963.

# 2 Labour Supply and Employment Trends

## by A. R. Thatcher*

### Introduction

In the summer of 1966 employment in the UK reached the highest level ever recorded. Since then there have been substantial falls in employment in the manufacturing industries, in the other industries which are included in the index of production (mining and quarrying, construction, gas, electricity and water), in agriculture, in transport and in the distributive trades. At the same time there have been substantial rises in employment in services, most notably in education, health and other local authority employment. However, between 1966 and 1976 the falls exceeded the rises by about 700,000.

All the various reasons put forward for this change are extensively discussed elsewhere in this book – the competitive failure of British manufacturing industry; shortages of skilled manpower; the rise in public sector employment; more 'voluntary' unemployment because of higher levels of social security benefits; the general progress in developed countries towards the 'post-industrial society'. Official statistics throw a good deal of light on the relative sizes of some of the factors, but the information is widely scattered. The purpose of this chapter is to bring together, in condensed form, a good deal of diverse information relevant to these issues.

The paper begins by describing the changes which have taken place in the size and composition of the labour force and the main employment trends. It then considers the extent to which the increase in unemployment since 1966 can be explained by these factors. Later sections summarise the available information about skill shortages, pay differentials and international comparisons of produc-

* This paper was prepared when the author was Director of Statistics at the Department of Employment, before becoming Registrar General, Office of Population Censuses and Surveys.

tivity. The implications of this evidence are discussed in the final section.

## The Size and Composition of the Labour Force

*Demographic changes*

The number of males in the labour force in Great Britain, including the unemployed as well as those in employment, but excluding those in full-time education, has been relatively stable throughout the whole of the postwar period. Since 1951 there have never been less than 15.6 million and never more than 16.4 million, and if the forecasts are right we shall still be in this range for the next five years. Of course, the numbers would have risen considerably if it had not been for the raising of the school-leaving age and the expansion of further and higher education.

The great change in the labour force has been in the number of women, particularly married women. This is almost entirely due to the tremendous increase in the proportion of married women working, particularly the proportion who return to work after having their families. The participation rates for married women in Britain are amongst the highest in the countries of the industrial West, and so far have confounded each successive forecast by rising even more than expected. This has been especially true within the last few years, when an unprecedented fall in the birth rate has made more married women available for employment, and when equal pay legislation has increased the incentive to seek work. The figures in Table 2.1 bring out the general trend.

*Table 2.1   Estimated labour force in Great Britain,[a] 1951–76 (thousands)*

|       | Males  | Females | | Total |
|-------|--------|---------|---------|--------|
|       |        | Married | Other   |        |
| 1951  | 15,879 | 2,658   | 4,304   | 22,841 |
| 1956  | 15,923 | 3,251   | 3,937   | 23,111 |
| 1961  | 16,227 | 3,886   | 3,854   | 23,967 |
| 1966  | 16,158 | 5,063   | 3,799   | 25,020 |
| 1971  | 16,037 | 5,799   | 3,387   | 25,223 |
| 1976  | 15,914 | 6,731   | 3,223   | 25,868 |

Source: see Appendix.
[a] Excluding those in full-time education.

Projections of the future size of the labour force are given in the *Department of Employment Gazette* for June 1977. Over the next few years unusually large numbers of young people will be entering the labour force because of the high birth rates in the 1960s; at the same time the number of workers retiring will be rather less than usual because of the low birth rates in the years 1914–18 and the losses in the second world war of many who would have been reaching retiring age; both these factors will tend to increase the labour force. The prospective changes for married women are much less certain, but on balance the forecasters are expecting a further increase in the numbers seeking work.

*Labour input*

The same increasing share of married women in the labour force has been accompanied by a substantial increase in the proportion of jobs which are filled by part-time workers. Although it could be argued that it may have been the existence of extra part-time jobs which provided the incentive which induced more married women to work, nevertheless it seems more likely that the main underlying causal relationship until recently has been in the opposite direction: in a period when the demand for labour was rising and when the supply of males was relatively static, extra labour could only be found by employing more married women. Since many of these married women were only prepared to work part-time, employers had an inducement to provide more part-time jobs where the nature of the work made this possible.

*Table 2.2   Proportion of female employees working part-time, 1951–76*
*(percentages)*

|      | In manufacturing | | In whole economy | |
|------|-----------|------------------------|------------------------|-----------------------|
|      | L-returns | Census of employment | Census of employment | Census of Population |
| 1951 | 12.2 | .. | .. | .. |
| 1956 | 11.8 | .. | .. | .. |
| 1961 | 13.7 | .. | .. | 25.0 |
| 1966 | 17.7 | .. | .. | 32.0 |
| 1971 | 18.7 | 20.1 | 33.5 | 37.8 |
| 1976 | 21.7 | 23.5 | 40.1 | .. |

Source: see Appendix.

Table 2.2 brings together data from various sources and shows the extent to which the proportion of women who are working part-time has grown, until it has now reached 40 per cent for the economy as a whole.

Concurrently with the increase in numbers working part-time, there was a fall in the average hours which were actually worked by those working full-time, and also in the 'normal hours' laid down in wage agreements (hours beyond which overtime rates become payable). The figures in Table 2.3 for the industries covered by the October surveys of the earnings of manual workers illustrate the trend for 'all workers' (full-time manual men and women, excluding juveniles).

*Table 2.3    Normal and actual hours worked by manual workers,[a] 1951–76*
*(hours per week)*

|      | Normal hours | Average actual hours |
|------|--------------|----------------------|
| 1951 | 44.4         | 46.3                 |
| 1956 | 44.3         | 46.8                 |
| 1961 | 42.3         | 45.7                 |
| 1966 | 40.3         | 44.3                 |
| 1971 | 40.0         | 43.2                 |
| 1976 | 40.0         | 42.6                 |

Source: see Appendix.
[a] Men and women working full-time, but excluding juveniles.

More people have been working part-time and full-time workers have been working for shorter hours. In addition, whereas two weeks' holiday with pay was the norm for manual workers in 1956, the average holiday entitlement in 1976 was well over three weeks. There are also more public holidays. For all these reasons, the total labour input to the economy, as measured in man-hours, has risen less (or fallen more) than the number of people in employment.

## Employment Trends since 1959

While the supply of labour has been continually rising, the numbers of employees in employment have followed a different pattern. In view of the various theories discussed in this book, it is interesting to see how employment has changed in the manufacturing industries, in the production sector as a whole (covering all the industries which are included in the index of production), in services, both public and private, and in the public and private sectors as a whole. However, it would only cause confusion to present the data in every possible way, so as a convenient compromise, Chart 2.1 illustrates the four main trends, distinguishing the manufacturing and production industries, public services and private services, and shows clearly how employment in the manfacturing and production industries fell between 1966 and 1976, while employment in the public services (here taken as employment which is in the public sector but not in any of the industries covered by the index of production) showed a steadily rising trend. Employment in private services showed variations.

There is another piece of evidence which is important, showing how the main changes in employment were divided between males

*Chart 2.1    Employees in employment, United Kingdom, 1959–78 (millions)*

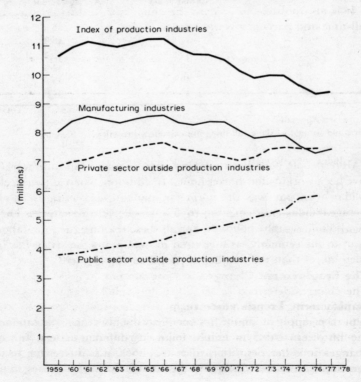

Table 2.4    Changes 1966–76 in United Kingdom employment
(*thousands*)

|  | Males | Females | Total |
|---|---|---|---|
| Index of production industries | − 1438 | − 536 | − 1975 |
| Other industries |  |  |  |
| Private sector | − 385[a] | + 213[a] | − 171 |
| Public sector | + 367[a] | + 1065[a] | + 1432 |
| *Total* | − 1456 | + 742 | − 714 |

Source: see Appendix.
[a] Estimates.

and females (Table 2.4). Thus most of the fall in employment in the production industries consisted of males, while most of the increase in employment in services, and particularly in the public sector outside the production industries, consisted of females.

It is also possible to analyse the changes to distinguish between full-time and part-time workers, as in Table 2.5.

Table 2.5    Changes 1971–6 in United Kingdom employment
(*thousands*)

|  | Full-time | | Part-time | | Total |
|---|---|---|---|---|---|
|  | Males | Females | Males | Females |  |
| Index of production industries | −585 | − 296 | + 11 | + 34 | −836 |
| Other industries | + 142 | + 186 | + 105 | + 820 | + 1253 |
| *Total* | −443 | − 110 | + 116 | + 854 | + 417 |

Source: see Appendix.

## The Employment Changes in Perspective

The changes described so far, including a fall of 15.6 per cent in manufacturing employment over a period of ten years, need to be kept in perspective. In this section we show how they compare with the historical trend in employment in manufacturing, with the changes in other countries, and with the normal level of labour turnover and labour flows which go on all the time.

## Historical perspective

Table 2.6 shows how the recent figures for employment in manufacturing from 1959 onwards, as given by the continuous series of employment statistics described in the Appendix, compare with some earlier statistics as recorded in the Censuses of Production between 1907 and 1951. The figures are not strictly comparable, partly because the definition of 'manufacturing' was changed from time to time, but nevertheless the general run of the figures is informative. It will be seen that the fall has taken place entirely since 1966; before then the trend was still upwards.

*Table 2.6   Employment in manufacturing, United Kingdom, 1907–76*
*(thousands)*

| | |
|---|---|
| 1907 | 4951 |
| 1924 | 5383 |
| 1930 | 5444 |
| 1935 | 5694 |
| 1948 | 7308 |
| 1951 | 7829 |
| 1959 | 8071 |
| 1966 | 8584 |
| 1976 | 7246 |

Sources: see Appendix.

It is well known that in most developed countries there has been a decline in the proportion of the workforce which is employed in the primary industries (agriculture, forestry, fishing, mining, and quarrying) and a rise in the proportion in services. Table 2.7 shows the proportions in Great Britain as recorded in the Censuses of Population between 1931 and 1971, with (almost comparable) estimates for 1976.

Viewed on this time-scale, the decline in the primary industries showed the expected long-term downward trend between 1931 and 1966, but over this period it was balanced by an expansion of the production industries, rather than services. It is only since 1966 that there has been a major contraction in the production industries and an expansion in services.

## International comparisons

The United Kingdom is not the only country in which employment in manufacturing has declined in recent years. The proportion of civil employment which is in the manufacturing industries is shown in

Table 2.7    Proportions of workforce employed in different sectors, Great
Britain, 1931–76 (percentages)

|        | Primary industries | Production industries[a] | Services | Not known |
|--------|--------------------|--------------------------|----------|-----------|
| 1931[b] | 11.9 | 37.0 | 50.6 | 0.5 |
| 1951   | 8.9 | 43.6 | 47.4 | 0.1 |
| 1961   | 6.6 | 44.3 | 48.7 | 0.4 |
| 1966   | 5.4 | 44.0 | 50.3 | 0.3 |
| 1971   | 4.3 | 42.9 | 52.8 | – |
| 1976   | 3.3 | 39.5 | 57.2 | – |

Source: *Department of Employment Gazette*, October 1975, p. 984.
[a] Here defined as manufacturing, construction, and gas, electricity and water.
[b] In this year there was high unemployment in industry and still many private
domestic servants (included under services).

Table 10.2 of the background paper. The decline in the UK manufacturing industries in the last decade has been shared by Belgium,
Denmark, Germany, Holland, the US and Sweden, but not by
France, Ireland, Italy or Japan. The percentage in manufacturing
in the UK is still higher than in all the countries listed above
except Germany and Italy.

*Labour turnover and labour flows*

Finally, we may compare the employment changes in 1966–76 with the
labour turnover and labour flows which go on all the time. Between
1966 and 1976 the net fall in employment in manufacturing was 1.34
million, an average of 134,000 per annum. This is large in comparison
with the previous net changes in manufacturing in the postwar
period, but it is still quite small in comparison with the *gross* flows of
labour which occur each year anyway. Some figures giving rough
orders of magnitude will illustrate this point.

In a typical year, there are about $9\frac{1}{2}$ million instances of people
leaving their employer. Of these, about $2\frac{1}{2}$ million are students leaving
vacation employment and people giving up second jobs. Of the
remaining 7 million, about $1\frac{1}{2}$ million move to another employer,
$3\frac{1}{2}$ million register as unemployed, $1\frac{1}{2}$ million become sick or in-
active and nearly 1 million die, retire or emigrate. These are
replaced by $1\frac{1}{2}$ million who find jobs after coming from other
employers, $\frac{3}{4}$ million who leave education, $3\frac{1}{2}$ million who find jobs
after being unemployed, and a balance which is largely women re-
entering the labour force and immigrants. (In the case of the manufac-

turing industries there are regular estimates of the numbers joining and leaving, which were recently summarised in the *Department of Employment Gazette*, June 1977, pages 608–9.)

The available information, admittedly somewhat out of date, suggests that in a given year about 10 per cent of employees change from one Industry Order to another and that, of those who leave their Orders in manufacturing, about half move to another Order in manufacturing, about a third move into services and the remaining sixth move to construction, public utilities, agriculture or mining (for further details see *Department of Employment Gazette*, December 1975, and April 1970).

## Employment, Unemployment and Vacancies

Until 1966 the numbers in employment moved fairly closely in parallel with the labour supply and unemployment stayed low. Since 1966 the supply of labour has gone on increasing, while the demand for labour in many industries has fallen. It is therefore not surprising to find that unemployment has risen. In this section we consider the extent to which the increase in unemployment can be accounted for by these known factors, or whether the size of the increase can only be explained on the assumption that there have also been structural changes. For this purpose we shall be comparing levels of employment and unemployment at dates (1966, 1971 and 1976) which were at very different points of the economic cycle, but it should be noted that this does not affect the validity of the argument. The relationships between changes in employment, unemployment and labour supply can be expected to hold between *any* pair of dates, not just between corresponding dates.

We observe, first, that if every person in the labour force were either in employment or registered as unemployed, then there would be a very simple identity of the form:

Change in employment + change in registered unemployment
= change in the labour force

However, in practice things are not quite as simple. There are students who work in vacations and who are counted as being in employment for some purposes, but as being in education in others; there are the 'unregistered unemployed', who say in household surveys that they are looking for work, but who do not register as unemployed; there are those who are sick, who are neither employed nor looking for work; there are also other complications like people with two jobs, retired people drawing pensions who also have part-time jobs, members of the forces overseas, and so on.

Although there are some difficult problems of measurement, a reconciliation between the census of employment, the unemployment statistics and the total labour force is possible but complicated (see *Department of Employment Gazette*, June 1977, page 588; also the December issue for earlier estimates of the 'unregistered unemployed'). For the present purpose, however, it is sufficient to look at changes in the main components for the period 1971–6, as shown in Table 2.8.

*Table 2.8    Changes 1971–6 in the total labour supply and its main components, Great Britain (thousands)*

|                          | Males  | Females |
|--------------------------|--------|---------|
| Total labour supply      | − 123  | + 768   |
|                          |        |         |
| Employees in employment  |        |         |
| Production industries    | − 565  | − 248   |
| Other industries         | + 238  | + 975   |
| *Total*                  | − 327  | + 727   |
|                          |        |         |
| Registered unemployed    | + 383  | + 208   |
| Unregistered unemployed  | − 34   | − 54    |

Source: see Appendix.

The simplest interpretation of these figures is that for males the dominant change was a very large fall in employment in the production industries (in which three quarters of all employees are males). The rise in employment for males in other industries was not large enough to offset this and the change in the labour supply was fairly small, so that registered male unemployment rose. For females employment also fell in the production industries, but the dominant changes were a very large increase in the labour supply and a very large increase in the employment of females in services. The concurrent increase in unemployment for females may have been partly due to an increased tendency to register as unemployed.

In the earlier period 1966–71 comparisons are more difficult, partly because there was a considerable increase in the number of self-employed and partly because employment in that period was measured from counts of national insurance cards. This introduced further complications, such as variations in the number of persons who had jobs in some weeks but not in others, which was one of the main reasons why the card counts differed from other sources such as the Censuses of Population. The most informative comparisons are those based on the Censuses of Population, as in Table 2.9.

*Table 2.9    Changes 1966–71 in the total labour force and its main components, Great Britain (thousands)*

|  | Males | Females |
|---|---|---|
| Total labour force | − 161 | + 273 |
| Numbers in civil employment*a* |  |  |
| Production industries | − 478 | − 196 |
| Other industries | − 65 | + 303 |
| *Total* | − *543* | + *107* |
| Registered unemployed | + 371 | + 43 |
| Unregistered unemployed | − 11 | + 107 |

Source: see Appendix.
*a* Employees, employers and self-employed.

The developments in 1966–71 which reduced the demand for labour in the production industries would seem to be the prime reason why there was a large rise in unemployment for males. We note, however, that the rise in unemployment was not quite as large as the fall in employment, because there was also a fall in the supply of males in the labour force. For females, on the other hand, the fall in employment in the production industries was more than offset by the rise in employment in services. Thus unemployment for females would not have risen if it had not been for the large increase in the number of married women in the labour force.

Some commentators have argued that the increase in registered unemployment between 1966 and 1971 may have been partly due to another factor, namely the introduction in December 1965 of statutory redundancy payments and the payment from October 1966 of an earnings-related supplement to national insurance benefits. These, by encouraging the unemployed not to take the first job which was offered, could have increased the number of unemployed, increased the number of vacancies and reduced the numbers in employment. An apparent change in the relationship between unemployment and vacancies seemed to support this theory and in 1974 the Department of Employment set up a working party to examine the evidence. Their report (summarised in the *Department of Employment Gazette* for October 1976) found, however, that the numbers actually receiving these new benefits were not large enough to have accounted for more than a relatively small part of the increase in unemployment between 1966 and 1971. Also, in an article on the unemployment statistics and their interpretation published in the *Department of Employment Gazette* for March 1975, it was concluded that, although changes in the economy might have made it more difficult to reduce unemployment to the levels observed before 1966, and although unemployment was not such a major hardship as in earlier years, there was nevertheless no strong evidence that the characteristics of unemployed persons had greatly changed.

Whether changes in social security benefits *other* than redundancy payments and earnings-related benefits may have affected the position is still a matter of some debate. There seems little doubt that there are certain categories of worker, particularly those with large families, who may not find it worthwhile to accept certain jobs. However, if the vacancy which they were offered is then filled by someone else, this will not necessarily affect the *total* numbers of persons who are employed or unemployed, though of course it will affect the composition of these totals. Even if there is a delay before a vacancy is filled, the resulting reduction in the number in employment cannot be more than the corresponding increase in the number of vacancies. Since vacancies have been consistently low since 1966, apart from a brief interlude in 1973–4, the numbers involved in such a process can only have been fairly marginal.

Broadly speaking, the calculations in this section seem to suggest that the observed changes in the *totals* in employment and unemployment can be largely explained without any need to suppose that there have been structural changes, other than the increase in the labour supply and the factors which have reduced the demand for labour. We observe, though, that the numbers of females in the labour force have increased much more than was originally expected. It is not impossible that changes in the social security system may have increased their incentive to register as unemployed, though only a proportion of females seeking work have been entitled to benefits. But this is very hard to disentangle from other factors, such as equal pay and the effect of the falling birth rate on the number of married women available for work.

## Skill Differentials and Skill Shortages

It is often suggested that the output of the manufacturing industries has been held back at critical moments by shortages of skilled manpower, and that this in turn may have been due, at least in part, to the compression of the differentials in earnings between skilled and unskilled workers. In this section we recapitulate briefly the general nature of the evidence on these points.

### The engineering industry

Most of the literature on skill differentials is concerned with the engineering industry, which is exceptionally well documented. Hart and Mackay [6] have summarised the statistics for 1914–66, and more recent data are available from Department of Employment surveys. The figures show, for example, that the ratio of pre-tax earnings of fitters to those of labourers in the engineering industry fell from 1.65 in 1914 to between 1.38 and 1.45 in the interwar period; fell further to about 1.25 during the second world war, gradually recovered to about 1.4 in the late 1960s and then fell back to 1.3 in 1974 and to 1.25 in 1977.

The narrowing of differentials during 1914–18 was presumably partly due to the 'dilution' of skilled labour during the expansion of the munitions industry. This and the further narrowing in 1939–45 may perhaps suggest that the differentials in 1914 and 1939 were partly a reflection of the conditions of entry to the industries at those times and of the methods of production. We may also note that 1914–18, 1939–42 and the 1970s were all periods of rapid inflation.

The compression in differentials since 1969 has been quite marked and perhaps rather more than might have been expected from the incomes policies of this period. The insistence of certain trade unions in engineering on flat-rate increases was also important. Perhaps both had a common origin in this particular case. Be that as it may, a major factor in the narrowing of differentials in engineering seems to have been the introduction of measured day work and other changes in pay systems, including the abolition of certain agreements which had previously governed the differential between skilled and unskilled workers.

In engineering, as in construction, skilled workers have declined since 1963 both in absolute numbers and as a proportion of the total labour force. Also, apprentices and other trainees have declined as a proportion of skilled workers. For many years, in the South East, notified vacancies for skilled workers persistently exceeded numbers registered as unemployed (particularly for tool-setters, tool-makers, draughtsmen and sheet metal workers).

In 1975 the NEDC and the Manpower Services Commission set up a joint committee to examine the problem of skill shortages in the engineering industry. Their report, published in 1977, included the following points:

(a) The numbers completing approved apprenticeship training had fallen by a third since the early 1970s.

(b) A survey of skilled workers who had left their companies within the previous two years showed that the most common reason given by the older workers was that they had left because of redundancy, while the most common reason for the younger workers was that they felt they had poor prospects for advancement. Only 11 per cent mentioned low pay as a reason.

(c) Many companies were not fully utilising the skills of their existing workers.

(d) The committee believed that the narrowing of differentials in engineering had gone too far and was now a disincentive to potential entrants (NEDO, [9]).

A further point, though this was not specifically mentioned in the report, is the change in the national education system. Many of the people who used to become apprentices are now going into further education. But according to many employers, the new products of the further education system do not have the same aptitudes and motivation as their predecessors. Whether the remedy lies in the education system or in industry is clearly an important question.

*Other shortages*

Not everyone who is looking for a job will register as unemployed, and certainly not every firm which has a vacancy will notify its local employment office. Indeed, surveys suggest that only about one third of total vacancies are notified, so that the ratio of notified vacancies to registered unemployment has no absolute meaning and varies between regions and between occupations. Nevertheless, the *change* in the ratio of notified vacancies to registered unemployment is still a useful indicator, indeed the best we have, of changes in the demand for labour in particular occupations.

For example, in September 1974 there were, overall, about two unemployed persons for every notified vacancy; by June 1976 there were nine unemployed persons for every notified vacancy. By any criterion, the shortage of labour in June 1976 must have been less than in September 1974. Nevertheless, even in 1976 there were several occupations in which there were at least 1000 unfilled vacancies and more vacancies than unemployed. Nurses, typists, sewing machinists and posts in catering and personal services were in this category; in engineering they were machine tool-setters, maintenance fitters and motor vehicle mechanics. Groups which were identified as in short supply at earlier dates included accountants, systems analysts, computer programmers, engineering draughtsmen and technicians, telephonists, postmen, salesmen, policemen, butchers, carpenters, toolmakers, fitters, electricians, assembly workers, coalminers, bus drivers and bus conductors.

If demand is raised very rapidly indeed, as in 1972–3, then it is only to be expected that the demand for skilled labour will outstrip supply until the latter has a chance to catch up. Such shortages may be temporary. Many other shortages are local and do not necessarily act as a serious constraint on output. It is worth noting that in the last few booms reported shortages of skilled labour did not reach their peak until after output had turned down, which, though certainly not conclusive, suggests that other factors such as capacity bottlenecks and failure of demand may have been just as important in determining the time at which the booms ended.

In general, apart from the shortages in the skilled engineering, construction and electrical occupations, the other shortages listed above may not be of the kind which would bring the growth of the economy to a halt. However, this does not detract from their importance. In the long run, what matters is how the skills and aptitudes of the British workforce compare with the skills and aptitudes of our competitors.

## Earnings Differentials Between Sectors

Some commentators have suggested that the manufacturing industries may have been deprived of labour because the services sector in general, and the public services in particular, may have been offering higher rates of pay. This section summarises the evidence on this point.

Earnings in Britain are exceptionally well documented and the overwhelming lesson of the statistics is that earnings in different industries tend to move very closely in parallel, within a few per cent (see 'Trends in earnings', *Department of Employment Gazette*, May 1978). The only really major exceptions in the postwar period have been dockers and coalminers, whose positions in the earnings league have shown notable changes.

The fact that earnings in different industries tend to move practically in parallel seems to imply that most shifts in employment in the economy – the decline of some industries and the expansion of others – normally occur in practice without any large inducements in the form of exceptionally higher earnings in the expanding industries. The main mechanism is simply that the expanding industries offer more vacancies than the declining industries, at the going-rate. This seems to be the reason why an OECD investigation [10] found as its main conclusion that 'large short-term changes in relative earnings do not seem to be necessary to bring about substantial changes in the pattern of employment'.

### Earnings in the public and private sectors

Before the institution of the *New Earnings Survey* in 1970, the official earnings statistics covered a very large part but not the whole of the economy, so that it was not possible to make precise comparisons between earnings in the public and private sectors. Such evidence as was available was analysed by Dean [5], who found little change in the ratio of private to public sector manual earnings in the years between 1950 and 1970. It was only after 1970 that the ratio changed significantly.

The official statistics from 1970 to 1977 are analysed in the *Department of Employment Gazette* for December 1977. The public sector gained on the private sector in the period 1970–5, while the private sector gained on the public sector in 1976–7. In both sectors manual women gained substantially on manual men and non-manual women gained on non-manual men. Over the period as a whole, the ratio of public to private sector earnings for men rose by 7 per cent, but fell for women.

*Earnings in manufacturing*

Corresponding to the changes between the public and private sectors, the *New Earnings Survey* also provides comparisons between earnings in manufacturing and in the rest of the economy. Between April 1970 and April 1977, the average earnings of full-time manual men increased by 161 per cent in manufacturing and by 175 per cent in non-manufacturing. Thus the non-manufacturing sector showed a relative gain of 5 per cent. The largest increase in earnings outside manufacturing was 210 per cent for manual workers in mining and quarrying, followed by manual workers in insurance, banking and finance, then, gas, electricity and water. Thus, much of the gain outside manufacturing was in the nationalised industries, but it was not confined to them. For non-manual men, the corresponding gain relative to the non-manufacturing sector was 4 per cent. These changes of 4 per cent and 5 per cent over the seven years 1970–7 are not really very large, considering the employment changes which took place in this period, and also how employment changed in the period 1966–70 when the earnings differentials were relatively stable. This seems to support the OECD findings.

## International Comparisons of Productivity

The literature on international comparisons of productivity is vast. For the purpose of the present paper it is sufficient to quote a few recent references which are particularly relevant.

Kravis [8] has given a most authoritative review of the subject, including a discussion of the economic reasons why some countries grow faster than others. Further studies have been summarised by Pratten and Atkinson [11].

A report by the Central Policy Review Staff [4] contained direct comparisons between almost identical plants in the UK, Belgium, France, Italy and Germany. Output per man was consistently lowest in the UK, for reasons which included frequent stoppages, quality faults and poor maintenance. The survey found many instances of identical machines which had more men operating and maintaining them in Britain than on the Continent.

The results of comparisons of productivity within the EEC and the trends since 1955 have been very conveniently summarised by Jones [7]. The UK's trend has been far flatter than all the rest. According to the latest estimates, output per man–hour in manufacturing in the UK is now only about two thirds of that in France and Germany, though for GDP per head the ratio is more like three quarters.

However, this is by no means a new phenomenon. Slower growth in Britain can be traced back to the 1870s. In the early 1900s an inquiry team found that America and Germany had far more efficient factories than Britain and observed that they had a faster 'natural pace of work'. The historian Correlli Barnett [2] describes the many previous inquests into the reasons for this, for example, by the Cabinet Defence Policy and Requirements Committee in the 1930s, the Balfour Committee on Trade and Industry in the 1920s, the 'Wake up England' campaign in the late 1890s and early 1900s, the Royal Commission on Technical Education in 1884, and indeed still further back to prescient forebodings by a Royal Commission in 1868. Barnett attributes the underlying causes to deep-seated British attitudes in both industry and education, with roots well back in the nineteenth century.

## Discussion

It was suggested above that in the particular industries in which employment was falling before 1966 the three main reasons were falling demand, growing competition and in some cases technological changes resulting in higher output per head. Since 1966 the first two factors have hit many more industries. Demand has failed to rise adequately and competition has become fiercer, not only from the developed but even more from the developing countries. These are the obvious explanations for the falls in employment, but we must also consider the alternative theories which were mentioned in the introduction.

### Shortages of manpower

If surveys show that a particular machine is operated by three men in France and Germany, while an identical machine is operated by four men in Britain, then it is really very hard to argue convincingly that output in British manufacturing industry is being held back by an overall shortage of manpower. International comparisons of productivity are not always as clear-cut as this, but nevertheless they appear at their face value to suggest that there are many British industries in which we have too many men rather than too few in relation to our competitors. There may be good social reasons for preferring it that way, but we cannot then be surprised if our competitors produce the goods more cheaply, unless our wages are also lower than theirs in proportion to our productivity. In effect, this is what has already been happening in many industries.

The theory that British manufacturing industries have been unable to expand as they should because of a shortage of skilled workers is a very different proposition from the theory that there is an overall shortage of manpower. The evidence discussed above suggests that skill shortages are important, particularly in the engineering, construction and electrical occupations, but they are only part of the problem.

It has been strongly argued by some economists that the expansion of public expenditure, or of employment in the public services, or alternatively the 'non-tradeable' sector, has had the effect of holding back the manufacturing industries at times when they might have expanded.

However, the argument about expenditure and finance is really rather different from the argument about manpower. We know that since the early 1960s there has been a very large expansion of public expenditure including transfer payments, rising indeed from 40 per cent to 60 per cent of GNP on the old definitions. This led to an increase in taxation, and many have thought that this was one of the reasons for the increase in wage-push inflation since 1969. There was also a very abrupt increase in public expenditure in the period 1971-4, by over 20 per cent in real terms, in a period when the real national income (as distinct from the real national product) rose by less than 1 per cent because of the change in the terms of trade. These events may well have affected inflation, profits, cash flows, investment and output, and hence by this route the demand for manpower. However, this is quite another matter from saying that output was directly held back because the manpower needed was being held in the public services.

This last possibility has been argued in particular by Bacon and Eltis [1]. They suggest that the public services have taken on more labour during slumps but have not released it again in booms, and that by this 'ratchet effect' the manufacturing industries have been deprived of labour. The evidence, however, shows that most of the expansion of employment in the public services consisted of women, while most of the contraction in the manufacturing and production industries consisted of men. Also the net changes were relatively small in comparison with the normal order of magnitude of labour turnover and labour flows, and the relative earnings changed by only a few per cent over several years. Although there may certainly be room for more than one view about the interpretation of these data, it still seems to the author, as a personal opinion, that one cannot rule out a much simpler explanation. This is that the demand for labour in manufacturing fell at a time when the demand for labour in the public services happened to be rising because successive governments had decided to increase public expenditure. These events happened at the same time; but there is no need to suppose that the second caused the first, except perhaps indirectly through the financial mechanism mentioned above.

A rather similar remark applies to the theory that higher social security benefits have caused a fall in employment. They certainly helped to make unemployment less unpleasant than it used to be, they may have affected the composition of the unemployed and they may conceivably have induced more people (particularly women) to register as unemployed and thus appear in the monthly statistics, but this does not prove that they caused a significant fall in the numbers in employment.

## *The post-industrial society*

We now turn to the theory that, irrespective of the actions of governments, there is an inevitable downward trend in employment in industry, as developed economies progress towards the post-industrial society.

The term 'post-industrial society' was coined in 1959 by the American sociologist Daniel Bell [3]. His ideas start from the theory of Colin Clark that, as a nation becomes more industrialised and productivity increases, there is an inevitable progression under which a large proportion of the labour force shifts first from agriculture into industry and then from industry into services. Productivity in agriculture has already increased so much that relatively few people are now needed to work the land; productivity in manufacturing still has a long way to go, but it is rising all the time, so that eventually the same thing will happen. Also, as a country gets richer one may expect it to spend more on services, and in particular on health and education. There will be corresponding occupational changes, ultimately more important than the fate of particular industries.

As the process proceeds, the government will become the largest single employer. The growing cost of the public sector will lead to higher taxes and hence to higher wage claims. If wages in the public services rise without compensating gains in productivity, they will give rise to additional claims on social resources. Increasingly there will loom the 'fiscal crisis of the state'.

There is no doubt that the increase in productivity in agriculture has led to a spectacular fall in the numbers employed on the land. But so far there is no such clearly established trend in industry. Table 2.7 shows the figures for Great Britain, where the proportion in production industries remained high until 1966 and is still higher than in 1931. Even in the US, the proportion of the labour force employed in manufacturing (26.9 per cent in 1920, 20.2 per cent in 1930, 23.9 per cent in 1950 and 22.5 per cent in 1970) shows only a very slow downward trend, of the order of 4 percentage points over a period of 50 years. Presumably this is because demand has risen almost as fast as output per head.

The 'de-industrialisation' since 1966 has not been confined to Britain, but equally it has not been universal: it has not happened at all in France, Ireland, Italy or Japan. Manufacturing employment is rising in the developing countries and it would be rash to forecast that there will be a permanent fall in total industrial employment in the world as a whole, at least for a very long time. What will happen to Britain's share is of course another matter; in the long run this will depend on how well we stand up to the growing competition from other countries.

## Effects of competition on employment

If the only way to stay competitive were to raise output per head very substantially, then there would be an unpleasant potential dilemma. Failure to raise productivity in this way could lead to further loss of markets and a fall in employment at some stage in the future. On the other hand, deliberate action to raise output per head, by de-manning or by labour-saving investment, will lead to a fall in employment now.

However, a reduction in employment in some industries will not necessarily reduce the total number of workers in employment in all industries. The extra competitiveness may add to exports or reduce import penetration, thus permitting a reflation of the economy and an expansion of employment in other sectors such as services. Neverthe-less, if the employment reduction in manufacturing consists largely of unskilled manual men, when the expansion in services consists largely of women, as happened in the period 1966–76, then there may still be a social problem.

It is very important to remember, however, that output per head is only one of the factors which affect competitiveness. Our costs relative to other countries depend on wages as well as on output per head. Moreover, costs and prices are not the only things which affect sales. There is plenty of evidence to suggest that non-price factors, such as design, quality, marketing, delivery dates and anticipating the demand for new products, are just as important. The future level of employment in manufacturing will depend crucially on these factors.

Until quite recently, it used to be widely believed that full employment could always be achieved by boosting demand and investment, and that the competitiveness of British industry could be improved by devaluing the pound and maintaining wage restraint. But the experience of the 1970s has shown that these things are not simple. It is not easy to maintain demand in the face of competition if most additions to purchasing power are spent on imports rather than the home product; it is not easy to find people to pay for investment if it does not pay for itself; it is not easy to maintain wage restraint when the pound is falling so that import prices are rising.

Other methods of increasing total employment include the further expansion of the public sector, subsidies on employment, or subsidies on such investment projects as will increase the demand for labour. These methods can be applied if people are prepared to pay for the subsidies, in particular by lending to the government or by paying higher taxes without asking for higher wages; otherwise they will eventually produce inflation. Thus it will be seen that these remedies, like those in the previous paragraph, ultimately involve a reduction in the real net wage after tax. If this can be accepted, then full employment is always possible, at least in principle.

From one point of view, we have already been accepting a slower growth in output per head and hence a slower growth in real wages than other countries. Purely as a description of the past, and not as a judgement or a prediction for the future, it seems possible that the desire to maintain employment may have been one of the motives behind these past choices. But achieving both full employment and a high standard of living is more difficult, perhaps depending ultimately on the long-term attributes discussed on page 45.

*Appendix: sources*

Tables 2.1, 2.8 and 2.9 were provided by the Department of Employment from the latest information currently available, on the basis used in the *Department of Employment Gazette* for June 1977. Table 2.2 brings up to date the information discussed in the *Department of Employment Gazette* for November 1973. Table 2.3 brings up to date table 84 in Department of Employment, *British Labour Statistics: historical abstract 1886–1968*, London, HMSO, 1971.

Statistics of numbers in employment in the UK were based from 1948 to 1970 on counts of national insurance cards. Since the cards were abolished the statistics have been based mainly on the census of employment, which is a direct annual return from employers. Articles in the *Department of Employment Gazette* (March 1975, December 1976 and June 1977) have given a consistent series of the numbers in employment in each industry since 1959, which was the year when the 1958 SIC was introduced. This consistent series was designed to remove, so far as possible, the discontinuities in the earlier published statistics which resulted from the changes in the SIC in 1968 and the change from the counts of national insurance cards to the censuses of employment in 1971. This consistent series is the primary source for Tables 2.4 and 2.5.

*References*

[1]  Bacon, R. W. and Eltis, W. A., *Britain's Economic Problem: too few producers*, London, Macmillan, 1976.
[2]  Barnett, C., *The Collapse of British Power*, London, Cassells, 1972.
[3]  Bell, D., *The Coming of Post-Industrial Society*, London, Heinemann, 1974.
[4]  Central Policy Review Staff, *The Future of the British Car Industry*, London, HMSO, 1975.
[5]  Dean, A. J. H., 'Public and private sector manual workers' pay, 1970–1977', *National Institute Economic Review*, November 1977.
[6]  Hart, R. A. and MacKay, D. I., 'Engineering earnings in Britain, 1914–1968', *Journal of the Royal Statistical Society* (series A), no. 1, 1975.
[7]  Jones, D. T., 'Output, employment and labour productivity in Europe since 1955', *National Institute Economic Review*, August 1977.
[8]  Kravis, I. B., 'A survey of international comparisons of productivity', *Economic Journal*, March 1976.
[9]  NEDO, *Engineering Craftsmen: shortages and related problems*, London, 1977.
[10]  OECD, *Wages and Labour Mobility*, Paris, 1965.
[11]  Pratten, C. F. and Atkinson, A. G., 'The use of manpower in British manufacturing industry', *Department of Employment Gazette*, June 1976.

# Comment

## by P. M. Jackson*

### Introduction

The past couple of years has witnessed a revival of interest in the supply-side of economic management. This is to be contrasted with the overwhelming dominance of Keynesian aggregate demand management which has characterised so much of economic policy in the postwar period. With the exception of a brief flirtation with economic planning in 1964–5 and frequent attempts to use selective controls to restore economic balance at the regional level, policy-makers have, in the main, relied upon the broad-based instruments associated with monetary and fiscal policies.

The concept of 'de-industrialisation' has served as a catalyst accelerating the current debate on the structural dimension of economic management. Thatcher's paper, which concentrates upon trends and structural changes in the labour market, is a welcome and useful contribution to the discussion. It usefully draws together data from a number of hitherto diverse sources, thereby enabling us to gain a better perspective of the changes which have taken place in the labour market over the postwar period. This is extremely valuable in view of the fact that unless we have adequate data it is impossible to evaluate the alternative competing accounts and explanations of these trends.

My comments will be directed first at some points of clarification in Thatcher's paper, second, at embellishments to his data and, third, at identifying a number of theoretical issues which might be developed from the paper.

### Employment Trends

The data presented show that, over the postwar period in the UK, whilst the supply of labour has increased (in terms of the total number of hours worked), a number of structural changes to the composition of the labour force have taken place. An increasing number of individuals have been working part-time, whilst the average number of hours worked per week per person has declined. The total number of

* I would like to record my thanks to Andrew Dean and W. Martin, with whom I have discussed at an earlier date some material contained in this note. Some of the data relating to employment in the public sector was collected with the aid of an SSRC grant.

persons in employment has fallen since 1966, but within the group significant changes have taken place: the number of part-time (married) women has increased; a decline in employment has taken place in the primary and secondary (essentially production) industries and within these it has been a decline in male employment; there has been a substantial growth in employment in the services sector, especially of females; within the services sector public employment has shown a rapid growth; finally, these trends are not confined to the UK but can be found in the majority of North American and West European economies.

## Unemployment

The total number of persons in employment has decreased since 1966, whereas at the same time the total labour force (all the people in a job or looking for one) has increased. These two trends have contributed to rising unemployment.

*Table 2.10    Trends in UK unemployment, 1951–76 (percentages)*

|                   | 1951–5 | 1956–61 | 1962–6 | 1967–71 | 1971–6 |
|-------------------|--------|---------|--------|---------|--------|
| Average rates     | 1.4    | 1.5     | 1.7    | 2.6     | 3.7    |
| Long-term/total   | 46.6   | 53.5    | 54.7   | 56.7    | 64.1   |

Source: Department of Employment.

Whilst there is little doubt of Thatcher's interpretation of the data relating to aggregate levels of unemployment, we do need to dig a bit deeper to pick up trends of structural changes other than those set out in his Tables 2.8 and 2.9. For various periods since 1950 the average unemployment rate was as shown in Table 2.10, which also gives the proportion of long-term unemployed in the total for similar periods. The duration of unemployment has increased substantially since 1951. The social implications of having 1 million persons unemployed all of whom find a job within a month are different from having half a million unemployed all of whom have been out of work for more than six months. In 1951–5 the time spent out of work was on average 6.1 weeks, whereas in 1967–74 it had increased to 11.9 weeks, and in 1974–6 it was about 16.0 weeks (Roberti, [7]). The average duration of unemployment, however, obscures the problem of the long-term unemployed, defined as those out of work for eight weeks or more. As a percentage of the total unemployed, they have also increased over the period (Table 2.10).

These figures underline the increasing severity of unemployment. An examination of the data would also suggest that peaks in the unemployment rate now correspond to peaks in the proportion of long-term unemployed. Recent interesting work by Nickell [6], whilst tentative, shows that the conditional probability of an individual obtaining work declines dramatically after the first six months of unemployment to very low levels. Nickell also reports that he found the impact of the levels of unemployment benefits on the conditional probability of obtaining work significant for the first twenty weeks or so, but insignificant thereafter. These results should be borne in mind when interpreting the data in Thatcher's paper.

Table 2.11   Unemployed school-leavers as proportion of total unemployed, United Kingdom, 1971–6 (percentages)

| 1971 | 1972 | 1973 | 1974 | 1975 | 1976 |
|------|------|------|------|------|------|
| 2.1  | 2.4  | 1.2  | 2.5  | 5.2  | 7.0  |

Source: Department of Employment.

Further, unemployed males are more likely to be middle-aged or above. However, in recent years, unemployment amongst the young has been increasing. Table 2.11 shows unemployed school-leavers as a percentage of total unemployment. Moreover, those aged 16–24 who are members of minority groups (people born in or with one or both parents in New Commonwealth countries and Pakistan) have also increased in proportion – from about 0.6 per cent of total unemployed in 1973 to 1.4 per cent in 1977 (CSO, [1], Chart 5.16). Whilst these changes have taken place recently and therefore cannot be thought of as a trend, many would argue that they constitute more than a short-term problem and may be expected to continue for some time into the future. Certainly, unemployment amongst the younger age groups is also causing concern in North America and Australia.

## Skill Differentials, Skill Shortages and Earnings Differentials

This whole area is generally unsatisfactory and Thatcher has done well to set out what limited information is available. We do not know very much about what factors generate the demand for skills, how this information is transmitted to the labour market, or how the labour-market information (wages and demand) is fed back into the education and training systems. We know even less about occupational choice. Studies from the US show that the markets in most skills are characterised by 'cobwebs' and there is every reason to believe that this is a general characteristic. This means that any attempts at manpower planning at the national level, in the absence of detailed knowledge of the leads and lags in labour markets, is more likely to be destabilising than helpful.

Recent work by Wabe and Leech [8] has indicated that any cross-section analysis of inter-industry differences in average earnings is fraught with difficulties, their study casting doubts on the validity of many of the previous studies of variations in the growth of average earnings over time. Clearly this is unresolved and we await further developments before we are in a position to know *why* relative earnings have changed.

A similar argument applies to the analysis of earnings differentials between the public and the private sectors. Dean [2] has thrown a great deal of light on this question, but as yet we are not in a position to know *why* earnings changed relatively after 1970 (see also Department of Employment, [3]).

A number of hypotheses can be advanced, but remain, as yet, untested:

(a) There was a once-and-for-all 'catching-up' by public sector employees after the incomes policies of the 1960s. The NBPI [5] had previously pointed out that most low-paid workers were in the public sector. An improvement in low absolute earnings would have narrowed the *relative* position of public and private sector earnings.

(b) Public sector employees more than just 'caught up'.

(c) The relative earnings of women improved most, due in part to the Equal Pay Act. Given the large number of women employed in the public sector, public sector average earnings rose relative to the private sector.

(d) Pay is made up differently in the two sectors. If (as seems to be the case) a greater proportion of public sector total earnings is basic pay (rather than overtime, bonuses, etc.) then public sector employees require a greater increase in basic pay, and this shows up as an apparent change in relative wages rates.

These hypotheses are not mutually exclusive.

## Public Sector Employment

One thing we have discovered from the 'Public Sector Employment Project' at Leicester University is that there is a surprising lack of useful data on public sector employees and their characteristics, and that those data which do readily exist are ambiguous. When account is taken of the importance of part-time employment in the public sector, it appears that many of the conclusions drawn by some commentators about the growth of public sector employment are misleading. In a recent study, Jackson [4] has examined in greater detail the changes in the composition of public sector employment. For example, over the period 1952–73 full-time male employment grew annually by 1.6 per cent and part-time male employment by 5.5 per cent, whereas the corresponding growth rates for females were 2.8 and 6.2 per cent.

The age composition of the public sector labour force also shows a significant difference in comparison with the private sector. The public sector has an older labour force biased towards those nearing retirement. The national average of public and private sector male employees in the age group 55–64 is 17.1 per cent; for education this figure is 18.2 per cent, for local government 20.4 per cent, for medical and dental services 22.1 per cent and for central government 26.3 per cent.

A question which is frequently asked is whether there are too many administrators in the public sector. Great play is often made of the increase in the number of administrators and clerical staff per doctor in the National Health Service, which was 2.2 in 1970 and 2.6 in 1976. However, the optimal mix of skills within any industry or sector of the economy is an extremely complex issue. An efficient allocation could be defined in terms of whether or not it would be possible to increase total output by reallocating labour between activities. However, this approach ignores the problem of measuring output, the trade-off between efficiency and other considerations such as distribution, and the elasticity of substitution between inputs.

A wider consideration of the post-industrial society reveals that within the majority of manufacturing industries the ratio of operatives to others (administrators, etc.) has declined over the period 1963–70. This represents a wider structural change, which is also reflected within the public sector.

## The Way Ahead

Thatcher's paper has set out data which help us to *account* for the changes which have taken place; in their present form they do not enable us to *explain* the trends. This requires much more careful modelling and subsequent testing of hypotheses. The following summary remarks are, therefore, speculative, but suggest possible means of proceeding:

(a)  The naive modern Physiocratic idea that public sector employment has directly crowded out private sector employment cannot be substantiated by the facts and ought to be dismissed; it confuses stocks and flows of labour.

(b)  We need to know why the manufacturing sector shed labour and also what kind of labour it shed (skilled, unskilled, etc.). Was its reduced demand for labour due to reduced demand for final output in both domestic and overseas markets (if so, why?), or was labour becoming too expensive relative to capital? And has recent investment been capital-deepening or capital-widening?

(c)  What factors have caused an increase in the demand for public sector employment? Do fiscal illusions cause an expansion, or is the public sector budget constraint too elastic?

These are a few of the questions which are being examined at Leicester and should throw some light on the issues in the near future.

## Concluding Remarks

Traditionally we have thought in terms of people being employed or unemployed. The position is, however, more complex; choices are made between work, non-market work and leisure; households make joint decisions with respect to the hours of work of husband and wife. For the individual, too, the life-cycle balance between education, work and retirement has become complex. These decisions and structural changes are at best only imprecisely reflected in broad employment and unemployment data.

If growth takes place in the tertiary sector, which tends to attract groups such as women and retired persons into the labour force, then unemployment may grow even when employment is expanding. Those who become unemployed in recessions may not be those who are hired when recovery comes.

*References*

[1] CSO, *Social Trends 1977*.
[2] Dean, A. J. H., 'Public and private sector manual workers' pay, 1970–1977', *National Insitute Economic Review*, November 1977.
[3] Employment, Department of, *Department of Employment Gazette*, December 1977.
[4] Jackson, P. M., 'The growth of public sector employment' in Institute for Fiscal Studies, *Fiscal Policy and Labour Supply*, London, 1977.
[5] NBPI, *Report no. 29: Pay and Conditions of Manual Workers in Local Authorities, the National Health Service, Gas and Water Supply*, Cmnd 3230, London, HMSO, 1967.
— *Report no. 169: General Problems of Low Pay*, Cmnd 4648, London, HMSO, 1971.
[6] Nickell, S., 'Estimating the probability of leaving unemployment' (LSE Discussion Paper), 1977.
[7] Roberti, P., 'Unemployment' in R. Klein (ed.), *Inflation and Priorities*, London, Centre for Studies in Social Policy, 1975.
[8] Wabe, S. and Leech, D., 'Relative earnings in UK manufacturing – a reconsideration of the evidence', *Economic Journal*, June 1978.

# 3  Technical Innovation and British Trade Performance

## by C. Freeman*

### Introduction

The fact that technical change plays a critical part in productivity growth is not in dispute among economists. The problems experienced in econometric work on the 'residual' in aggregate production functions do not affect this consensus. Despite the heroic efforts of Denison [3] it is certainly difficult (and probably impossible) to *measure* statistically the precise contribution of technical change (and many other factors) to the process of economic growth and international trade performance. It is even quite difficult to establish for any one country, such as Britain, whether relative weaknesses in technical innovation and the management of technical change have contributed to a relatively poor performance or not. This paper nevertheless attempts to make such an assessment, although without recourse to production functions or residuals.

It concentrates on relative trade performance rather than the growth of the economy as such, and this is for two reasons. First, in a comparatively open trading system, such as that prevailing in OECD countries for the past quarter of a century, export shares and the capacity to compete with imports in the home market provide a relatively objective, straightforward and convenient test of comparative efficiency in each industry for each country. To paraphrase Hegel: 'Die Weltmarkt ist das Weltgericht' – 'World history is the world court of judgement'. Secondly, in Britain's case there is a close link between trade performance and overall economic performance. It is not the purpose of this paper to investigate the precise nature of this link, but clearly Britain has faced and still faces major difficulties

* In making this analysis I draw heavily on the work done at the Science Policy Research Unit in preparation of a new book on *Technical Innovation and British Economic Performance* [15]. I am particularly indebted to Keith Pavitt, the editor of this book, as well as to other colleagues who have contributed chapters on particular sectors of British industry.

in attempting to achieve a higher growth rate in the face of chronic weakness in the balance of payments.

In order to discuss specifically *British* problems it is first necessary to establish the role of technical innovation in trade performance in general terms. The first part of this paper summarises some previous work in this field, reports some new work and seeks to demonstrate that technical innovation is now a well-established explanatory factor for a large part of international trade, although its role in relation to capital goods differs from its role in consumer goods and materials. The second part of the paper concentrates entirely on specific identifiable weaknesses in Britain's management of technical innovation and the ways in which these are reflected in trade performance and more generally in the performance of the economy.

## The Role of Technical Innovation

During the 1960s international trade theory underwent a profound change. This began with Posner's [17] seminal article in 1961 and culminated in Johnson's [8] paper at the Montreal Conference of the International Economic Association, in which he suggested a synthesis of the new 'technology gap' theories with traditional theories of factor costs and comparative advantage.

Posner, starting from the fairly obvious fact that a country which first introduces a new product may export it at least until imitators come into the market, developed a set of concepts which suggested that a large part of foreign trade might be explained by this mechanism, rather than by traditional factor-cost advantages. As long as the 'imitation lag' was longer than the 'demand lag', technology-gap trade would tend to persist and there were several factors which would tend to maintain this gap for fairly long periods. Among the most important of these were the quality and scale of commitment to R and D, the 'clustering' of technical innovations and dynamic economies of scale. Posner's paper was written in theoretical terms, but soon afterwards Hufbauer [7] provided an excellent empirical illustration in his work on international trade in synthetic materials. He measured imitation lags in many countries for some 60 products and demonstrated a strong relationship between export performance and innovative leadership. He was careful, however, not to throw out the baby with the bath water. He recognised that as a new product technology matured and became internationally established traditional factor-cost elements in comparative advantage could become increasingly important. His theory was thus a combination of 'technology gap' explanations and what he called 'low wage' explanations, and he correctly anticipated that the standardised bulk synthetics would cease to be mainly technology-gap commodities. This led in turn to the development of 'product-cycle' theories of international trade, in which the comparative advantage of countries gradually changes over time as an innovation is diffused through the world economy. Hirsch [6] was a pioneer of this approach.

Although Hufbauer showed convincingly that technical innovations in PVC, nylon, polystyrene, synthetic rubbers and many other materials had contributed very substantially to the export perform-ance of the German and US chemical industries, he did not investigate the sources of these innovations other than by identifying the firm which first introduced them. Several studies at the National Institute in the 1960s (Freeman, [4]) attempted to relate the innovative performance of firms to their investment in scientific research and experimental development (R and D). The results of this work lent support to the view that the innovative leadership of German chemical firms had rested to a great extent on their exceptionally heavy investment in R and D over a long period. Similarly in the world market for electronic capital goods, the dominant position of United States firms was also related to their enormous commitment to R and D, both in industry and in government. Patent statistics confirmed the technical leadership of the relevant German and US firms in com-parison with their competitors elsewhere and also indicated a further mechanism to reinforce this leadership.

These studies and Hufbauer's work were important also in demon-strating the importance of static and dynamic economies of scale in relation to new products and processes. The imitation lag could be prolonged if R and D threshold costs of entry were particularly high. The innovator would also be more able to retain his comparative 'technology gap' advantage if the learning curve was steep, in terms of either volume of production or learning time. Moreover, would-be imitators could repeatedly be put at a disadvantage if innovators could sustain a flow of technical innovations or new 'generations' of products and processes. All of these mechanisms were shown to be important in some sectors of the electronics and chemical industries, and other studies also demonstrated their importance in the aircraft industry. Studies by Golding [5] and Sciberras [22] showed that dynamic economies of scale were particularly important in the elec-tronic components industry.

Although this work offered firm empirical evidence on the importance of technical innovation in interpreting patterns of trade performance by particular firms and countries, it was confined to specific industries, which could be dismissed as atypical. The first attempt to relate these sector studies to the overall pattern of R and D expenditures and international trade performance was made by Vernon [24], Keesing [9] and their colleagues at Harvard in the mid-1960s. In their work they provided a plausible resolution of the 'Leontief paradox' which was later incorporated by Johnson [8] into his new theoretical synthesis at the Montreal Conference.

Leontief [10] had shown that, contrary to the predictions of the neo-classical theory of comparative advantage, US exports were actually more labour-intensive than US imports. Vernon, Keesing and their colleagues demonstrated that there was a fairly strong association between the ranking of US shares of world export markets by product groups and the R and D intensity of each group. World export performance was exceptionally good in aircraft, electronics, scientific instruments and drugs, which, although far from capital-intensive in the traditional sense of the term, were all characterised by an exceptionally high investment in R and D. Such industries were 'labour-intensive', but extremely skill-intensive. Thus it only remained for Johnson to take over the concept of 'human capital' to develop his revisionist version of comparative advantage in capital-intensive industries. In doing so, he took into account (as Vernon did also) the large numbers of professional and skilled people working in management, production, marketing and technical services, as well as in R and D itself. His theory thus put the main emphasis on human capital generally rather than just on R and D or innovation.

Whilst 'technology-gap' and 'human capital' theories appeared to offer useful explanations of some aspects of US trade performance and also had obvious relevance to the trade between industrialised and less developed countries, it was more difficult to apply them to consumer goods industries and to the production of basic materials.

In fact there are important distinctions to be made between the nature of technical innovation and R and D investment in these three different types of industry. In the capital goods and chemical industries technical effort is directed mainly to the design and development of new products which have superior technical characteristics and all-round performance. These industries are the most research-intensive in industrialised countries (Table 3.1).

In the basic materials industries, on the other hand, technical effort is directed mainly to cost reduction through factor-saving innovation.

*Table 3.1    Research and development expenditure as a proportion of net output. US and UK. 1958 (percentages)*

|  | US | UK |
|---|---|---|
| **Group 1:  Capital goods and chemicals** | | |
| Aircraft and aero-engines | 30.9 | 35.1 |
| Electronics | 22.4 | 12.8 |
| Other electrical | 16.3 | 5.6 |
| Vehicles | 10.2 | 1.4 |
| Instruments | 9.9 | 6.0 |
| Chemicals | 6.9 | 4.5 |
| Machinery | 6.3 | 2.3 |
| Total | *13.0* | *6.3* |
| **Group 2:  Basic materials** | | |
| Rubber | 2.7 | 2.1 |
| Non-ferrous metals | 2.0 | 2.3 |
| Metal products | 1.3 | 0.8 |
| Stone, clay and glass | 1.2 | 0.6 |
| Paper | 0.9 | 0.8 |
| Ferrous metal | 0.8 | 0.5 |
| Total | *1.3* | *0.9* |
| **Group 3:  Consumer goods** | | |
| Food | 0.5 | 0.3 |
| Textiles and apparel | 0.2 | 0.3 |
| Lumber and furniture | 0.2 | 0.04 |
| Other manufacturing | 0.9 | 0.4 |
| Total | *0.5* | *0.3* |

Source: C. Freeman, 'Research and Development: a comparison between British and American industry', *National Institute Economic Review*, May 1962.

Much of the output is standardised and produced by capital-intensive flow processes exploiting production economies of scale and resource endowments. Many of the process innovations are launched as a result of technical effort on the part of equipment suppliers in the capital goods industries, but a modest level of in-house R and D is usually important both for the efficient introduction of process innovations and for the development of more specialised 'tailor-made' materials. Indeed, those firms which concentrate more on 'speciality' materials – special alloys, new synthetics, special grades of paper, etc. – may have high research-intensity and resemble more closely the first category of industries, whilst the chemical industry is actually increasingly divided between those sections operating like the steel or aluminium industries and supplying standard bulk materials on a large scale, and those sections like drugs based on product innovation.

Finally, in the third group of industries supplying consumer goods, fashion-based design and advertising are often more important than technical innovation in products. Consequently, these industries are generally of very low research-intensity, although some have high capital-intensity. Technical change in terms of lower production costs is of course extremely important in these industries too, but such change tends to occur largely as a result of the R and D activities of the suppliers of capital goods and materials, rather than through in-house R and D.

Taking these variations into account it is not surprising that third world industrialising countries are sometimes able to compete effectively in the third and second groups of industries, but find it much more difficult to do so in capital goods. It is in the capital goods category that comparative advantage in human capital and R and D intensity is most firmly established and where it matters most, whereas traditional price competition is critical in the second category and often the third. One would thus expect that attempts to explain trade performance by the relative scale and direction of R and D activity (or other measures of in-house effort directed towards technical innovation) would prove most successful in relation to the first category of industries (and to a smaller extent the second). Keesing's and Vernon's correlations might largely reflect these differences. This does not mean that technical change is negligible in consumer goods industries, but that its relative importance is less and it would not in any case usually be picked up by the conventional measures of in-house R and D or patents.

Ideally, in order to test the validity of hypotheses which attempt to relate trade performance to technical innovation, one would thus need a classification system which distinguished clearly between these three different types of industry, and moreover one which reconciled on a consistent basis the various measures of technical effort, commodity trade and industrial output.

Such problems of classification and data collection have proved a major barrier to further work in this field. A pioneering attempt to relate R and D expenditures (normalised by country) to export shares was made by Curnow [2] in the late 1960s. But this study had to make drastic simplifying assumptions to reconcile the divergent national classification systems for statistics on R and D and on trade.

It did, however, provide a preliminary demonstration of the importance of comparative advantage in technical innovation for several other OECD countries in various industries, as well as for the US. Keesing and Vernon's results had only established such a relationship between R and D performance and trade performance for the US itself, yet it was becoming increasingly obvious that the US was far from unique in this respect.

The sector studies carried out for the OECD 'technology gap' project [13] had already made it clear that, although the US at that time continued to enjoy a clear technical lead in some key sectors with close affinities to military and space technology, several European countries had either already closed or were rapidly closing the gap in such industries as vehicles, machinery and chemicals. In total, of course, these latter industries were far more important components of international trade and production; not only were other countries (including increasingly Japan) competing effectively with the US in product innovation in these 'mainstream' industries, but they also had caught up or were catching up in the technical improvement of processes in the consumer goods and basic materials industries. Indeed, despite continuing US technological leadership in a few specialised industries, several European countries have now attained the goal which seemed so remote in the 1940s and have closed the overall industrial productivity gap in output per man employed. Clearly the transfer of technology through multinational corporations has been one important factor in this process, but OECD statistics [14] show that those countries which have closed the gap or have nearly done so have also been characterised by a steep rise in their R and D investment in industry.

It thus became a matter of particular interest to make a renewed attempt to overcome the statistical difficulties and to find a way to get comparable series which could provide some measure both of the innovative effort of firms in various industries in various countries, and of their trade performance.

One way around these difficulties is to use a different measure of technical effort – patent statistics. These have their advantages, which were powerfully argued by Schmookler [21], but also their disadvantages. They cannot be used directly for international comparisons because of the variations in national patent systems, but they can be used where two or more countries are operating essentially within the same set of rules, as for example, in taking out patents in a third country. It is a fair assumption that patents still represent a major part of innovative activity and that any firm with a major patentable invention will tend to take out a US patent as well as a domestic patent. This is partly because the US is the largest and most important single market and partly because competition is likely to emanate from that source. In addition the costs of patenting there are relatively low. It is therefore exceptionally fortunate that the Office of Technology Assessment and Forecasting in the US Department of Commerce has recently begun to make available long-term series of US patent statistics classified by country of origin for 40 industrial sectors. These statistics are fairly closely related to R and D statistics (Table 3.2), but there are some important differences. Firms in machine building (including engines) and metal manufacture tend to patent more than might be inferred from the level of their R and D expenditures, while firms in the aircraft industry patent proportionately much less than their R and D expenditures might suggest. This is partly because of the very high cost of prototype development and testing in the aircraft industry.

*Table 3.2    Shares of R and D expenditure and US patents by country (percentages)*

|  | Shares of total industry-financed R and D[a] | Shares of patents taken out in US in 1976 |
|---|---|---|
| United Kingdom | 14.6 | 14.5 |
| France | 11.9 | 11.8 |
| Germany | 25.1 | 29.6 |
| Italy | 5.6 | 3.7 |
| Netherlands | 4.1 | 3.6 |
| Japan | 35.4 | 31.7 |
| Sweden | 3.3 | 5.2 |

Source: Pavitt [15].
[a] For 1975 at 1970 prices. Excludes government expenditure.

The new statistics have been used by Soete [23] and Pavitt [15] to make a new assessment of the relationship between technical inventive effort and export performance for 22 OECD countries. For each of the 40 industrial sectors, 1974 exports *per capita* for each country were regressed against US patents *per capita* over the period 1963–76 (Table 3.3). The US itself is omitted from the analysis, because patenting by US firms in their own home market is obviously on a different basis from that of foreign firms.

In general the results offer fairly strong confirmation of the view

| | US SIC | Equation | |
|---|---|---|---|
| | | t-value b coeff. | r² |
| *Significant results*[a] | | | |
| Special industrial machinery | 355 | 12.13 | 0.89 |
| Drugs | 283 | 12.12 | 0.89 |
| Metalworking machinery | 354 | 11.99 | 0.88 |
| Engines & turbines (incl. aero) | 351 | 8.40 | 0.79 |
| Instruments | 38–3825 | 8.24 | 0.78 |
| Electrical transmission & distribution equipment | 361, 3825 | 7.88 | 0.77 |
| Ordnance, guided missiles | 348, 376, 3795 | 7.50 | 0.75 |
| Electrical industrial apparatus | 362 | 7.30 | 0.74 |
| Industrial inorganic chemicals | 286 | 5.86 | 0.64 |
| Office & computing machinery | 357 | 5.42 | 0.61 |
| Communications & electronic equip. | 366, 367 | 4.49 | 0.52 |
| Electrical lighting, and equipment | 364 | 4.17 | 0.48 |
| Construction machinery | 353 | 4.13 | 0.47 |
| Soaps, cleaning products, etc. | 284 | 4.07 | 0.47 |
| Miscellaneous chemical products | 289 | 3.68 | 0.42 |
| General industrial machinery | 356 | 3.52 | 0.40 |
| Fabricated metal products | 34 ⎱3462 ⎰3463 | 3.48 | 0.39 |
| Industrial organic chemicals | 281 | 2.92 | 0.31 |
| Motor vehicles | 371 | 2.81 | 0.29 |
| Petroleum products | 13, 29 | 2.79 | 0.29 |
| Railroad equipment | 374 | 2.71 | 0.28 |
| Miscellaneous machinery | 359 | 2.67 | 0.27 |
| Refrigeration & service machinery | 358 | 2.51 | 0.25 |
| *Non-significant results* | | | |
| Aircraft | 372 | 2.34 | 0.22 |
| Miscellaneous electrical equipment | 369 | 2.24 | 0.21 |
| Plastic materials | 282 | 2.21 | 0.20 |
| Radio & TV receiving equipment | 365 | 2.20 | 0.23 |
| Electrical household appliances | 363 | 2.16 | 0.20 |
| Rubber products | 30 | 1.82 | 0.15 |
| Farm machinery | 352 | 1.62 | 0.12 |
| Textiles | 22 | 1.59 | 0.12 |
| Misc. transportation equipment | 379–3795 | 1.53 | 0.11 |
| Non-ferrous metal products | 3336, 3398, 3463 | 1.33 | 0.09 |
| Stone, clay, glass products | 32 | 1.32 | 0.08 |
| Ferrous metal products | 331, 332, 3399, 3462 | 1.30 | 0.08 |
| Agricultural chemicals | 287 | 1.08 | 0.06 |
| Food | 20 | 0.99 | 0.05 |
| Motors and bicycles | 375 | 0.61 | 0.02 |
| Paints & allied products | 285 | 0.52 | 0.01 |
| Ship and boat building | 373 | 0.47 | 0.01 |

Source: Soete, [23].                                     [a] Significant at the one per cent level.

that the relative scale of inventive and innovative activities is related to export performance in the capital goods industries for all major industrial countries, not only as the US. These results are, of course, subject to all the usual caveats about the nature of the correlation, the direction of causality and the possibility of both sets of measures being influenced by a third factor, such as quality of management.

What is particularly interesting is that this relationship does not hold for most consumer goods or basic materials. Clearly there are some anomalies. While there is a strong correlation for aero-engines, there is no significant correlation for aircraft as such. The omission of the US is an important factor here; another is the continued high level of German patenting in the 1960s at a time when production and exports of German aircraft were very low. Finally the military security aspects of patenting for such countries as Britain and France are a further complication. Farm machinery is another anomaly and in this case the strongly multinational character of the industry and the patenting policy of the leading Canadian and US firms is the probable explanation. 'Agricultural chemicals' might be expected to be in the first group, but here it must be remembered that, while pesticides and herbicides almost certainly resemble drugs, this group as a whole is dominated by the bulk fertiliser trade. While most sectors of the chemical industry are in the first group, some of the standardised products are in the second.

It could be maintained that firms which have been successful in their exports indulge in patenting activity in the US mainly as a protective measure to secure their position. In this case the direction of causality would be to some extent the reverse of that postulated. The relationship is in any case probably reciprocal, but it would be difficult to deny that for most capital goods and chemicals the capacity to take out US patents is one of the characteristics of successful exporters, and that this is in turn fairly closely related to R and D activity.

## Technological Innovation in Britain

The case of Britain, which today ranks relatively far down the international 'league table' for industrial R and D and is far surpassed in absolute terms by Germany and Japan (Table 3.2) as well as by the US, is complex. In terms of R and D intensity Britain also now ranks well below several smaller European countries such as Sweden and Switzerland, so that currently the picture is consistent with relative trade performance. But in the 1950s and early 1960s Britain ranked much higher in the R and D league table and at that time apparently devoted greater resources in absolute terms to industrial R and D than either Germany or Japan. Allowing for a time lag of two to five years in the application of the results of most industrial R and D, this might have been expected to find some reflection in a better economic and trade performance in the 1950s and 1960s.

Williams [25], in pointing to the paradox of the lack of any clearly observable relationship between R and D investment and economic growth, has even suggested that there might be a problem of 'over-investment' in R and D in Britain. He points out some of the obvious fallacies in any attempt to relate the performance of an economy directly to the level of its investment in R and D: while improved efficiency is certainly related to technical change, formal R and D is by no means the only source of such change. The transfer of technology is often the most important source and this offers the obvious explanation for the fact that many countries in the process of industrialisation may enjoy high productivity growth rates for long periods with much lower investment in R and D than the established industrial countries. Moreover, R and D may be performed with greater or with less efficiency, and it may sometimes be directed to objectives which have little or no relevance to the improvement of economic performance.

It is thus important to examine both the absolute magnitude and the distribution of British R and D activities over time in comparison with our principal industrial competitors. Secondly, it is essential to attempt some assessment of the relative efficiency of these R and D activities and, in general, of the British record in management of technical change. Only in the light of such an analysis is it possible to draw conclusions about this 'British paradox'.

In examining the pattern of British R and D expenditures and comparing them with other industrial countries, two peculiarities stand out: first, the extraordinarily high concentration of British effort in the aircraft industry in comparison with Germany and Japan (Table 3.4); second, the very high proportion of total British R and D which is government-financed and directed to a few areas of high technology – especially military technology, aero-space and military electronics. The counterpart of these peculiarities is the relatively low (and declining) proportion of British expenditure directed to R and D in machinery.

Thus the distribution of British R and D effort in the 1950s and 1960s was radically different from that of Japan, Germany,

Table 3.4   Estimated industrial distribution of R and D expenditure,[a]
1962 (percentages)

| | United Kingdom | France | Germany[b] | Japan[b] | United States |
|---|---|---|---|---|---|
| Aircraft | 35.4 | 27.7 | – | – | 36.3 |
| Vehicles | 3.0 | 2.6 } | 19.2 | { 7.4 | 7.4 |
| Machinery | 7.3 | 6.4 } | | { 5.3 | 8.2 |
| Electrical machinery | 21.7 | 25.7 } | 33.8 | 28.0 | { 21.6 |
| Instruments | 2.3 | .. } | | | { 3.9 |
| Chemicals | 11.6 | 16.8 | 32.9 | 28.3 | 12.6 |
| Steel and metal products | 2.9 } | 3.2 | 6.6 | { 7.0 | 2.0 |
| Non-ferrous metals | 1.2 } | | | { 2.7 | 0.6 |
| Stone, clay, glass | 1.3 | 1.2 | 0.8 | | 1.0 |
| Rubber | 1.2 | | 1.0 | | 1.1 |
| Paper | 0.9 | 5.0 | 0.6 | 17.9 | 0.6 |
| Food and drink | 1.9 | | 0.6 | | 0.9 |
| Other manufacturing | 3.4 | | 1.9 | | 2.0 |
| Transport, energy | 4.4 | 9.0 | 0.6 | ..[c] | .. |
| Other non-manufacturing | 1.6 | 2.4 | 2.0 | ..[c] | 1.9 |

Source: C. Freeman and A. Young, *The Research and Development Effort in Western Europe,
North America and the Soviet Union*, Paris, OECD, 1965.

[a] Analysis by Industry Group, with companies in the industry of their principal
activity. Industrial classifications vary between countries, so this table indicates broad
outlines only.

[b] For 1963.

[c] Excluded from total.

Switzerland, Netherlands, Italy, Belgium and most of our other
European competitors. It did however closely resemble that of the US
and it is therefore particularly interesting to find that the US has now
also been seriously challenged in world export markets by Germany
and Japan in those product groups in which Britain's technical
effort was relatively weak – machinery, metal products and chemicals.

Britain in the 1950s and 1960s was thus in the peculiar position
of putting in an extremely strong innovative effort in a very few
selected industries. In these industries she was performing far more
R and D than any of her European competitors (with the partial
exception of France), both absolutely and relatively. Yet such was the
scale of US investment in these very same industries, that is was
extraordinarily difficult for the UK to emerge successfully from this
competition. Both absolutely and relatively US firms have an

enormous commitment to aircraft, electronic, nuclear, and instrument R and D, buttressed by very heavy supporting military R and D and procurement expenditures by the Federal government. In this extremely unequal competition it is astonishing that British firms had any success at all, particularly as the EEC market offered no advantages to Britain in the 1950s and 1960s. No other country has succeeded in challenging US supremacy in these specialised fields either.

Empirical studies of the aircraft industry and the computer industry, especially the work of Golding [5] and Sciberras [22], have all demonstrated conclusively the colossal economies of scale operating in these industries. Research, development and design costs exceeding £100 million are by no means uncommon for a new generation of products and they have been known to reach £1000 million. If these costs cannot be spread over a fairly high sales volume, they inevitably impose an extraordinarily unfavourable burden and commercial failure is the almost inevitable and predictable outcome, as British (and French) firms have found to their cost time and time again. The *Plowden Report* [1] long ago pointed out this inexorable logic for the UK aircraft industry.

In these circumstances, despite its 'bankruptcy', the performance of Rolls-Royce was and remains highly creditable, and so too was the performance of several British firms in radar and communications equipment. Nevertheless, despite these successes in terms of the overall contribution to export volume, the returns from this heavy British R and D investment were relatively meagre. Furthermore, the opportunity cost of this one-sided effort must also be considered. By and large the more exotic technologies and research-intensive organisations attracted the cream of the industrial scientific and engineering talent in the 1950s. Government laboratories in similar fields, such as Farnborough (aircraft), Malvern (radar) and the Atomic Energy Authority, also took a large share of the brightest engineers, scientists and technicians. The available stock of technical manpower was inadequate in the 1950s and as Peck [16] has argued the opportunity cost of this diversion of talent may have been extremely high. A country like the US, with much greater numbers of engineers and scientists, may have been more able to absorb such extra claims, but Britain clearly could not.

Not only are absolute R and D threshold levels often high and dynamic economies of scale very important, but in addition the risk of failure in particular projects is inevitably present. These problems were exacerbated by some extraordinarily inept public decision-making in relation to 'big' technology throughout the 1950s and 1960s. Concorde is the extreme example of unproductive but huge investment. Commercial and market factors were frequently ignored, and even the most elementary project evaluation procedures were honoured more in the breach than in the observance. It took a long time before any government was prepared to stand up to the expert but special pleading of a high technology lobby in full cry. This applies particularly to aircraft and nuclear reactors, where prototype development and testing can be very expensive. The limited British technical resources were also stretched over too many firms and government organisations. There were at one time as many as five consortia in the nuclear construction industry in an oddly misguided attempt to sustain domestic 'competition'. The consequences of this strange approach have recently been analysed in relation to the advanced gas-cooled reactor by Rush *et al.* [19].

The reverse side of the coin was the deplorable state of many sectors of the mechanical engineering industry, some of which scarcely had any graduate engineers in R and D (or in any other function) before the 1960s. Even today they have relatively few, and perhaps the most disquieting trend of all in British technical effort is the steady decline of R and D in mechanical engineering, after a brief upturn in the 1960s. This means that with scarcely any military or big technology projects German and Japanese firms, even in the 1950s, had more and better engineers and technicians working in such industries as machinery, shipbuilding, and steel and metal products than the UK. Today the disparity is enormous. Both Germany and Japan now take out twice as many patents in the US per annum as Britain. The Japanese rise is relatively recent, but Germany first overtook Britain in this respect before the first world war.

Perhaps the biggest single long-term contrast between British and German industry has been in the number and quality of engineers deployed in all managerial functions in manufacturing. For more than a century engineering was a Cinderella discipline in British universities, and a Cinderella profession in status and attractions in comparison with Germany (and other countries with a similar cultural tradition). The few really good engineers tended to enter the public sector or the national laboratories or a few prestigious private firms. Many engineers had only part-time and a very inferior level of training and qualification, and their contribution to manage-

engineering were prestigous in Germany

ment often reflected this. In Germany in contrast the normal professional route to most senior management positions across a broad range of industry was through six years of full-time intensive engineering education, and professors of engineering would typically have ten or more years of industrial experience. This contrast applies at all levels of the system, from apprentices, through technicians and 'HNC-engineers' to graduate and doctoral level. Despite a series of attempts at reform over the past 30 years, the contrast remains very strong.

The long-standing relative weakness of British technical effort in mechanical engineering, metal products, steel and shipbuilding has been empirically verified both by detailed case studies of particular sectors (Pavitt, [15]) and by statistical studies of trade performance. Perhaps the most telling evidence emerged from Saunders' [20] comparative study of British and German engineering exports, and similar studies by NEDO [12]. These demonstrated that the value–weight ratio of Germany machinery exports was about twice as high as the British in almost every product group, thus confirming conclusively the evidence from case studies that the outstanding German export position (and that of other competitors such as Sweden and Switzerland) was based primarily on quality, design and technical performance.

The peculiar British paradox of the postwar period was thus one of a completely inappropriate allocation of government and industrial R and D resources at a time when the total British R and D effort was temporarily greater than that of any of our major competitors except the US. Whereas the US at least derived substantial trade advantages from its world dominance in military-related technologies, British trade and industrial performance gained little from the heavy UK investment in these areas and may indeed have been weakened by it. Even the considerable British R and D work in military electronics did not provide the basis for exploitation of civil electronic markets to any great extent, although the potential here was and remains enormous.

In product groups which were decisive for world trade in the 1950s and 1960s British technical effort was relatively poor in comparison with Germany and several other countries. Whereas machinery, vehicles, metals and metal products accounted for about half of world exports of manufactures in this period, aircraft exports accounted for only about 4 per cent and nuclear reactors for even less. The quality and number of engineers was woefully inadequate for the needs of British industry in the 1950s, and despite various reforms the quality remains inadequate.

Belatedly, the misallocation of R and D resources began to be recognised in the 1960s, but little has been done to rectify it. The former Chief Scientist of the Department of Industry, Sir Ieuan Maddock, on many occasions emphasised the lop-sided pattern of our R and D expenditures [11], but the structural rigidities in the system seem to be very great. The reasons for this rigidity are on the side of demand as well as supply. It was not just a question of good engineers being in short supply. Many sectors of British industry were also unwilling to employ them and some still are. This was particularly evident in such key sectors as machine tools. Nor was it just a question of under-investment in R and D. Weaknesses in quality and quantity of technical resources were equally apparent and just as important in marketing, production and technical services. Short-term accountancy considerations still frequently dominated management decision-making in British firms, rather than the long-term strategic emphasis on product design and development, process innovation, marketing organisation and technical service so characteristic of much Japanese industrial planning and our more successful European and American competitors. Whereas professional engineering and economic qualifications were the normal requirements for senior management in Germany and Japan, this was far less true in British firms.

As we have seen, in-house R and D is not a major determinant of competitive trade success outside the capital goods industries. In the basic materials industries and in the consumer goods industries it is, however, essential for management to have the capacity to identify relevant process innovations and to deploy adequate production engineering and other technical resources to introduce and exploit process innovations quickly and efficiently. New ideas and new techniques may come from anywhere in the world and it may often be more sensible to import know-how than to re-invent.

Even if much greater technical resources had been allocated to design and development, to research and to process innovation in the British engineering, materials and consumer goods industries, this would not in itself solve some of the more deep-rooted problems, such as the national cultural lag in attitudes to professional engineering. There is good empirical evidence that even when British firms have used precisely the same technology as foreign competitors they have often had substantially lower labour productivity. Ray [18] has shown that in general British firms have not been quick to introduce process innovations by international standards, but even when they were they have still not succeeded in deriving much competitive advantage from this lead. The improvement of UK performance depends both on an improved allocation of resources for invention and innovation and on a much more efficient exploitation of the potential advantages to be derived from technical innovation. The alternative is that increasingly adopted by some sectors of the UK engineering industry and reflected in the low value–weight ratio of our exports – low-wage competition. This, however, may be even less of a 'solution' than trying to maintain technological competition, since there are many third world countries who can beat the UK in that league.

## References

[1] Aviation, Ministry of, *Report of the Committee of Inquiry into the Aircraft Industry* (*Plowden Report*), Cmnd 2853, London, HMSO, 1965.

[2] Curnow, R. C., 'On the association between research and development inputs and shares of international trade' (mimeo.), 1968.

[3] Denison, E. F., *The Sources of Economic Growth in the United States and the Alternatives before Us*, New York, Committee for Economic Development, 1962.

[4] Freeman, C., 'The plastics industry: a comparative study of research and innovation', *National Institute Economic Review*, November 1963.
　　—'Research and development in electronic capital goods', *National Institute Economic Review*, November 1965.
　　—'Chemical process plant: innovation and the world market', *National Institute Economic Review*, August 1968.

[5] Golding, A. M., 'The semi-conductor industry in Britain and the United States' (D.Phil. thesis, Sussex), 1972.

[6] Hirsch, S., *Location of Industry and International Competitiveness*, Oxford, Clarendon Press, 1967.

[7] Hufbauer, G., *Synthetic Materials in International Trade*, Cambridge (Mass.), Harvard University Press, 1966.

[8] Johnson, H. G., *Comparative Cost and Commercial Policy Theory for a Developing World Economy*, Stockholm, Almquist & Wiksell, 1968.

[9] Keesing, B., 'The impact of research and development on United States trade', *Journal of Political Economy*, February 1967.

[10] Leontief, W., 'Domestic production and foreign trade: the American capital position re-examined', *Proceedings of the American Philosophical Society*, September 1953.

[11] Maddock, I., 'End of the glamorous adventure?', *New Scientist*, 13 February 1975.

[12] NEDO, *International Price Competitiveness, Non-price Factors and Export Performance* by D. K. Stout, London, 1977.

[13] OECD, *Gaps in Technology* – Sector Reports and *General Report*, Paris, 1968–9.

[14] OECD, *International Statistical Year for Research and Development* – Reports, Paris, 1967, 1971 and 1974.

[15] Pavitt, K. (ed.), *Technical Innovation and British Economic Performance* (forthcoming).

[16] Peck, J., chapter 10, 'Science and technology' in R. E. Caves (ed.), *Britain's Economic Prospects*, Washington (DC), Brookings Institution, 1968.

[17] Posner, M. V., 'International trade and technical change', *Oxford Economic Papers*, October 1961.

[18] Ray, G. F., 'The diffusion of new technology: a study of ten processes in nine industries', *National Institute Economic Review*, May 1969.

[19] Rush, H. J., McKerron, G. and Surrey, J., 'The advanced gas-cooled reactor: a case study in reactor choice', *Energy Policy*, June 1977.

[20] Saunders, C. T., 'Engineering in three countries' (mimeo.), 1978.

[21] Schmookler, J., *Inventions and Economic Growth*, Cambridge (Mass.), Harvard University Press, 1966.

[22] Sciberras, E., *Multi-national Electronic Companies and National Economic Policies*, New York, JAI Press, 1977.

[23] Soete, L., 'Technical change and international trade performance' (mimeo.), 1978.

[24] Vernon, R., 'International investment and international trade in the product cycle', *Quarterly Journal of Economics*, May 1966.

— (ed.), *The Technology Factor in International Trade*, New York, National Bureau of Economic Research, 1970.

— Gruber, R. and Mehta, D., 'The R and D factor in international trade and international investment of US industries', *Journal of Political Economy*, February 1967.

[25] Williams, B. R., *Technology, Investment and Growth*, London, Chapman Hall, 1967.

— 'Research and economic growth: what should we expect?', *Minerva*, Autumn 1964.

# Comment

## by G. F. Ray

Professor Freeman mentions the 'British paradox' of the lack of relationship between earlier relatively high expenditure on research and economic growth or trade performance. Elsewhere he quotes Hufbauer as saying that 'as a new product technology matured and became internationally established in a range of countries, traditional factor cost elements in comparative advantage could become increasingly important' and thus arriving at the 'low-wage' explanation of trade success.

This introduces yet another 'British paradox'. Already towards the end of the 1960s Britain was a low-wage country (Ray, [7]) and, despite the frequently mentioned wage explosion in the few years prior to the recent wage restraint, the gap between British wages and those in other industrial countries has widened to the extent that, according to recent German estimates, total labour costs in Germany and the Benelux and Scandinavian countries (as well as in North America) are now twice as high as in Britain; elsewhere in Europe and in Japan they are also markedly higher (Table 3.5).

*Table 3.5   International comparison of labour costs[a]*

| Ranking | 1970 | DM | Indices UK = 100 | 1977[b] | DM | Indices UK = 100 |
|---|---|---|---|---|---|---|
| (1) | USA | 15.80 | 270 | Germany | 18.50 | 231 |
| (2) | Sweden | 11.12 | 190 | Belgium | 18.50 | 231 |
| (3) | Germany | 9.42 | 161 | Sweden | 18.00 | 225 |
| (4) | Denmark | 8.75 | 149 | Denmark | 17.50 | 219 |
| (5) | Belgium | 7.84 | 134 | Switzerland | 16.50 | 206 |
| (6) | Switzerland | 7.72 | 132 | USA | 15.50 | 194 |
| (7) | Italy | 6.93 | 118 | Austria | 12.00 | 150 |
| (8) | France | 6.45 | 110 | France | 11.00 | 138 |
| (9) | United Kingdom | 5.86 | *100* | Italy | 11.00 | 138 |
| (10) | Austria | 5.22 | 89 | Japan | 10.00 | 125 |
| (11) | Japan | 3.94 | 67 | United Kingdom | 8.00 | *100* |

Source: Institut der Deutschen Wirtschaft, Cologne.
[a] Total cost of labour involved in production (manufacturing) at current exchange rates.
[b] At exchange rates of December 1977.

British industry has been singularly unable to exploit its labour-cost advantage, probably for many reasons: low productivity offsetting the cost advantage used to be considered first on the list; lack of capacity and entrepreneurship cannot be far behind. The extent of lagging productivity has been assessed by several scholars (for example, Jones, [3]), but many of their studies are restricted to the symptoms without analysing the causes in depth. There cannot be much doubt that slow adoption of technological innovations is one of the causes. Earlier studies at the National Institute (Nabseth and Ray, [4]), including those by Freeman (see his own references), have clearly shown that other countries were quicker than Britain to reach a substantial measure of diffusion of new techniques. Dissemination of international 'best-practice techniques' has been slow in British industry, even in branches where there are quite a few pioneering firms, some of them worldwide technological leaders, whose performance is well above the industry's average.

In the period 1953–76 UK investment amounted, on average, to 17.3 per cent of GNP. Apart from the US this was by far the lowest figure among industrial countries and it relates investment to the slowest growing GNP. In view of the investment requirements of most innovations, this low level of investment may provide a partial explanation for the slow spread of new techniques, but there is also evidence of a relatively low utilisation of new capacity. In other words, the GDP growth achieved in the UK has been considerably less than would have been expected on the basis of actual investment, applying the capital–output ratios of some other countries (OECD, [6]).

The eventual outcome can best be seen in the penetration of imports of all types of products into the UK market, probably manifesting itself most clearly in consumer goods. To take just two examples: the British audio industry, which had been significant, lost most of its markets because it neglected the growth areas of the tape-recorder, the cartridge and the cassette; in the past five years about 10,000 jobs have been lost in the television industry through lack of R and D (or the adoption of progress resulting from R and D elsewhere) and other factors depressing competitiveness (Baker [2]). Digital watches and hand-held calculators are other examples, but the best illustration can be found in the pathetic record of the UK motorcycle industry, which totally failed to recognise consumer needs; its market was first flooded with Italian scooters and mopeds and later by Japanese models which offered better performance at very competitive prices. The outcome is the virtual disappearance of the British industry.

The narrowness of the industrial base – reflecting, among other things, lack of entrepreneurship – is of course affecting areas and products which have little to do with innovations. For example, it was already known by about 1964 that thousands of miles of large-diameter pipe would be needed for the nationwide natural gas network (apart from oil developments which became common knowledge only later), but no capacity was built to manufacture such pipes; they have all been imported.

Another point which is likely to be relevant to unsatisfactory performance is the relative scarcity of small firms in the UK.

In his report to the Bolton Committee (Department of Trade and Industry, [9]) Freeman estimated the contribution of small British firms to postwar innovations at about 10 per cent – markedly more than their share in total spending on R and D. His findings, besides the well-known American example concerning the contribution to innovation of the small firms along 'Route 128' in Massachusetts and also in California, indicate the importance of small firms from this particular angle.

The number of small plants or firms in Britain is much smaller than in most industrial countries of comparable size. Preliminary studies at the National Institute indicate that, in Germany, for example, they may be as much as five times as frequent as in Britain. Thus, the scope for innovations coming from the 'small sector' is limited *a priori* by the size of that sector – but there are other restraining factors as well. The NRDC, an obvious source of support for small or new technology-based firms, finds itself 'more limited by opportunity than by resources' and argues that there are serious gaps in the provision of financial support for technological innovation in Britain, that the mortality rate of small companies is high and that there is a general lack of encouragement for new technology-based firms (NRDC, [5]).

*Table 3.6   Proportion of qualified engineers and scientists in the total workforce of the metal-working industries, 1974 (percentages)*

| | |
|---|---|
| Sweden | 6.6 |
| West Germany | 5.7[a] |
| France | 5.3 |
| United Kingdom | 1.8 |

Source: Engineering Employers Federation, *Graduates in Engineering*, London, 1977.
[a] 'Ingenieurschulen' graduates and holders of THS diplomas in the ratio 4:1.

Finally, whilst Freeman's international comparisons use R and D expenditure as a yardstick, a similar comparison based on qualified manpower points more sharply to the backwardness of British industry (Table 3.6). This is not a new phenomenon – its roots go back a long way in history (Albu, [1]) – but its consequences are especially obvious in the context of innovations.

Much less is known, however, in the under-researched area of general education – the vocational education and training of the 'unqualified' labour force as a whole. The educational standard on the shopfloor may be just as important as, or more important than, the quantity and quality of the élite. Secondary education is of obvious importance from this point of view; unfortunately, Britain has 'one of the lowest participation rates in full-time education of those aged between 16 and 18 of any country in western Europe, comparable only to the rates in Portugal and the Republic of Ireland' (*The Times*, [8]). As Albu writes, 'there is considerable evidence that a great part of our industrial labour force, in spite of the Industrial Training Act, is still worse educated and trained than that of our main competitors. Only well trained technicians, craftsmen and operators can get the best out of sophisticated equipment. A competitive technically advanced industry is only as strong as the pyramid of skills which supports it.'

## References

[1] Albu, A., 'British attitudes to engineering education: a historical perspective' (mimeo.), 1978.

[2] Baker, K., 'A trade unionist's view' in Society of Business Economists, *The Re-industrialisation of Britain*, London, 1978.

[3] Jones, D. T., 'Output, employment and labour productivity in Europe since 1955', *National Institute Economic Review*, August 1976.

[4] Nabseth, L. and Ray, G. F. (eds), *The Diffusion of New Industrial Processes*, Cambridge University Press, 1974.

[5] NRDC, 'Evidence to the Committee to Review the Functioning of Financial Institutions', London, 1978.

[6] OECD, *The Growth of Output 1960–1980*, Paris, 1970.

[7] Ray, G. F., 'Labour costs and international competitiveness', *National Institute Economic Review*, August 1972.

— 'Labour costs in OECD countries, 1964–1975', *National Institute Economic Review*, November 1976.

[8] *The Times*, 13 May 1978, Statement by the Secretary for Education in 'Government plans grants for pupils of 16 to 18'.

[9] Trade and Industry, Department of, Bolton Committee, *Research Report No. 6: The Role of Small Firms in Innovation in the UK since 1945* by C. Freeman, London, HMSO, 1971.

# 4 Foreign Manufacturing by UK Firms

## by Ann D. Morgan*

## Introduction

The object of this paper is to answer two questions: first, do large British firms manufacture abroad to a greater extent than German or Japanese firms? Secondly, if they do, does this have unfortunate consequences for the balance of payments and for employment in the United Kingdom? International comparisons of this kind are notoriously difficult. None the less, it is clear that the answer to the first question is yes, British firms do manufacture abroad more than German firms and much more than Japanese. A survey of the available evidence on foreign direct investment and on the overseas manufacturing activities of large firms provides ample support for this view, but it also suggests that there are a number of special features in the British situation which should be taken into account and, further, that the pattern of investment by large British and German firms may be tending to converge.

## The Available Evidence

Tables 4.1 to 4.3 summarise the salient features of the estimated stock of British, German and Japanese foreign direct investment in manufacturing in 1971; US figures are included for comparison. The sources and methods used in making these estimates are briefly described in an Appendix to this paper, but a word should be said here about their quality: it is regrettably poor. Absolute values are not comparable from country to country, and even the British and American figures, which both refer to book values, are not directly

*I am grateful to R. D. Pearce of Reading University for supplying the data for the sample of British and German firms on which the alternative estimate of comparative overseas production on page 82 is based.

*Table 4.1    Estimated stock of foreign direct investment, 1971[a]*
*($ millions)*

|  | United Kingdom (book values) | Germany (transactions) | Japan (approvals) | United States (book values) |
|---|---|---|---|---|
| **All sectors:** |  |  |  |  |
| Developed countries | 12,526[b] | 4,430 | 2,317 | 58,571 |
| Developing countries | 4,844[b] | 1,713 | 2,118 | 23,358 |
| *Total* | 24,207 | 6,143 | 4,435 | 86,198[c] |
| **Manufacturing:** |  |  |  |  |
| Developed countries | 8,260 | 3,318 | 184 | 29,633 |
| Developing countries | 1,991 | 1,284 | 783 | 5,999 |
| *Total* | 10,251 | 4,602 | 967 | 35,632 |

Sources: see Appendix.
[a] End-year figures, except Japan end-March 1972.
[b] Excludes oil, banking and insurance, in which total investments were valued at $6840 million. No breakdown by areas is available.
[c] Includes $4270 million 'international, unallocated'.

*Table 4.2    Distribution of foreign investment in manufacturing by main regions and countries, 1971 (percentages)*

|  | United Kingdom (book values) | Germany (trans-actions)[a] | Japan (approvals)[b] | United States (book values) |
|---|---|---|---|---|
| **Developed countries** |  |  |  |  |
| North America | 25 | 17 | 6 | 30 |
| (of which US) | (16) | (9) | (..) | (−) |
| Europe | 20 | 52 | 5[c] | 44[c] |
| (of which EEC-6) | (18) | (31) | (..) | (24) |
| Australia, New Zealand, |  |  |  |  |
| South Africa | 33 | 2 | 6 | 7 |
| *Total* | 81 | 72 | 17 | 83 |
| **Developing countries** |  |  |  |  |
| Asia | .. | 3 | 43 | 2 |
| Latin America | 5 | 15 | 37 | 14 |
| *Total* | 19 | 28 | 83 | 17 |

Sources: see Appendix.
[a] Percentages refer to geographical distribution of all foreign investment.
[b] End-March 1971.
[c] Includes developing countries in Europe.

Table 4.3   Distribution of foreign investment in manufacturing by industry, 1971 (percentages)

| | United Kingdom (book values) | Germany (transactions) | Japan (approvals) | United States (sales) |
|---|---|---|---|---|
| Chemicals | 17.4 | 30.8 | 6.8 | 16.5 |
| Metals | 3.6 | 8.1 | 19.2 | 7.4 |
| Mechanical engineering | 6.7 | 9.6 | 9.5 | 15.7 |
| Electrical engineering | 12.7 | 15.5 | 10.2 | 10.0 |
| Motor vehicles and other transport equipment | 2.4 | 12.2 | 12.2 | 22.4 |
| Other | 57.2 | 23.8 | 42.1 | 28.0 |
| (of which food, drink and tobacco) | (28.1) | (3.8) | (7.1) | .. |
| (of which textiles, etc.) | (7.6) | (2.6) | (26.4) | .. |
| Total manufacturing | 100.0 | 100.0 | 100.0 | 100.0 |

Sources: see Appendix.

comparable because of differences in coverage and in the timing and method of valuation. The German figures relate to cumulative transaction values and exclude, notably, investments financed by undistributed profits. It has been estimated that in 1969 the total was understated in consequence by 25 per cent (Krägenau, [7]). German estimates may be further biased downwards since they do not allow for the revaluation of existing assets. On the other hand, the estimates for manufacturing quoted in the tables refer to all investment overseas by manufacturing enterprises, including expenditure on distribution facilities and the like, thus involving an overstatement of the total invested in manufacturing of, probably, around 20 per cent. The Japanese figures are based on approvals, not realised investments, and so considerably overstate the value of existing assets. There are also differences in the geographical and industrial classification of investments. However, even after making every allowance for the imperfections of the data, it is clear that at the beginning of the 1970s the state of foreign investment differed radically between the three countries, and also between them and the US – a warning not to argue without qualification from American experience to British, German or Japanese practice.

The British stake in foreign manufacturing facilities was between two and three times as large as the German, and many times larger than the Japanese. British and German investments, like American, were concentrated in developed areas, Japanese in the developing countries. However, a very high proportion of Britain's overseas manufacturing assets were to be found in Canada, Australia, New Zealand and South Africa – the developed Commonwealth countries – which accounted for over 40 per cent of the total British stock, whereas German investments were concentrated in Europe, more especially in the EEC and neighbouring countries. Data on the manufacturing subsidiaries of large firms – those appearing in the *Fortune* list of the 200 largest non-US industrial corporations (including oil and mining companies) in 1970 and some others – collected by Vaupel and Curhan [10] broadly confirm this pattern. The only significant difference between subsidiary numbers and asset data is in the proportion of British and German firms' activities in North America, which is higher for assets than for numbers, probably because of the above-average size of subsidiaries located in the US.

The difference between Britain and Germany in the industrial distribution of their investment stock (Table 4.3) was also striking. German investment is concentrated in chemicals and in the engineering and motor vehicle industries, that is tending towards the American pattern of investment in sophisticated high-technology industries. British investments were predominantly in more traditional industries. Further illustration of this point is provided by the Vaupel and Curhan data. Over 80 per cent of the number of German subsidiaries listed (excluding oil firms) were in chemicals, engineering and vehicles, but fewer than half of the British subsidiaries. Furthermore, 70 per cent of German subsidiaries covered were owned by firms whose expenditure on R and D exceeded 4 per cent of the value of sales. For subsidiaries of British firms the comparable proportion was only 26 per cent, a difference that can hardly be due solely to a lower propensity on the part of British firms in general to invest in R and D. The most exceptional feature of the British pattern was the very large foreign stake in the food, drink and tobacco industry, which accounted for over a quarter of estimated foreign assets in manufacturing. Hence, despite the difference in the value of total foreign assets in manufacturing, it appears that the British stake in the newer high-technology industries, though larger than the German, was not perhaps so very much larger; indeed in the motor vehicle industry it was probably much smaller. As for Japan, its investments too were concentrated in traditional industries, notably textiles and metal manufacturing.

There is one other curious feature of British overseas investment, that is the apparent tendency of medium-sized firms to invest overseas much more than do their peers in other industrial countries apart from Japan, which has its own peculiarities. The Vaupel and Curhan data show that German parent firms with sales in excess of $2 billion in 1970 had almost as many manufacturing subsidiaries as British firms with comparable sales, but below that level the number of German subsidiaries fell dramatically to only about 15 per cent of the British figure. Of German subsidiaries covered, 66 per cent belonged to the very largest firms, but only 23 per cent of the British. Thus, even within the firms big enough to make the *Fortune* list, the connection between size and direct foreign investment was far more pronounced in Germany than in the United Kingdom. Unfortunately there is no information directly available on the overseas assets of medium-sized German and British firms. However, it is indicative of the difference between them that for a sample of large British and German firms drawn from the *Fortune* list of the 300 largest non-US enterprises in 1972 whose total sales were approximately equal in value, overseas production by the British firms was only one and a half times as large as by the German firms – not two to three times as large as implied by the asset data. The inference is that a larger proportion of British than of German firms falling outside the *Fortune* list have overseas manufacturing assets.

The origins of the differences between British, German and Japanese foreign direct investment are matters of history, but clearly suggest that many of the more striking features of the British position were the consequence of first the creation and then the disintegration of the Commonwealth trading system. British firms trading with the Commonwealth tended to establish local manufacturing facilities there when tariffs and other forms of protection were raised against them. This was a major motive not only before the last war but also after it, both in the older Dominions and in the newly-independent Commonwealth countries. Once established those facilities were maintained largely out of reinvested profits. This accounts for a high, though diminishing, proportion of what is recorded as direct foreign investment in the balance of payments. There is no comparable investment flow for Germany, still less for Japan. German firms followed a similar policy between the wars, but the assets thus created were confiscated by the allies (Franko,

[5]). However, there is a curious parallel here with the behaviour of Japanese investors in the 1960s. A high proportion of the Japanese enterprises established then were in industries requiring little technical skill and were established by small or smallish firms to protect markets in developing countries in South East Asia whence they might otherwise have been wholly excluded as local industries developed. This was a purely defensive strategy which is changing rapidly under the pressure of events (Yoshiro, [11]). British investors in the Commonwealth were able to play the same game, but for very much longer.

*Table 4.4    Net foreign direct investment overseas on a balance-of-payments basis, 1971–6*

|  | 1971 | 1972 | 1973 | 1974 | 1975 | 1976 |
|---|---|---|---|---|---|---|
|  | ($ million) | | | | | |
| **United Kingdom** | | | | | | |
|  Total | 1984 | 1996 | 5250 | 4454 | 2964 | 4514 |
|  Manufacturing | 934 | 881 | 2048 | 1930 | 1370 | 2184 |
| **Germany** | | | | | | |
|  Total | 1048 | 1564 | 1654 | 1915 | 2008 | 2452 |
|  Manufacturing | 661 | 627 | 994 | 1203 | 1175 | 1577 |
| **Japan** | | | | | | |
|  Total | 360 | 723 | 1904 | 2012 | 1763 | 1991 |
|  Manufacturing | 106 | 152 | 783 | 686 | 504 | 657 |
| Retained profits/total | (percentages) | | | | | |
|  United Kingdom | 48.7 | 63.1 | 51.8 | 54.0 | 79.8 | 66.4 |
|  Germany | 24.1 | 18.7 | 19.2 | 23.4 | 22.5 | 21.1 |

Sources: see Appendix.
*Note*: All figures include retained profits of overseas enterprises.

The 1970s have seen an increase in the recorded flow of direct investment from all three countries (Table 4.4). British investment rose very sharply in 1973, in part because of very large investment by the food, drink and tobacco industries in the US and Germany, but fell back subsequently. Measured at constant dollar prices, net investment in overseas manufacturing assets in 1975 was considerably lower than in 1971, though in 1976 it probably rose again above that level. German investment has risen more steadily and more steeply, to over 50 per cent above the 1971 level in constant dollar terms by 1975 and higher still in 1976, when the estimated outflow was approaching the UK figure. (The margin of error in these estimates is very large, but the trend is unmistakable.) The biggest proportionate increase came in Japanese investment (partly because controls were relaxed), but it still remains in absolute terms far below the British or German level.

British foreign investment, however, involves far less transfer of capital from one country to another than does German or Japanese. A very high proportion of UK investment is financed by retained profits (Table 4.4). Because of exchange controls, most of the balance has been financed by funds borrowed abroad. Indeed, according to the latest Balance of Payments 'Pink Book', reinvested earnings plus foreign borrowing have latterly been larger than net foreign investment (excluding oil company transactions), so that far from foreign direct investment entailing the export of capital it is estimated

*Table 4.5   Industry and area distribution of net foreign investment 1972–5 cumulative (percentages)*

|  | United Kingdom | Germany | Japan |
|---|---|---|---|
| *Areas*[a] | | | |
| North America | 32.4 | .. | 31.7 |
| (of which US) | (24.7) | (10.6) | (29.1) |
| Western Europe | 30.4 | 40.8 | 21.5 |
| (of which EEC-6) | (21.8) | (26.9) | (5.4) |
| Other developed | 22.9 | 25.7[b] | 3.2 |
| Other | 14.3 | 22.9 | 43.6 |
| | | | |
| *Industries*[c] | | | |
| Chemicals | 22.5 | 24.3 | 21.3 |
| Metals | 2.1 | 16.9 | 16.4 |
| Mechanical engineering | 8.3 | 15.1 | 8.6 |
| Electrical engineering | 10.8 | 16.0 | 11.4 |
| Transport equipment | 2.1 | 5.4 | 7.0 |
| Other | 54.3[d] | 22.3 | 35.4 |

Sources: see Appendix.
[a] UK figures for manufacturing only; Germany and Japan total foreign investment.
[b] Including Canada.
[c] German percentages are based on cumulative transaction values and Japanese on cumulative approvals for 1972 to 1976 inclusive.
[d] Of which food, drink and tobacco 31.7.

to have made a net addition to the reserves (CSO, [3]). German profits reinvested are less than a quarter of the total investment flow.

Table 4.5 shows the estimated distribution by area and industry of foreign investment during the period 1972–5. The geographical pattern of German investment shows little change, but in Britain the tendency, dating from the 1960s, to invest more in Europe and the US and less in the old Commonwealth has strengthened, while the Japanese have drastically reduced the proportion of their investment going to the developing countries. Thus, there has been a slight convergence of the location of overseas investment from the three countries. Changes in the industrial pattern of investment by UK firms are less striking, although a slightly higher proportion has recently been invested in the newer industries, principally because of a rising share for chemicals and allied industries. Additional German investment has been directed more to metals and mechanical engineering, less to chemicals and motor vehicles, but it still remains heavily concentrated in the newer industries. The Japanese investment pattern has been transformed.

*Table 4.6*   *Relationships between foreign investment in manufacturing[a] and domestic activity (percentages)*

|  | 1971 | 1972 | 1973 | 1974 | 1975 | 1976 |
|---|---|---|---|---|---|---|
| Ratio to GNP at factor cost |  |  |  |  |  |  |
| United Kingdom | 0.77 | 0.63 | 1.29 | 1.10 | 0.66 | 1.10 |
| Germany | 0.34 | 0.27 | 0.32 | 0.38 | 0.31 | 0.39 |
| Japan | 0.04 | 0.05 | 0.20 | 0.16 | 0.11 | 0.12 |
| Ratio to GDFCF |  |  |  |  |  |  |
| United Kingdom | 3.65 | 3.03 | 5.91 | 4.87 | 2.99 | 5.16 |
| Germany | 1.13 | 0.92 | 1.18 | 1.44 | 1.35 | 1.71 |
| Japan | 0.12 | 0.15 | 0.54 | 0.46 | 0.34 | 0.39 |
| Ratio to GDFCF in manufacturing |  |  |  |  |  |  |
| United Kingdom | 17.55 | 17.23 | 36.53 | 26.19 | 17.82 | 30.55 |
| Germany | .. | .. | .. | .. | .. | .. |
| Japan | 0.53 | 0.79 | 2.79 | .. | .. | .. |

Sources: see Appendix.
[a] Foreign direct investment in manufacturing on a balance-of-payments basis.

Although German foreign direct investment is catching up on British in absolute terms, it still remains very much less important in relation to domestic activity, while Japanese foreign investment is relatively trivial. Table 4.6 shows estimated annual investment in recent years as a proportion of GNP, of domestic fixed capital formation and (where possible) of domestic investment in manufacturing. For the UK this last figure is very high – never less than 17 per cent and rising in 1973 to over 36 per cent. Unfortunately, comparable figures are not available for Germany, but on a reasonable estimate for the proportion of domestic capital formation going to manufacturing, foreign investment was equivalent to 5.0–7.5 per cent at the beginning of the 1970s, rising more recently to between 9 and 12 per cent. Once again, the available evidence suggests that the gap between Germany and the UK is narrowing fast.

Data on the relative size of overseas production by British, German and Japanese firms are available only for a sample of large firms in the early 1970s. Buckley and Pearce [1] analysed by country and industry the performance in 1972 of 156 of the world's largest industrial companies for which were able to obtain figures of group sales, overseas production and exports. Inevitably the sample was dominated by American firms, of which 75 were included; there were 28 British, 11 German and 17 Japanese. The authors calculated a number of performance ratios, of which the most interesting for present purposes are shown in Table 4.7.

*Table 4.7    Overseas production and export ratios in a sample of large firms, 1972 (percentages)*

|  | United Kingdom | Germany | Japan | All firms (inc. US) |
|---|---|---|---|---|
| Overseas production/group sales | 34.7 | 28.8 | 2.4 | 35.6 |
| Parent exports/parent production | 30.5 | 39.3 | 17.4 | 19.1 |
| Overseas production/overseas production *plus* parent exports | 63.5 | 50.7 | 12.4 | 74.4 |

Source: Buckley and Pearce [1].
*Note:* see text for composition of the sample.

It is possible that the overseas production ratios for British firms are biased by differences between the importance of overseas production in different industries. The firms covered included oil companies, which by their nature are heavily engaged in overseas production, while a number of other industries where British investment is large (including food, drink and tobacco) are also more than usually involved in overseas production. However, it is most unlikely that allowance for these factors would affect the ranking of the three countries. The overseas production ratio calculated from a larger sample of firms, excluding the oil companies, was 29.1 per cent (59 firms) for the United Kingdom, 19.5 per cent (42 firms) for Germany and 3.9 per cent (73 firms) for Japan – this last figure involving much estimation. For firms in the same industry (excluding diversified firms), the UK and German ratios were for chemicals 33 and 45 per cent, for mechanical engineering 29 and 9 per cent, for electrical engineering 24 and 15 per cent and for motor vehicles 15 and 12 per cent. Thus it is unlikely that the industry pattern of the smaller sample used by Buckley and Pearce distorted their results, though it does appear to have yielded inflated indicators of the degree of reliance on overseas production by both British and German firms.

In three out of four major industries then, and also of course in traditional industries such as food and textiles, British firms in the early 1970s were more heavily engaged in overseas production than were German firms and on average they supplied a higher proportion of foreign markets by local production rather than exports. Judging from the growth of foreign direct investment, the gap between the two groups has narrowed since then but has not disappeared.

## The Consequences

We now turn to the question of whether this greater involvement of British firms in overseas enterprises has unfortunate consequences for the balance of payments and employment in the United Kingdom. One line of approach to such questions derives from the older theory of the effect of international capital movements, appropriately modified but still assuming an unrestricted world economy with full employment, unchanging technology and knowledge of all kinds freely available to all investors. This is not the world we live in and, moreover, the model ignores the essence of direct investment. It is not a matter of whether to invest a finite sum and nothing else in A or B. It involves a combination of ownership, or at least control, technology and skill; to put them together involves organisation. Foreign direct investment is a package deal and the package, as we have seen, does not necessarily involve the export of capital.

A more realistic approach was adopted by Hufbauer and Adler (US Treasury, [9]) and Reddaway [8] on the balance-of-payments effects of American and British foreign direct investment.

The elements taken into account (apart from the initial capital flow) were associated exports of capital goods; associated exports to the overseas subsidiary; profits and fees for services. The American report also included secondary trade effects, which are all positive for the home (investing) country, and export-displacing effects, which are negative. It turns out that the latter are crucial. If it is assumed that the output of the foreign plant could instead have been supplied as exports by the home plant, then the balance-of-payments effects are unfavourable. If, however, exports from the home plant were going to be displaced by production in the host country in any case, then there is a gain to the balance of payments of the investing country as a result of making the investment. For employment, too, the question of export displacement is crucial, since if foreign production is substituted for exports domestic production will be reduced, but if exports were going to be displaced anyway, then the associated exports generated by the overseas operation will increase production and employment at home. Both reports concluded that foreign investment had, in practice, a beneficial effect on the balance of payments of the investing country.

This approach does not, however, distinguish overseas operations that are straightforward export-substituting or import-replacing ventures from those which might be described as making the best of a bad job, and it is in any case too limited. There are other motives for foreign investment in manufacturing. These have been explored in a number of empirical studies (see, for example, Horst, [6]; Caves, [2]) and surveys of firms (Dunning, [4]) designed to elicit them. The results are not conclusive and, unavoidably but unfortunately, fail to distinguish between different motives and hence different effects. It seems desirable therefore to list and consider separately the possible kinds of foreign direct investment in manufacturing and their relevance to the British position.

There are very many possible motives for foreign direct investment in manufacturing, but only seven are of real significance in the present context. The first four are, at least in principle, quite distinct:

(1)  to obtain captive supplies;
(2)  to secure access to knowledge;
(3)  to provide a physical base for serving a market;
(4)  to avoid being wholly excluded from a given market by government action.

The remaining three are more difficult to distinguish because they are so often found in association and to some extent they overlap:

(5) to exploit firm-specific knowledge;

(6) to keep up with the competition;

(7) to obtain higher returns from association with other factors of production, characteristically labour, that are cheaper abroad than at home.

The first motive is generally discussed only in connection with primary production, but in fact it operates in some sectors of what is classed as manufacturing. A significant part of British overseas investment in the manufacture of food, drink and tobacco, of non-ferrous metals and of paper, for example, is of this kind. The alternative to such investment – dependence on supplies bought in the open market – involves greater risk to the firm in the home country.

The alternatives to investment intended to secure access to knowledge are to go without, or to purchase it in some other fashion at greater cost. In terms of the investment involved it is probably not important, but it is mentioned for the sake of completeness.

The third category, providing a physical base for serving a market, is so obvious that it would hardly seem worth mentioning were it not so often forgotten. Here the typical overseas operation is a plant assembling parts and components imported from the home country, but classed as manufacturing just as much as any plant where the raw materials go in at one end and the finished product emerges at the other. In this case overseas 'manufacturing' is a necessary condition for exporting to a large foreign market. The mind boggles at the thought of international trade conducted exclusively in goods fully finished and packaged for the sale to the final consumer. Just how important such assembly-type operations are in the context of overseas manufacturing is unknown, but they probably account for a sizeable proportion of the assets involved.

The case of defence against exclusion from a market generally involves some kind of industrial promotion programme by the host country, coupled with tariff protection or even an outright ban on imports. There is a great deal of such investment around: American enterprises in Canada; British firms in the old Commonwealth; American, Swiss and (in the 1960s) British investment in the EEC; a high proportion of all foreign investment in the developing countries. The alternative for any firm abstaining from such a venture is that someone else invests – whether another firm foreign to the host country or a local entrepreneur does not matter – so that it loses not only the market for the particular product, but also any market it might be able to supply with intermediates and the associated exports, whether of the same product of a higher quality or of other goods in its product range. By investment it can maintain a larger flow of exports from its domestic operations, at least for some time and possibly for many years to come than it would otherwise, which thus benefits domestic employment and the balance of payments. In the long run the association between the overseas operation and domestic exports is likely to weaken, but the parent firm and the home country are still left with a useful source of foreign income. (The host country, of course, may view the matter rather differently.) This in fact appears to be the nature of a very large part of the stock of British foreign investment in overseas manufacturing facilities, particularly, of course, in the Commonwealth. There seems to be only one possible source of damage to the home country from investment of this type – that scarce managerial skills will be unduly preoccupied with developing existing local markets for overseas plants rather than new export markets for domestic plants. That, however, is a problem associated with all foreign investment, and is more appropriately dealt with later.

The definition of the next category of foreign direct investment, (that associated with firm-specific knowledge), derives from the product-cycle theory of trade. Because of its importance in American overseas operations (and because so much professional economists' ink has been lavished on it on both sides of the Atlantic) it has come to be considered *the* characteristic pattern of multinational enterprise investment. It is typically regarded as being undertaken by firms in industries distinguished either by a high degree of R and D, or by product differentiation (or of course both) which cannot exploit their knowledge capital fully by exports or by licensing. For example, it may not be possible to exploit the market at a distance because of the physical nature of the product, or by licensing because of problems of quality control. A pure export operation involving a sophisticated product may require to be associated with overseas production of simpler, more standardised versions in order to build up customer loyalty and obtain reliable information about the market. It has been observed that many American, and indeed other, firms with overseas production facilities tend to supply the simpler, more standardised range of their output from such facilities and to export the newer products from their home base. In their judgement the export operation is not viable without the overseas production operation.

Again it turns out that it is not a case of either home production or foreign production, but of both or neither. The home country benefits by higher exports and employment and, of course, by securing the rent from the firm-specific knowledge involved. The gains from this kind of overseas production should be more lasting than in the purely defensive case, provided the investing firm maintains a flow of new products and processes, since the firm creates an effective framework for a continuous development of new ideas at home, with its associated export flow and a continued shifting of other production overseas to secure rent. Without a case by case study it is impossible to determine how much direct foreign investment in manufacturing falls into this category, but at a guess it applies strictly to a range of chemical and engineering products sold by industry to industry. UK activity in this category appears to be undesirably limited, judging by the industrial distribution of foreign investment.

Industries producing differentiated consumer goods are another matter. There does not seem to be any justification, in terms of benefits to the home country, for their overseas operations on grounds of exploiting firm-specific knowledge; if this were the only or the true motive for overseas production of differentiated products it might legitimately be claimed that overseas production has 'unfortunate consequences' for domestic employment and the balance of payments. But of course it is not.

The main motive is 'to keep up with the competition'. In oligopolistic industries, a firm must match the actions of its competitors if it is to stay in business, and it does so. It has been demonstrated from US and Japanese evidence that the timing of overseas investment projects is influenced by the action of competitors and that there is bunching by industries and markets (which is not, incidentally, confined to investment in the developed countries). If there are half a dozen or a dozen major firms in an industry worldwide and all but one of these firms produce in overseas markets, then the firm that does not produce there is likely to be at a disadvantage. It will know less about the market; it will be in less close contact with its customers and less able to adapt to changing tastes and fashions; it will be slower to counter moves by its competitors. This weakness will feed back to the home base. It is by no means impossible that the end-result will be the disappearance of the exclusively home-based firm and of the industry in question from its home country.

But what about the Japanese? Since the war they have established themselves in oligopolistic industries and have built up a large export trade without recourse to overseas production. The answer to that is twofold: first, the Japanese built up these industries on the basis of a large, rapidly growing and rigorously protected domestic market; they developed their export trade by exploiting scale economies in a way that competitors could not (or would not) match, and all this was made possible because their currency was until recently very much undervalued. Second, now that the yen is undervalued no longer, Japanese enterprises are rapidly expanding their overseas production facilities.

Oligopolistic concerns invest in each others' home markets for the same reasons that they invest in third countries, so that the net effect on a country's exports and employment depends partly on the balance of inward and outward investment, partly on the effect of outward investment propping up (so to speak) the home base. In the end it may have no 'unfortunate effects' on foreign payments and employment (except of course for the country without any sizeable firms in oligopolistic industries). Even so the whole business is undesirable, but this is not a 'foreign investment' problem; it is a problem of the existence of worldwide oligopolies and requires a worldwide solution. Until then the country that does not have overseas enterprises is the loser. Britain is hardly a loser, but its position in this category again appears to be weak, except in food, drink and tobacco, not only relative to the US but also possibly to the Germans.

Finally there is the type of foreign investment which is undertaken because domestic production costs have become too high. An overvalued exchange rate entails domestic costs generally too high for competition and may promote foreign rather than domestic investment. Some British investment overseas in the 1960s may have been induced by the overvaluation of sterling (certainly some American investment was due to overvaluation of the dollar). Again, however, this is not a 'foreign investment' problem but a symptom of something wrong in the economy at large.

The emigration of specific labour-intensive industries is another matter and does involve loss of employment in the industries concerned as well as not so much smaller exports – they will be in decline already – but higher imports. This kind of foreign investment follows shifts between countries in comparative advantage, and that is a tide it is foolish to swim against. Such industries can only be kept at home by restrictions and protection that may help the industry itself but are a burden on the rest of the community. Short-term protection may be desirable, but in the long run it is less painful to redeploy domestic resources into other industries or to upgrade domestic output, meanwhile exporting activities that are no longer viable and, if possible, developing the kind of pattern already described that is geared to the product cycle and will preserve some kind of efficient domestic operation. Whether or not such foreign investment in search of cheaper labour or other factors of production is deemed harmful depends not on the investment itself but on the entire reaction of the firm to changing world circumstances.

It is, perhaps, particularly true in this case that the preoccupation of scarce managerial talent with overseas enterprises could be damaging to the development of industry at home, though it is one that could arise in connection with any kind of foreign investment. The difficulty is not, however, the distraction but the scarcity of managerial talent. In any case, it appears that in practice this is a problem that does not arise. Those firms with extensive overseas operations are also those firms that are most expansive and most export-minded, in Britain and in other countries.

I conclude, therefore, that there is no reason to believe that the overseas manufacturing activities of British firms have unfortunate effects on the balance of payments or on employment – rather the reverse. They may sometimes appear in association with such effects, but the trouble stems from the conditions that give rise to the investment, not the investment itself. The social and political consequences of foreign direct investment may be another matter. That, however, is largely a problem for host countries and outside the scope of this paper.

*Appendix: sources for Tables 4.1–4.6*

United Kingdom: book values – *Business Monitor M4: Overseas Transactions 1972*, Part II: Census of overseas assets at end-1971; foreign investment flows – *United Kingdom Balance of Payments 1966–76* and *Trade and Industry*, 9 June 1978; GNP and domestic investment – *National Income and Expenditure 1976*. The distribution of certain manufacturing assets between host countries in 1971 and net foreign investment in manufacturing in 1976 were estimated from data for all assets and investment. Asset figures were converted to dollars using IFS end-year rates; all other figures were converted at annual average rates.

Germany: transaction values – data collected by the Bundesministerium für Wirtschaft; foreign investment flows, GNP and domestic investment – Monthly Reports of the Deutsche Bundesbank, except retained profits from IMF, *Balance of Payments Yearbook*, Vol. 28. Transaction values of investment in manufacturing up to 1970 were estimated from incomplete data for major industries and for 1971–5 from data for major industries and for all industry (including mining, etc.); actual figures were available for 1976. The proportion of foreign direct investment on a balance-of-payments basis going to manufacturing was estimated by reference to the proportion of manufacturing to all transaction values in each year. Transaction values and foreign investment were both converted at IFS annual average rates.

Japan: approvals – data collected by the Ministry of Finance; foreign investment flows – Bank of Japan, *Balance of Payments Monthly*; GNP and domestic investment – OECD. The proportion of foreign investment in manufacturing in each calendar year was estimated by reference to the proportion of manufacturing to all investment approvals in the preceding financial year, for example, 1970–1 for 1971. Original data were in dollars.

United States: all data – *Survey of Current Business*.

*References*

[1] Buckley, P. J. and Pearce, R. D., 'Overseas production and exporting by the world's largest enterprises – a study in sourcing policy' (University of Reading Discussion Paper), 1977.

[2] Caves, R. E., 'The causes of direct investment: foreign firms' shares in Canadian and UK manufacturing industries' (Harvard Institute of Economic Research Discussion Paper), 1973.

[3] CSO, *United Kingdom Balance of Payments 1966–76*, London, HMSO, 1977.

[4] Dunning, J. H., 'The determinants of international production', *Oxford Economic Papers*, November 1973.

[5] Franko, L. G., *The European Multinationals*, London, Harper & Row, 1976.

[6] Horst, T., 'The industrial composition of US exports and subsidiary sales to the Canadian market', *American Economic Review*, March 1972.

[7] Krägenau, H., 'Wie hoch sind die deutschen Auslandsinvestitionen?', *Wirtschaftsdienst*, November 1970.

[8] Reddaway, W. B., *Effects of UK Direct Investment Overseas: final report*, Cambridge University Press, 1968.

[9] US Treasury, *Overseas Manufacturing Investment and the Balance of Payments* by G. C. Hufbauer and F. M. Adler, Washington (DC), US Government Printing Office, 1968.

[10] Vaupel, J. and Curhan, J., *The World's Multinational Enterprises, Source Book of Tables*, Boston (Mass.), Harvard Business School, 1973.

[11] Yoshiro, M. Y., *Japan's Multinational Enterprises*, Cambridge (Mass.), Harvard University Press, 1976.

# Comment
## by Stuart Holland

Mrs Morgan's paper is very useful in its analysis of the disproportion between British, Japanese and German foreign investment, and of the relative changes between them over time. However, it is not clear that her rather emphatic conclusion 'that there is no reason to believe that the overseas manufacturing activities of British firms have unfortunate effects on the balance of payments or employment – rather the reverse' follows either from her own analysis or from factors which she has not considered.

*Chart 4.1    UK companies' foreign production relative to exports compared with that of Germany and Japan (percentages)*

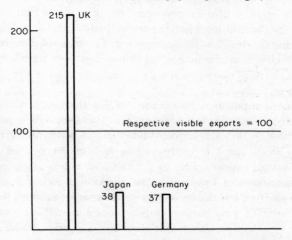

Source: United Nations, *Multinational Corporations in World Development*, New York, 1973.

For instance, the disproportion in the ratio of the value of foreign production by UK, German and Japanese companies to British, German and Japanese visible export trade is dramatic. As shown in Chart 4.1, the value of foreign production by British business abroad in 1971 was more than double visible export trade, as against ratios of less than two fifths of such trade for Germany and Japan. For American business abroad the ratio was even more dramatic at 4:1 but, as

Sir Alec Cairncross has observed in his paper (Chapter 1, above), the export tail of the US economy is shorter and stubbier than the British, with less capacity to wag the dog of the domestic economy.

The disproportion cannot be explained simply in imperial terms. Channon [2], while apparently oblivious to the macroeconomic implications of his findings, has shown that the nature of the multinational expansion of UK capital changed over the period 1950–70, with the number of firms operating six or more subsidiaries abroad increasing from about a fifth to around a half. He chose to call this increase 'dramatic' and added that by lower indices of 'multinationalisation' effectively all the top 100 British manufacturing companies by the early 1970s were multinational in operation.

On the analytical side, one should not neglect the extent to which the multinationalisation of British capital in 1950–70 paralleled a trend towards monopoly in British big business. Prais's research [6] has shown that the share of the top 100 companies in British net manufacturing output increased from around a fifth to nearly a half between 1960 and 1970 – almost precisely the increase which Channon analysed for the multinational spread of British capital (on his higher six-subsidiary index) for the same period. The increased share in such firms' proportion of manufacturing output has been paralleled by an increased share of manufacturing employment – by 3.8 million to a total of 7.25 million in 1975.

Even more important in the context of this analysis, account should be taken of the fact that UK visible export trade was very significantly concentrated by the early 1970s. While some 10,000 firms were regular exporters from the UK, only 220 such firms accounted for two thirds of visible export trade, 75 for half and as few as 31 for 40 per cent (Department of Trade, [8]). In this kind of scenario, one has a situation where a few dozen very large companies account for half of British manufacturing output, employment and visible export trade, with the clear consequence that they also are price-leaders for the dominant share of manufacturing output.

It is against such a background that the multinational range and spread of such companies becomes an important issue in relation to export performance and de-industrialisation. In essence, to gain meaningful judgements at this level of analysis, one has to move from facts to analysis. It is important to stress an alternative paradigm or perception of the facts as known. This is important in the area of export trade, export pricing, devaluation and foreign production as a substitute for exports.

Analytically this alternative was outlined by Bertil Ohlin in his work in the 1930s on international and interregional trade, cited recently when he received the Nobel prize (Ohlin, [5]). Essentially, he drew attention to the extent to which conventional models of international trade assumed an immobility of factors of production. The modern theory of comparative advantage, based on relative factor proportions, assumed that neither capital nor labour were mobile between countries. However, he pointed out that, to the extent that factor mobility occurred, direct investment in different countries and regions of the world economy would tend to be substituted for trade, as firms produced locally rather than exporting from another national or regional base. Mrs Morgan has cited the Reddaway report [7] on this issue. However, whatever the strengths and weaknesses of that report, it was clear enough in stating that the indirect trade for the capital exporting country tended to be short-term and virtually 'once off'. In other words, there was a minor gain during the period of foreign investment provided that the capital equipment involved meant export orders for firms in the country of origin of the investment. It was more agnostic on Ohlin's question of foreign production versus national exports in the long run.

One of the methodological problems in such judgement arises from knowing what would or might have been the case in the event of less foreign investment. Basically, the problem shows the difference between economics as a presumed social science and the physical sciences. In the latter one can establish test conditions in many cases which enable the scientist to run or re-run the hypothesis under different conditions. In economics, we cannot stop and restart the real world on different assumptions in order to adjust the model.

None the less, if one does not wish to miss the wood for the trees in such an issue, it is significant to consider the overall position of successful exporting economies such as Germany and Japan relative to the UK, in terms not only of the previously cited ratio of foreign production of multinationals to national exports, but also of foreign export resources put in the field by leading companies. A study by the British Export Trade Research Organisation in 1975 [1] found to its surprise that leading British companies had either one or no one as a permanent export representative in key foreign markets, compared with an average of eleven for German and Japanese companies.

Similarly, an analysis of the low price responsiveness of British exports to the 1967 devaluation undertaken by Hague *et al.* [3] concluded that British firms were not wholly rational – in terms of the conventional export paradigm – in their reluctance to decrease foreign prices, increase volume exports and enlarge their command of foreign markets.

However, a more appropriate analysis of the underfielding of foreign export representatives and the low response of firms to devaluation should take account of the massively greater foreign production by British firms than by their German and Japanese 'competitors'. If foreign production has followed exports, in the sense that it has occurred in those markets where British firms already had some export base and 'brand attachment', the Ohlin model suggests that it will tend to be substituted for export trade. Thence there are two probable effects:

(i) firms will place less emphasis on exports and export teams than on foreign production;

(ii) they will tend not to follow through devaluation with lower export prices, because they are in key markets their own 'foreign' competitors and would be undercutting their own prices and cash flow abroad by responding significantly to devaluation.

Chart 4.2 illustrates this disincentive to respond to devaluation in basic terms. In the conventional international trade model, firm A

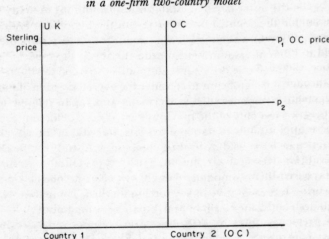

Chart 4.2    *Qualification of exchange-rate change
in a one-firm two-country model*

Key: see text.

located in 'Country 1' (for example the UK) would be able to reduce prices in other countries (or another country) OC from $p_1$ to $p_2$, while retaining the same receipts in sterling terms. However, if firm A is also already producing in OC, it would thereby need to reduce its foreign production price for the product or products concerned from $p_1$ to $p_2$. Inversely, by maintaining its price at $p_1$ for both some foreign production and some exports, it would preserve the cash flow of its foreign plant and reap higher sterling receipts through no price response to the devaluation.

Alternatively, of course, as anyway one would expect in terms of the Ohlin model, the multinational firm may decide to substitute foreign production for exports, and adopt a policy of either no exports or low exports. A Labour Research Department paper on multinationals [4] gives data on the very low share of exports in national production for leading multinationals in the UK (less than 10 per cent in many cases and as low as 2 per cent in the food industry). In the motor industry, which has a higher ratio in the cases of Ford, General Motors (Vauxhall) and Chrysler, this tends to be on components more than finished models, and anyway to be offset by high import ratios.

Moreover, multinational companies have now broken down the convenient symmetry of the old model. These firms do not employ significantly more labour-intensive production techniques in the developing countries they favour, but they are able to allocate the most efficient and modern techniques of production – on the capital side with 'x-efficiency' – through their global allocation of management, at the same time gaining a high 'y-efficiency' from labour (despite its frequent illiteracy or semi-literacy), since technical progress has tended to lower the labour skill required in the blue-collar sector. In practice, therefore, multinational capital can now gain the lowest net costs through a combination of cheap labour with modern capital and management skills on a global scale, reinforced by its command of sales outlets in developed countries.

These brief arguments are not intended to suggest that developed economies such as the UK should look only to themselves in a world desperate for development. But it is worth observing that those countries favoured by multinational capital are not the least developed in the world, but rather intermediate in product per head between Bangladesh and Britain. It also is worth stressing that the implications of the previous arguments do not necessarily mean advocating either import controls or a siege economy. What they stress is that the conventional models of export trade have been transformed in recent decades, and that Britain has been more subject to this transformation than any world economy other than the US.

There is a range of alternative policies between unconfident *laissez-faire* and an improbable command economy with major political costs. For one thing, no government of an economy as concentrated and as multinational as Britain can sensibly afford to be as uninformed on the real nature of cost and profit structures in big business as the British government today.

It has been argued elsewhere that big enterprises now constitute a new power bloc, or a mesoeconomic sector between the small-scale national enterprise of conventional models and the macro level of either statistical aggregates or government economic policy. At least the British government should inform itself systematically on the character and performance of such companies by disaggregating macro aggregates (either for manufacturing and services as a whole, or for individual sub-sectors) in such a way as to identify the share of trade represented by big business in the upper half of SITC categories. To assess the extent of transfer pricing and the nature of export trade in such companies, it would need to follow the path pioneered in Belgium and France by the *contrats de programme* introduced in 1968. It would also need to learn the lessons of that experience by adopting powers to oblige such mesoeconomic companies to reveal in standardised form just what they are doing, not only in trade but also in the related areas of cost and price scheduling in trade and foreign investment, in such a way that their activity can be related systematically to macroeconomic performance.

Ironically, a new approach to the nature of economic power in a multinational era need not prove the banana skin between the present mismanagement of the economy and a wholly managed system. In relation to the economic problems of Chad, Niger and Mali, Britain need have no economic problems, and certainly none in international trade. The very concentration of economic power represented by the trend to monopoly, with its related dimensions in terms of multinational command of trade, could be transformed within a democratic framework, provided that such power is made accountable to the democratic process rather than avoided by representative institutions. Thus, if planning agreements were endorsed by government, rather than considered the thin edge of Wedgwood Benn, or some other personification of Britain's real problems, their negotiation could give sufficient leverage to the British government to make possible a command of the strategic aggregates of not only trade, but also the related areas of investment, output and employment.

Leverage on these very few firms, either to reverse trends in foreign investment, or to reverse a given import–export ratio in their subsidiary trade with companies and plant abroad, could register a very sizeable effect on the aggregate trade balance of the UK. It makes possible an unconventional policy, with minimum numbers of mesoeconomic firms registering a maximum macroeconomic difference in investment, employment and trade aggregates. Whether the public leverage takes the form of planning agreements, competitive public enterprise through state holding companies, or something different, any government wishing to avoid either industrial degeneration or pressures for a siege economy can only ignore such new factors at its own peril.

## References

[1] British Export Trade Research Organisation, *Export Concentration*, London, 1975.
[2] Channon, D., *The Strategy and Structure of British Enterprise*, London, Macmillan, 1973.
[3] Hague, D. C., Oakeshott, E. and Strain, A., *Devaluation and Pricing Decisions*, London, Allen and Unwin, 1974.
[4] Labour Research Department, *Multinational Companies*, London, 1975.
[5] Ohlin, B., *Interregional and International Trade* (revised edn), Cambridge (Mass.), Harvard University Press, 1967.
[6] Prais, S. J., 'A new look at the growth of industrial concentration', *Oxford Economic Papers*, July 1974.
[7] Reddaway, W. B., *Effects of UK Direct Investment Overseas*, Cambridge University Press, 1968.
[8] Trade, Department of, *Trade and Industry*, April 1974.

# 5 UK Performance in Services

## by J. R. Sargent*

This paper falls into three sections. The first examines the UK's record since 1960 in foreign trade in services. The second considers some arguments which bear upon the case for and against placing greater reliance on services as a contributor to balance of payments equilibrium. The final section broadens the perspective from foreign trade to the capacity of the services industries to absorb investment. Throughout, the term 'services' excludes those attributable to general government, but is not necessarily confined to those provided by the private sector; some may be included which are attributable to public corporations. Although services do not include – and the term as used excludes – that part of total invisible trade which consists of interest, profits and dividends, it is not possible to exclude reference to these; in the case of financial institutions the services for which they charge fees or commission are often part and parcel of the operations which also provide them with investment income.

### The Record of Foreign Trade in Services

It is well known that, as the UK's share of world exports of manufactures has declined over the last decade and a half, her share of world exports of services has fallen with it. There was a period between 1967 and 1971 when the latter stabilised while the share of exports of manufactures continued to decline; but subsequently the parallel decline of the UK's share of services was resumed. The Bank of England drew attention to this in 1973. Since then the share of exports of manufactures has shown signs of stabilising, while that of services has continued to decline at an undiminished rate. Nevertheless, while

* I am grateful for assistance from the Midland Bank Economics Department.

with these variations the trends of their performance in world markets have been broadly similar for exports of services and of manufactures, the positive net contribution of services to the current account has been outpacing that of manufactures, especially since the middle of the 1960s. As Table 5.1 shows, in 1966 the import surplus on foods, materials and fuel was nearly all covered by the export surplus on manufactures, with a useful but comparatively minor contribution from that on services. By 1976 the latter's contribution had expanded markedly as the former's declined to not much more than a half of net imports of food, materials and fuel. In 1966 the positive contribution of the export surplus of services was less than one seventh of that of manufactures in absolute size; in 1976 it was slightly bigger than one half.

Table 5.1    Composition of the UK balance-of-payments current account, 1966 and 1976

|  | 1966 | | 1976 | |
|---|---|---|---|---|
|  | (£m) | (%) | (£m) | (%) |
| Visible deficit: food, materials and fuel | 2245 | *100.0* | 8980 | *100.0* |
| Visible surplus: manufactures | 2070 | *92.2* | 5049 | *56.2* |
| Surplus on services[a] | 275 | *12.2* | 2598 | *28.9* |
| Surplus on other current items | 4 | *0.2* | − 72 | *− 0.8* |
| Current account deficit | − 104 | *− 4.6* | 1405 | *15.7* |
| *Total surplus* | 2245 | *100.0* | 8980 | *100.0* |

Source: CSO, *United Kingdom Balance of Payments 1966–76.*
[a] Excluding general government.

The declining capacity of manufacturing to maintain an export surplus commensurate with the deficit on food, materials and fuel reflects the fact that, as the UK's share of world markets in manufactures as an exporter has shrunk significantly, the share she accounts for as an importer has done so only marginally. The declining relative size of the UK in the world economy would lead one to expect a decline in both shares, but this has not happened, for reasons with which this paper is not concerned. The major difference which distinguishes services from manufacturing is that as the UK's share of world exports has fallen, her share of world imports has fallen along with it to a much greater extent. This suggests that services have not been so affected by the increasing import penetration which has become so evident with manufacturing. It is not possible to track this in the same way for services. Instead Table 5.2 sets out year by year the extent to which for the main categories of services the UK's share of world exports has exceeded her share of world imports. Since world imports and exports do not quite tally statistically, the percentages are not exactly the same as the UK's net foreign income from services as a percentage of world trade, but they approximate to it fairly closely.

*Table 5.2   UK share of world receipts less UK share of world payments (percentages)*

|      | Transport | Travel | Other services | Total services[a] | Investment income | Manu- factures |
|------|-----------|--------|----------------|-------------------|-------------------|----------------|
| 1960 | + 1.0     | − 1.4  | + 8.5          | + 2.2             | + 11.4            | + 7.4          |
| 1961 | + 2.3     | − 1.3  | + 9.5          | + 3.1             | + 11.3            | + 7.2          |
| 1962 | + 2.6     | − 1.3  | + 8.8          | + 3.0             | + 12.1            | + 6.8          |
| 1963 | + 2.4     | − 2.2  | + 6.9          | + 2.2             | + 13.1            | + 6.9          |
| 1964 | + 0.5     | − 2.7  | + 7.4          | + 1.4             | + 11.1            | + 5.6          |
| 1965 | + 1.7     | − 3.2  | + 6.3          | + 1.3             | + 11.1            | + 5.6          |
| 1966 | + 1.2     | − 2.4  | + 6.5          | + 1.5             | + 10.3            | + 5.3          |
| 1967 | + 0.7     | − 1.4  | + 6.8          | + 1.8             | +  9.6            | + 3.8          |
| 1968 | + 1.4     | − 0.3  | + 7.4          | + 2.5             | +  7.5            | + 3.3          |
| 1969 | + 1.2     | + 0.2  | + 7.6          | + 2.7             | +  9.0            | + 3.5          |
| 1970 | + 1.1     | −      | + 7.7          | + 2.4             | +  7.8            | + 3.2          |
| 1971 | + 1.1     | + 0.3  | + 6.6          | + 2.3             | +  5.8            | + 3.4          |
| 1972 | + 1.1     | − 0.1  | + 6.4          | + 2.2             | +  5.3            | + 2.2          |
| 1973 | + 1.2     | − 0.2  | + 6.1          | + 2.1             | +  7.2            | + 1.2          |
| 1974 | + 2.8     | + 0.9  | + 6.0          | + 2.9             | +  5.2            | + 1.1          |
| 1975 | + 3.3     | + 1.3  | + 5.1          | + 3.2             | +  4.7            | + 1.8          |
| 1976 | + 3.5     | + 2.6  | + 4.7          | + 3.4             | +  4.6            | + 1.5          |

Sources: CSO, *United Kingdom Balance of Payments 1966–76*; Departments of Industry, Trade, Prices and Consumer Protection, *Monthly Review of External Trade Statistics*, June 1978; Committee on Invisible Exports, *World Invisible Trade*; GATT, *International Trade Yearbooks*.
[a] Excluding general government.

Compared with the worsening position for manufactures – though this was slightly better in the latest two years – total services have maintained their positive contribution over the period as a whole. During the first half of the 1960s it showed signs of slipping, in the second half it improved and, after some relapse in the early 1970s, it was restored to much the same as at the beginning of the period or somewhat better. Looking at the three major categories of services, the most successful recently has clearly been travel. After deteriorating in the first half of the 1960s, the travel account then turned around, first eliminating its deficit and lately achieving growing surplus. It is the only one of the three categories in which a declining share of world imports has, in recent years, been associated with an actual rise in its share of world exports – from 5.0 per cent in 1970 to 6.5 per cent in 1976. The travel account includes the expenditure which tourists and other visitors make within the UK, but not their costs of getting here. This element of the tourist boom accounts for the recent improvement in the transport account's net surplus, which is mostly attributable to civil aviation. The net contribution of sea transport tends to fluctuate around zero, the deficit on tankers absorbing the surplus on dry cargo.

Table 5.3   *'Other services'*[a]: net foreign earnings on current account, 1976

|  | Amount 1976 (£m) | Ratio to 1966 value = 1 |
|---|---|---|
| Insurance | 458 | *11.7* |
| Earnings on construction overseas | 456 | *11.4* |
| Banking | 169 | *7.7* |
| Brokerage | 212 | *7.3* |
| Commodity trading and merchanting | 247 | *7.1* |
| Expenditure by overseas students and journalists | 235 | *5.1* |
| Services associated with North Sea oil and gas | − 490 | – |
| Other | 405 | *3.8* |
| *Total of above* | 1692 | *5.3* |
| (Manufacturing) | (5049) | (*2.4*) |

Source: CSO, *United Kingdom Balance of Payments 1966–76.*
[a] Major items included in third column of Table 5.2.

The biggest net contribution to the current account comes from the third category of 'other services', which comprises financial services and a miscellany of others. It is not possible to relate these individually to corresponding figures of world trade, but it may be useful to set down the net contribution to the UK's current account of the major services included in the third column of Table 5.2. This is done in Table 5.3, which lists them in order of the increase in their net contribution between 1966 and 1976. In the case of financial services, this excludes their net income from interest and dividends.

These services taken together are more substantial net contributors than transport and travel combined, both absolutely and in relation to world trade; but at the same time they appear to have been less successful in holding, let alone improving, their position. Their decline since 1970 is exaggerated, however, by the substantial growth since then of consultancy and other fees paid in connection with the development of North Sea oil and gas, which (as Table 5.3 shows) rose to £490 million in 1976 from nothing in 1969. Excluding this item, the 1976 figure for 'other services' in Table 5.2 would be 6.1 per cent instead of 4.7 per cent. Obviously, if it had not been paid, there would have been less oil and a less favourable oil account later if not then. But some of it may be of a once-and-for-all nature, and in any case it would seem better to regard it as a debit to the oil account rather than to services in general. On this basis, services other than transport and travel have been losing some ground, but the loss has been comparatively slow and their net contribution remains a large one.

## The Contribution of Services to the Balance of Payments

Past performance in foreign trade in manufacturing and in services, then, supports the claim that the UK has been developing a comparative advantage in services. The claim is strengthened by the experience of the latest four years, 1972–6, in which the recovery in manufacturing appears more tentative than for services. Furthermore, the growth of services' net contribution to the current account to its present size of about half that of manufactures suggests that the advantage may be more than marginal in its significance. But the case for capitalising on the apparent comparative advantage has to be evaluated against the likely growth of the market. The case for switching resources to something in which there is a comparative advantage in a static sense, assuming that there is some feasible way of doing so, is less appealing if it involves a commitment to a less dynamic source of demand. How does the growth of the market for services compare? Table 5.4 sets out the ratios of world exports of services to world exports of manufactures.

For services as a whole the tendency has been for the market to grow somewhat less rapidly than for manufactures. Cyclical effects are evident, the ratio of exports of services to those of manufactures falling in periods of boom. This suggests that the market for services has the attractions of greater stability to set against somewhat slower growth. The latter, however, is a characteristic of the market as a

Table 5.4 Ratio of world exports of services to world exports of manufactures (percentages)

| | Transport | Travel | Other services | Total services |
|------|------|------|------|------|
| 1960 | 15.5 | 9.5 | 10.3 | 35.3 |
| 1961 | 19.6 | 9.8 | 10.2 | 39.6 |
| 1962 | 18.8 | 10.0 | 10.5 | 39.3 |
| 1963 | 18.8 | 10.4 | 10.7 | 39.9 |
| 1964 | 14.9 | 10.5 | 10.5 | 35.9 |
| 1965 | 14.1 | 10.9 | 10.9 | 35.9 |
| 1966 | 14.1 | 11.0 | 10.9 | 36.0 |
| 1967 | 14.9 | 11.4 | 12.5 | 38.8 |
| 1968 | 14.1 | 10.2 | 10.6 | 34.9 |
| 1969 | 12.8 | 9.6 | 10.3 | 32.7 |
| 1970 | 13.6 | 10.9 | 10.3 | 34.8 |
| 1971 | 13.5 | 10.0 | 11.5 | 35.0 |
| 1972 | 12.5 | 10.0 | 11.8 | 34.3 |
| 1973 | 12.0 | 9.3 | 10.4 | 31.7 |
| 1974 | 12.3 | 7.8 | 9.5 | 29.6 |
| 1975 | 11.9 | 8.5 | 10.8 | 31.2 |
| 1976 | 11.1 | 8.0 | 11.4 | 30.5 |

Sources: Committee on Invisible Exports, *World Invisible Trade*; GATT, *International Trade Yearbooks*.

whole which does not apply to all of its components. It is true of transport, but of travel only during the second half of the period, and taking account of cyclical fluctuations the growth of the market in other services seems to have kept pace with that for manufactures. (It has been faster than the growth of total visible trade, but this is of less relevance for the UK.)

These comparisons, however, may be biased against services by the fact that manufactures have so far been the main beneficiaries, as compared with services, of the tendency during most of the period for the freedom of international trade to be increased within regional groupings such as the EEC, and by means of multilateral tariff concessions and generalised preferences. As a result trade in manufactures has received a stimulus which may not be repeated in the period ahead. Within the EEC at any rate the emphasis will be shifting towards freeing trade in services. Thus the market for services, although it has not been particularly buoyant compared with manufactures in the past, may well be more so in the future. At least it should remain relatively immune for some years to come from the challenge of the more advanced developing countries, whose manufacturing capacity and ability to export manufactures is now growing rapidly. In the immediate future the growth of protectionism has to be reckoned with and, if there were grounds for thinking that this is likely to fall more heavily on goods than on services, the case for the latter would be further strengthened. But there are plenty of instances of protectionist arrangements for services, such as the shipping conferences and the IATA cartel, and they could be replicated in other spheres. There have, for example, recently been attempts by some American banks to prevent margins on Euro-currency lending from falling below 1 per cent.

While it is difficult to show convincingly that the world market for services either has been or will be more dynamic than for manufactures, the problem facing the UK is that her exports of services already command a relatively large share of what is still a relatively small market. To illustrate this by the position in 1976, imagine that the UK's share of world exports of manufactures had been smaller than it was by one percentage point. This would have meant a loss to the current account of £3.1 billion. To compensate for this by rising exports of services by the same sum would have involved increasing the UK's share of world exports of services by about a third, from 9.7 per cent to 13.0 per cent. If allowance is made for the relatively low import content of services compared with exports, the magnitude of the task would be less, but it would still be considerable.

This raises the question of the scope for expansion of particular services which might contribute to such a switch. As far as shipping and air transport are concerned, present protectionist arrangements and the past record of net foreign earnings do not offer much encouragement except in connection with tourism. We have, however, noted the improvement that this has recently brought about on the travel account. OECD estimates, now a few years out of date, suggest a fairly high income elasticity for the demand for travel in Continental countries which, at least until recently, have had high growth rates compared with the UK. These factors have no doubt combined to push the balance in our favour, aided for short periods by an undervalued pound. But it may be that there has been a once-and-for-all element in the improvement, stemming from the previous backwardness of our hotels and restaurants and our provision for foreign tourists generally. The correction of this has enabled us to break through into the tourist market in quite a big way, but once this has been achieved there may be less scope for continuous development at the same pace. This belief is reinforced by the 'positional' character of tourist attractions. While two railways from London to York may be no better than one, two hundred tourists in York Minster are much worse than one from the tourists' point of view, though there may be marginal benefits for the restoration fund. In other words, many of the things which tourists come to see and hope to enjoy have a capacity which is limited in a fundamental sense and cannot be expanded to meet the increase in demand. There are also limits to the tolerance of the natives. The tourist industry may well have some unexploited possibilities for spreading the demand outside the major centres, but it ultimately depends upon natural resources which are not – like those of extractive industries – exhaustible, but are to a considerable extent non-expansible.

One of the most impressive of the foreign earnings performers in Table 5.3 has been the construction industry, including the fees of architects, consulting engineers and quantity surveyors. The main growth here has taken place after 1973 and is connected with the jump in oil producers' income. This was followed by, and aggravated, the recession at home, in which the construction industry was hit hard; this forced it to look overseas. On the assumption that the oil price rise was a once-and-for-all adjustment not likely to occur again on the same scale, or at any rate not until the late 1980s, it is likely that there is also a corresponding once-and-for-all element in overseas earnings from construction. Although the demand will tend to be spread forward in time by the physical and financial problems which oil producers have met in trying to do too much at once, and some of the demand will be of a continuing nature, it would be realistic to look to a slackening in the years ahead of the rate of growth of earnings under this heading, and there is the possibility of an absolute decline in real terms. This will be more likely to the extent that there is a sustained recovery in the UK domestic demand for construction. Nevertheless, the example set by the industry, one which a few years ago would have been seen as having very little exporting capacity, in successfully marketing its skills abroad, is one which could be followed by others, and even include the export of technical services by manufacturing industry itself.

Turning to financial services, it is necessary to repeat the point that their contribution depends not simply upon net earnings from commissions and fees, but also upon the margin earned in lending. Only the former are included in the third column of Table 5.2; the latter are in the fifth column. The practicality of bringing about an improvement in the interest, profits and dividends element of the invisible account is sometimes dismissed as requiring a prior export of capital. Quite apart from the fact that this may on occasion be desirable – for example, to help check an excessive appreciation of the exchange rate, as in 1977 – it does not arise for financial institutions which both lend and borrow abroad and make a turn from these operations which is a net credit to the current account in the form of interest. It is true, of course, that there are credit risks attached to the lending and liquidity risks from financing it at somewhat shorter term, and, if these are miscalculated or inadequately provided against, the authorities acting as lenders of last resort might have to use the official exchange reserves to enable the obligations of British banks to non-residents to be discharged. But this is a contingent liability, which the system of supervision of financial institutions should minimise, if recent memories are not enough.

*Table 5.5    The City's banking earnings,[a] 1970 and 1976 (£ millions)*

|  | 1970 | 1976 |
|---|---|---|
| Net interest and discounts on borrowing and lending in sterling[b] | 16 | 85 |
| Net interest on borrowing and lending in foreign currencies | 16 | 266 |
| Net investment income from foreign branches | 23 | −112 |
| *Total* | 55 | 239 |

Source: CSO, *United Kingdom Balance of Payments 1966–76.*
[a] Excluding those from financial services.
[b] Including export credit.

The activities referred to above are mainly those of the banking part of the financial services sector. As Table 5.5 shows, they arise largely from operations in the Eurocurrency markets in foreign currencies, where the major growth has been. In itself the growth of net interest earnings on foreign currency lending has been substantial in the last six years, but the development of the London Eurocurrency market over that period has attracted many foreign banks to London – 285 were directly represented in October 1977 by a branch, subsidiary or representative office – and as a result the net earnings of British banks on their investments located overseas have been over-taken by those of foreign banks in the UK.

Over the last few years British banks' share of the London Eurocurrency market has declined only to a very small extent, but recently London has been tending to lose its share of the total Eurocurrency market. This has been partly because of the growth of offshore banking centres, but also because of the growing experience and expertise of the Continental banks, especially the German, which have forged ahead in the Eurobond or longer-term foreign currency lending business. Recently the decline in the US dollar has worked against London, in which the dollar segment of the market has been relatively predominant. There is no reason to think that London will be unable to respond to the challenge as regards maintaining the scale and growth of its business. It adapted it previously to the decline in sterling with speed and success. The more doubtful question concerns the terms on which it can be done. Since the middle of 1977 spreads between borrowing and lending rates from medium-term Eurocredits have been subject to downward pressure, pushing them recently towards $\frac{1}{2}$ per cent, while maturities have lengthened from five years to ten in a number of cases. This is not unprecedented; it occurred in 1973–4 and was reversed. But in the longer perspective the market appears more likely to be a borrower's than a lender's. A resumption in the developed countries of the rates of growth which prevailed in the 1960s seems increasingly unlikely, and the consequent slackening of domestic loan demand will push banks to seek more business in the international markets, which will continue to be overhung by the OPEC surpluses. While spreads are pressed to the minimum sustainable level, bad debts will grow as the slacker growth of the developed world reduces the buoyancy of the exports from which the less developed borrowers hope to service them. This is not to predict any kind of widespread or unmanage-able default, against which lenders are now better provided and better informed. It is simply to say that they may find it harder to earn an income, if conditions do turn out as outlined above.

The previous paragraphs have been about the contribution which banking in particular makes to the surplus on interest, profits and dividends, along with its contribution to the services account as defined. As far as the general business of financial services is concerned, there are now some rumbles on a distant drum beating out messages of potentially intensifying competition. There are proposals to establish an insurance market in New York modelled on Lloyds. The Chairman of the Federal Reserve System is reported to be in favour of legislation to remove advantages which foreign banks enjoy in the United States with regard to certain banking activities across State boundaries. A number of less developed commodity producers are uneasy about their dependence upon London's commodity markets. On the other hand, the next stages of the development of the EEC may see the opening up of the market in services. In general it seems likely that a number of the less developed countries in Latin America and South East Asia will move on sooner or later from displacing imports of manufactures to displacing imports of financial services. But there is a difference here, in that these countries are developing a manufacturing capacity which has the ability to displace not merely imports but the exports of more highly developed competitors in third markets. It seems likely that it will take them some time yet to reach this second stage in the market for financial services, although the rapid development of financial centres in Singapore and Hong Kong, and perhaps Brazil, leaves no room for complacency. It would be fatal if complacency were to sap the undoubted competitive strength which London derives from its unique combination of financial services – insurance, banking, shipping, air freight and commodity markets; also a variety of professional services – and from its recently developed ability to harness them together in support of large projects.

As the experience of manufacturing has shown, performance is no less important in the home market than overseas. The British banks have also suffered from competition in their own back yard in the last twelve years, losing market share in sterling advances to UK residents. In the early part of the period this could be explained by the application of quantitative controls on advances to the London Clearing Banks (although their subsidiaries escaped them). But the loss of market share continued after quantitative controls were abolished in 1971, largely owing to the increasing involvement of American banks in the sterling lending market. There are signs that the situation has been stabilised in the last year or so, and, since overdraft facilities – which are less common in the foreign banks – have expanded more than actual lending, it could begin to be retrieved as these are taken up.

This section has been mainly concerned with the growth of the market, but it would also be relevant to consider the terms of trade and whether they have moved less unfavourably for services than for goods. Separation of volumes and unit values is particularly hazardous for services, but the CSO have attempted this with their usual combination of academic caution and statistical enterprise. The figures in Table 5.6 are derived from theirs. For services there has

*Table 5.6    Movements of relative volumes and unit values for foreign trade in goods and services, 1966–76 (indices, 1966 = 100)*

|  | Volume: exports/imports | Unit values: exports/imports |
|---|---|---|
| Goods | 101.8 | 87.1 |
| Services: transport, travel, and other non-government | 129.1 | 91.6 |

Source: CSO, *United Kingdom Balance of Payments 1966–76* (especially Table 4.1).

been a somewhat smaller deterioration in the terms of trade than for goods. But what is more significant is that this has been associated with a much larger increase in the volume of exports relative to imports. A somewhat larger deterioration in the terms of trade for goods has been required to keep export volume more or less in line with import volume. This suggests that the price of a given improvement in the current account may be less if it is pursued via services than via goods. The latter, as pointed out above, would require a smaller enhancement of the UK's share of the world market; however, despite this initial disadvantage of services, the experience of the last decade indicates that they offer a superior trade-off.

## Investment in the Service Industries

So far we have been concerned with service industries' contribution to trade. We conclude with some remarks in a wider context, which relate to the declining profitability of manufacturing industry. This decline can be observed directly from figures of net income and net assets derived from company returns. But it is more illuminating to approach it via the National Income 'Blue Book' figures for profits, output and stock of capital, which make it possible to separate out movements in the profit-share and in the capital–output ratio. It is clear that the rate of return on capital in manufacturing has been pinched from both ends over the last decade and a half, by a decline in the profit-share and a rise in the capital–output ratio (or alternatively phrased, a decline in the productivity of capital). The corresponding movements are difficult to establish for the services industries. There is some evidence that the ratio of net income to net assets has dropped less sharply in distribution than in manufacturing, but comparable figures are not available for other services. Capital-stock estimates for the service industries are not disaggregated between them, and are confused by the substantial growth of leasing since the beginning of the 1970s. This means that since then part of the additional capital equipment installed and operated by manufacturing industry is owned by the financial services industry and appears in the latter's capital stock. This may conceal the extent of decline in the productivity of capital in manufacturing, while exaggerating the growth of the capital stock in services. The latter seems to have been quite large in relation to the growth of the labour force, and in relation to real output per head, although figures for real output in services have to be treated with caution. But what does appear to distinguish services from manufacturing is that services have avoided the decline in the profit-share which has contributed to declining profitability in manufacturing. Some figures for services are set out in Table 5.7. In the aggregate, the profit-share has remained remarkably stable over the last ten years. It has tended to sag in the last five years or so in the distributive trades, while rising in financial services, and in other services it has tended to rise for most of the period.

A theoretical explanation of the declining profitability of manufacturing might be that it represents an adjustment to a decline in the cost of capital (or required rate of return) brought into effect in the late 1950s and early 1960s by a combination of government investment incentives and the mood of confidence which developed at that time. There was certainly an accelerated growth of capital stock per head in manufacturing in the 1960s which continued into the early 1970s. In terms of both net and gross capital stock per labour–hour, the annual rate of growth was over 4 per cent by the early 1970s compared with less than 2 per cent in the late 1950s. As a result the marginal productivity of capital declined towards its reduced real cost. When technical progress is substantially embodied in new equipment, increased investment in new equipment tends (other things equal) to mean more scrapping of old equipment. As the scrapping process moves further within the original margin, enhancement of average productivity declines. For example, when it is decided also to

Table 5.7    Profit-shares in services: gross profits'[a] contribution to GDP[b]
(percentages)

| | Distri-butive trades | Banking, insurance, finance and business | | Other services | Total services | |
|---|---|---|---|---|---|---|
| | | Including rent | Excluding rent | | Including rent | Including rent, excl. capital consumption |
| 1966 | 38.9 | 44.1 | 32.9 | 28.1 | 35.4 | 33.2 |
| 1967 | 39.2 | 44.0 | 32.8 | 27.9 | 35.5 | 33.2 |
| 1968 | 37.8 | 44.3 | 33.0 | 28.7 | 35.3 | 33.0 |
| 1969 | 38.1 | 43.7 | 31.4 | 29.4 | 35.6 | 33.2 |
| 1970 | 35.7 | 43.5 | 31.1 | 29.9 | 35.0 | 32.4 |
| 1971 | 39.1 | 44.6 | 32.7 | 31.9 | 37.5 | 35.0 |
| 1972 | 37.6 | 44.3 | 32.8 | 33.4 | 37.6 | 35.2 |
| 1973 | 34.4 | 47.6 | 36.6 | 36.3 | 38.8 | 36.2 |
| 1974 | 30.1 | 48.0 | 35.9 | 35.9 | 37.1 | 34.1 |
| 1975 | 26.7 | 45.7 | 33.6 | 32.8 | 33.9 | 30.5 |
| 1976 | 26.5 | 49.7 | 38.3 | 33.6 | 35.2 | 31.6 |

Sources: CSO, *National Income and Expenditure*, Tables 3.1, 1.11, 12.1, 12.2 and 11.3.
[a] Including other non-employment income.
[b] Excluding stock appreciation.

scrap fifteen-year-old equipment and transfer its crew to new equipment, the differential in labour productivity between the new and old equipment is smaller than when twenty-year old equipment only is scrapped. Thus, the marginal productivity of capital declines with the scale of new investment. At the same time the accelerated scrapping will allow and encourage real product wages to rise, diminishing the profit-share.

For the services industries this has been avoided. It seems likely that they have also experienced a rising capital–output ratio, although it is not yet possible to establish by how much, and on the whole they have not enjoyed the same investment incentives as manufacturing. Their ability to avoid a decline in the profit-share prompts the theoretical explanation that the marginal productivity of capital has held up better in relation to the average than has been the case for manufacturing. To put the matter another way, the service industries may have a greater elasticity of substitution of capital for labour than is the case for manufacturing; opportunities for capital accumulation are less rapidly exhaustible through the process of accumulation itself.

These suggestions are tentative and based on evidence which is incomplete. Their implications are correspondingly speculative. They are that, while the accelerated rate of accumulation of capital in manufacturing may now be coming to an end as the return on capital reaches the minimum which is acceptable, there may still be some way to go before this happens in the services industries. They still retain a capacity to absorb capital which manufacturing may have exhausted. If this is so, it may lead to a slackening in the rate of de-industrialisation as far as employment is concerned. Reversion to a slower rate of accumulation of capital per head in manufacturing will mean a slower growth of labour productivity – indeed, this seems to be present now – so that to meet a given growth of demand for manufactures a faster growth of the manufacturing labour force will be required. While this is happening, it will not be matched in the services industries, where greater opportunities for capital accumulation appear to remain. Although these will mean a smaller growth of the labour force in services than would otherwise have been the case, there is no particular reason to think that it will be smaller than it has been. Consequently the rate of growth of employment in manufacturing should at least rise relatively to services, even though it remains smaller or negative. De-industrialisation, in other words, will decelerate.

# Comment

## by T. M. Rybczynski

This brief note must be considered complementary to the main paper, which was not available before the meeting and not as a comment upon it. It was prepared at short notice and therefore does not discuss the issues arising with the detail the writer would wish. It examines in a summary way the section of Chapter 10 dealing with the subject, as well as a similar section in Singh [1]. The main thesis put forward is that the statistical and the analytical basis of both papers as regards 'invisibles' and 'private services' are subject to important qualifications, which consequently affect the conclusions at which they arrive.

The treatment accorded to services by both papers is very brief – each of them deals with the topic in two pages – and their tables are on a highly aggregated level using the balance-of-payments classification. The arguments advanced disregard the relationship of their classification to the national accounts classification; they do not consider the analytical issues which arise when the whole subject is looked upon in the context of a growing world economy.

Both papers rightly make a distinction between invisibles as a whole and private services. The latter, using the IMF classification, comprise freight, merchandise, insurance, other transport, travel and other services; the former include in addition the earnings of foreign investment, portfolio as well as direct investment (including re-invested earnings), government receipts and private transfers.

Both papers state that a rise in interest, profits and dividends requires a prior increase in the outflow of capital. Although on the face of it peripheral to the main thesis of the two papers – but in fact forming one of its basic elements – this statement is not entirely correct. A rise in the profits and dividends components does not require additional outflow of capital if such an outflow is defined to exclude re-invested earnings. To force business overseas to remit all earnings is tantamount to a death sentence and the liquidation of overseas assets, and it raises the important issue of foreign investment in an increasingly interdependent world, where comparative advantage tends to alter. This topic is outside the scope of this note. A point, however, not irrelevant here is that nowadays, more so than in the past, only a very modest outflow of capital is needed, sometimes negligible or indeed nil, to support large investment overseas, simply because the funds required can be borrowed in countries where the investment is made, or in international capital markets or other domestic capital markets.

In evaluating the UK's position in invisibles and private services, Brown and Sheriff in Table 10.8 of their paper point to a decline in the UK's share of 'world trade' in these transactions. They define 'the total of world trade' in these transactions as the total of receipts (credits) accruing to eleven industrial countries (the US, Canada, Japan, the UK, Germany, France, Italy, Belgium–Luxembourg, the Netherlands, Sweden and Switzerland). Disregarding the problems of asymmetry between receipts and payments (credits and debits), the comments on changes in the UK's share of the 'world total' as defined also ignore the facts that the share of invisibles of these eleven countries in total world receipts (defined to include all countries – that is, all industrial and developing countries) has been declining, that the share of the eleven countries in total world private services (on a wide definition) has been declining even faster, and that their share in the world's total of interest, profits and dividends, government receipts and private transfers has been rising.

The question of definitions used is not only technical. It has important analytical implications if the whole problem is looked upon in the context of a (growing) world economy and, associated with it, changes in comparative advantage.

The second point to be made in relation to comments by Brown and Sheriff on the fall in the UK's share in the 'world total' of private services – using their definition – is that the UK's loss (from 26.3 per cent in 1955 to 15.0 per cent in 1976) accompanied by a marked decline in the US share (from 24.8 to 19.3 per cent in the same period) was also accompanied by a rise in the share of Japan (from 1.5 to 9.1 per cent), of France (from 6.5 to 13.1 per cent) and of Germany (from 9.4 to 12.0 per cent). Their combined increase from 17.4 per cent in 1955 to 35.3 per cent in 1976 represented losses suffered by the UK and the US, as well as by the remaining six industrial countries (making Brown and Sheriff's 'world total' of 1.7 per cent).

Of the three countries, Japan, France and Germany, which improved their share of the eleven industrial countries' total receipts, Japan improved its position in four groups of transactions making up private services as classified by the IMF – freight, other transport, other services and merchandise insurance. The only category in which Japan did not make any advance was travel. France increased its share in all five categories, as did Germany, although in the last seven years or so its additional improvement was restricted to 'other services' and 'travel'.

Changes in the share of receipts are, of course, of limited value in an evaluation of the competitive position of the individual countries. For this purpose it is necessary to look at the development of credits and debits. Two very general observations in relation to the changes in the shares of 'private services' as described above might, however, be helpful. The first is that an increase in the shares of Japan, France and Germany represented to a large extent a once-and-for-all adjustment associated with the rebuilding of their economies after world war II, and accompanying it there was a rapid rise in the movement of trade and capital. Secondly, 'private services' comprise a very large number of heterogenous transactions with different economic characteristics (in relation to factor intensity, income and price elasticity, substitution, etc.). Above all they differ enormously as regards being 'fully-freely tradeable'. Apart from the fact that some of them are natural monopolies of the countries providing them (railway services, postal services, etc.), a large number are subject to government protective devices, such as cargo preference schemes and restrictions on movements of foreign aircraft. While unfortunately it is impossible to obtain sufficient statistics about the share of non-fully tradeable and fully-freely tradeable services, there is reason to believe that the share of the latter has been declining and that probably quite an appreciable part of the fall in the UK's (and also the US's) share of private services can be attributed to this.

Indeed, the emphasis of policy in all industrial countries on the liberalisation and the freedom of visible trade and almost a complete disregard for services must have been an important contributory factor. It can be said to have been tantamount to accepting the principle of comparative advantage as regards goods, and not only ignoring it but helping to build impediments against it in relation to services.

Singh measures competitiveness (of manufactures and private services) by using the so-called trade ratio, that is to say the ratio of net receipts or payments to the total value of receipts and payments. (The maximum degree of competitiveness is $+1$ and of uncompetitiveness $-1$.) In a table in his article he shows that the competitiveness of private services as a whole rose between 1966 and 1975 from $+0.08$ to $+0.13$. In the last two years the increase continued, raising it in 1977 to $+0.18$.

In the context of the world economy it is, however, helpful to see how the components of private services have behaved, what are their main characteristics and the reasons why these characteristics have affected them. The development of trade ratios (and actual net receipts or payments) shown in Table 5.8 for the main five groups of private services, according to the classification used by the CSO, indicates that the UK has had, and continues to have, a significant 'comparative advantage' ($+1.0$) in financial services, that it has had a modest comparative advantage in other services and civil aviation (fluctuating around $+0.20$ and $+0.09$ respectively), that it has a very

Table 5.8   *Private services: balance of payments and trade ratios[a]*
1966–77

| | Sea travel | Civil aviation | Travel | Financial services[b] | Other services | Total |
|---|---|---|---|---|---|---|
| | | | (£ million) | | | |
| **Balance[c]** | | | | | | |
| 1966 | + 5 | + 31 | − 78 | + 125 | + 192 | + 275 |
| 1967 | − 17 | + 30 | − 38 | + 179 | + 229 | + 165 |
| 1968 | − 35 | + 34 | + 11 | + 254 | + 234 | + 568 |
| 1969 | + 33 | + 49 | + 35 | + 332 | + 231 | + 614 |
| 1970 | − 76 | + 50 | + 50 | + 413 | + 247 | + 567 |
| 1971 | − 52 | + 57 | + 47 | + 435 | + 319 | + 679 |
| 1972 | − 75 | + 77 | + 19 | + 492 | + 378 | + 899 |
| 1973 | − 98 | + 75 | + 1 | + 551 | + 440 | + 1193 |
| 1974 | − 18 | + 96 | + 154 | + 691 | + 444 | + 1269 |
| 1975 | + 64 | + 116 | + 255 | + 914 | + 350 | + 1263 |
| 1976 | + 45 | + 241 | + 620 | + 1086 | + 600 | + 1663 |
| 1977 | − 74 | + 214 | + 1011 | + 1294 | + 857 | + 2489 |
| | | | | | | |
| **Trade** | | | (ratio) | | | |
| 1966 | −[d] | + 0.09 | − 0.20 | + 1.00 | + 0.22 | + 0.08 |
| 1967 | −[d] | + 0.04 | − 0.08 | + 1.00 | + 0.24 | + 0.10 |
| 1968 | − 0.02 | + 0.08 | + 0.02 | + 1.00 | + 0.22 | + 0.13 |
| 1969 | + 0.02 | + 0.09 | + 0.05 | + 1.00 | + 0.20 | + 0.12 |
| 1970 | − 0.03 | + 0.09 | + 0.06 | + 1.00 | + 0.19 | + 0.12 |
| 1971 | − 0.02 | + 0.09 | + 0.05 | + 1.00 | + 0.23 | + 0.12 |
| 1972 | − 0.02 | + 0.10 | + 0.02 | + 1.00 | + 0.24 | + 0.12 |
| 1973 | − 0.03 | + 0.09 | + 0.01 | + 1.00 | + 0.21 | + 0.11 |
| 1974 | −[d] | + 0.05 | + 0.10 | + 1.00 | + 0.19 | + 0.13 |
| 1975 | +[d] | + 0.08 | + 0.13 | + 1.00 | + 0.11 | + 0.13 |
| 1976 | + 0.01 | + 0.13 | + 0.24 | + 1.00 | + 0.16 | + 0.16 |
| 1977 | −[d] | + 0.09 | + 0.31 | + 1.00 | + 0.19 | + 0.18 |

Sources: CSO, *United Kingdom of Payments 1966–76* and *Economic Trends*.

[a] Defined as (exports *minus* imports)/(exports *plus* imports).

[b] Excluding receipts from lending in sterling and from borrowing and lending in other currencies.

[c] Surplus = +, deficit = −.

[d] Between + 0.01 and − 0.01.

minute comparative disadvantage in sea transport (less than $-0.01$) and that its comparative disadvantage in the mid-1960s in travel has changed into a comparative advantage (from $-0.20$ to $+0.31$).

The main economic characteristics of travel are that such expenditures tend to be price-sensitive (that is, the elasticity is very important) on the supply-side, that its income elasticity is likewise high and that, as far as all industrial countries are concerned, such spending tends to fall into a category of freely tradeable services, but not completely so because of the restrictions that some countries can impose and from time to time do. Of these three characteristics price sensitivity is most important and the improvement in UK competitiveness can be attributed primarily to the decline in the external value of sterling. The fact that travel expenditure tends to be labour-intensive places it in a special class of its own.

Sea transport – which on the UK definition includes receipts and expenditure on freight, charter incomes and expenditure on passenger fares and spending by ship operators at home and overseas – is price-sensitive and its substitutability as concerns air transport is growing, but above all it is only 'quasi' freely tradeable. Indeed, sea transport is one industry where protective devices proliferate and have been increasing rapidly. In addition to developing countries now increasingly resorting to cargo preference schemes, there is in existence a bewildering variety of operating and construction subsidies, special tax privileges and other measures designed to offset 'comparative disadvantage' and turn it into a 'comparative advantage'.

Civil aviation in some ways resembles sea transport. Operating and capital-cost subsidies are common, enabling inefficient operators to continue in business; scheduled international traffic is subject to inter-governmental agreement, including prices; it is possible and not uncommon to levy discriminatory charges for airport facilities. The really freely tradeable proportion of this market (comprising mainly charter business) is probably small.

The group of 'other services' where there has been a fractional decline in the UK's competitiveness comprises miscellaneous transactions extending from those which are not freely tradeable at all to those which are freely tradeable, whose economic characteristics differ enormously. Non-freely tradeable goods include telecommunications and postal services, which are subject to inter-governmental agreements, and which are frequently in the hands of governmental monopolies; royalties and services among group companies are a return on 'human capital' and tend to be related to existing and new foreign investment; payments and receipts relating to films and television are again subject to special policies in regard to these industries. The only transactions that can be described as being freely tradeable or nearly so are earnings of construction work, comprising professional fees, where the UK has been consistently in a comfortable and growing surplus (with a trade ratio of 1.0) as well as 'others'. The latter includes professional fees, subscriptions, etc., which are subject to market forces.

It is the last category, financial services, which comprises fully-freely tradeable services, where the UK has had and continues to have a significant comparative advantage (a trade ratio of 1.0) and where net receipts have been growing rapidly. The official statisticians distinguish in this group five sub-groups: insurance, banking, commodity trading, merchanting of goods and brokerage, etc.

Insurance comprises income relating almost entirely to the underwriting of risks other than life risk and includes, of course, reinsurance. Such estimates as are available indicate that the income elasticity (the relation of GNP to such spending) is high and that it is also price-sensitive. Although it is labour-intensive, it is rapidly becoming less so. Above all, such services are freely tradeable. Earnings from banking, which exclude net interest on sterling lending to non-residents and net earnings on foreign currency deposits (Eurocurrency markets), although in official statistics they appear under interest, profits and dividends, are likewise income and price elastic and are fully and freely tradeable. (Incidentally, such banking receipts, especially from Eurocurrency deposits, have been growing rapidly and in 1976 (the last year for which statistics are available) amounted to £351 million and accounted for nearly 20 per cent of the private sector's net receipts of £1831 million under interest, profits and dividends.) Commodity trading, other merchanting, and brokerage income display similar characteristics. They respond strongly to a rise in the world's income, are price-sensitive and are becoming rapidly less labour-intensive.

To sum up: in total the UK's private services have been doing well. Their competitiveness as measured by the trade ratio has been improving. The improvement is to a large extent due to the expansion of fully-freely tradeable services, where the UK enjoys high competitiveness with favourable income and price elasticities and which are labour-intensive but becoming less so. Financial services are in this class. The UK's performance has been less impressive in services which are not freely tradeable because of impediments restricting competition in one way or another. These services include 'other services' and above all civil aviation and sea transport.

If this view is correct, the UK's private services and external accounts could benefit from a policy of reducing impediments to invisible transactions. While the freedom of movement of goods has played a central part in the UK's external economic policy, services tended to be forgotten.

The realisation that the process of balanced growth of the world economy requires a freedom of movement of services as much as a freedom of movement of goods would be of benefit to all and, above all, to mature countries such as the UK.

*References*

[1] Singh, A., 'UK industry and the world economy: a case of de-industrialisation?', *Cambridge Journal of Economics*, June 1977.

# 6 De-industrialisation in the Netherlands?

## by C. A. van den Beld

**Introduction**

In November 1977 the *Financial Times* published a special edition on the Netherlands, with some emphasis, naturally, on the Netherlands economy. This included the statement that the Netherlands had succeeded in building up over the last 25 years one of the 'world's most prosperous and enlightened welfare states', with minimum wages higher than in any other industrialised society, labour productivity also high, remarkably few strikes, and a social security system covering a very wide field. In sharp contrast, however, the industrial base (defined as the whole business sector) was seen as having been badly undermined in recent years.

There is, indeed, reason for serious concern about developments in the Netherlands; not over inflation, which is levelling off, nor about the balance of payments, which still shows some surplus on current account, but in terms of low profitability in industry, lack of international competitiveness, rising unemployment and falling employment.

The purpose of this paper is to consider how economic welfare was built up since the war and what factors led to the weakening of the industrial base. This is investigated first in macroeconomic terms and then as trends towards de-industrialisation in a narrower sense. In describing the past, variables and policies are emphasised which still seem relevant to the problems now confronting the economy.

**Macroeconomic Trends**

*Developments since the war*

The relevant period can roughly be divided into three: the 1950s,

1960–73, and the years since the very considerable rise in oil prices at the end of 1973.

The 1950s were a period of reconstruction – with Marshall Aid – and expansion. Before 1950 profits had been low and unemployment high, but the recovery was fast and remarkable. In general, the propensity to invest was high and external demand was strong.

Government policies which contributed significantly to the expansion of the economy included:

(a) devaluation of the guilder in 1949, in order to improve international competitiveness;

(b) up to 1953, wage increases permitted only on grounds of price increases, in order to restore the profitability of industry;

(c) after 1953, nominal wage increases still controlled, but real wages allowed to follow productivity trends;

(d) tax burdens gradually reduced, with specific measures to stimulate business investment.

The 1950s were thus characterised by a strong industrial base and rapid growth. Profits were high and in foreign markets Dutch industry was very competitive. In consequence, its export performance was good, with a growing share in the volume of world trade, which was itself being freed from quantitative restrictions. The low level of (real) wages meant that labour-intensive activities shared in the general expansion of the economy; unemployment fell to a low level.

Proceeding to the 1960s: the Treaty of Rome in 1958 gave new impulse to the economy, raising the propensity to invest even higher than it was already. International trade continued to grow rapidly and after 1965 natural gas became an important element in the overall expansion, which continued to gather momentum. On the labour market unemployment fell below 1 per cent and a wage explosion following the well-known Phillips' mechanism occurred in 1964 (the government having abandoned its policy of strict wage control in 1959). This initiated a period of large wage and price increases, and since then – in contrast to the 1950s – the government has favoured a relative expansion of public expenditure, so that taxes too have risen. More pronounced still was the increase in social security contributions due to a vast extension of the social security system. These increases were passed on in wages to a considerable extent, thus reinforcing the spiral of wage and price increases in the 1960s and the early 1970s.

All transfer payments by the government, including social security payments, were in some way or other linked to wages, which, of course, protected many kinds of incomes, but not profits. In fact, unit labour costs rose faster in the Netherlands than abroad, implying a considerable deterioration in international competitiveness. Entrepreneurs could not pass on the increase in full, so that there was a sharp rise in real wage costs and profit incomes were severely affected.

Throughout the 1960s production expanded largely in capital-intensive industries, partly because of the sharp rise in real wage costs. Labour-intensive activities, therefore, had a limited share in the expansion of the economy, again in contrast to the 1950s. From 1964 registered unemployment started to rise, slightly but definitely, but in subsequent years the rise was a poor reflection only of what was happening on the labour market. In 1967 the Labour Unfitness Act was passed, under which many people of working age were declared unfit to work, and therefore not registered as unemployed.

These trends continued, more or less, into the early 1970s. Undoubtedly, therefore, the factors which have weakened the industrial base (still broadly defined) were already strong by 1973.

The rise in oil prices at the end of 1973 intensified the international recession of 1974–5. In 1976 there was an upturn in international trade, but its trend appeared to be slow, and it still is.

Many industrialised (and other) countries were confronted with balance-of-payments problems because of the rise in oil prices. The Dutch economy, however, maintained a considerable surplus, being rich in energy, and whereas other currencies depreciated the guilder appreciated. This had a favourable influence on inflation, but it led to a further deterioration in international competitiveness, affecting imports as well as exports. Again the industrial base became weaker: there was a considerable increase in unused capacity, profit levels were severely affected, and exports both suffered from the slow trend in international trade and could not maintain their volume share, which fell from 1974 onwards. The competitive position was also reflected in the capital account of the balance of payments. Since 1974 capital exports in the form of direct investment abroad have been substantial, in contrast to reduced investment at home.

Government policy has remained in favour of a relative expansion in public expenditure. Additional revenue could be obtained from the exploitation of natural gas, but increases in taxes and social security contributions were less than in the past; fiscal encouragement to investment was considerably extended, also government contributions to the social security system. In total these tax concessions and contributions amounted to 3.5 per cent of national income in 1977, thus counterbalancing to some extent the weakening of the industrial base, but the underlying upward trend in public expenditure was strong and was reinforced by rising unemployment. Large sums, too, are nowadays spent on supporting industries and individual firms, which again indicates the difficulties which many businesses are encountering.

## Some data

The story of the past can be illustrated by statistical data as in Table 6.1. This reveals very considerable rates of growth in production and in labour productivity in the 1960s. But after 1973 production grew slowly and there was a fall in employment. The trend in unemployment was downward until 1963 (when it reached 0.8 per cent), but then upward until the present. The proportion of the active in the total population became strikingly low.

The weakening of the industrial base can be seen from labour's share in total business income, which has shown a considerable increase after some decline in the 1950s. The present level appears to be extremely high, and is a result of both high costs and under-utilisation of capacity, the latter being due partly to the low level of international trade combined with a poor export performance. Nevertheless, the balance of payments still shows some surplus on current account.

There has been a very marked rise in the burden of taxes and social premiums over the last twenty years. Combined with non-tax revenues (which include those from natural gas), this illustrates the strong upward trend in public expenditure. The increase in the collective burden contributed to the wage–price spiral as explained above, but inflation has levelled off in recent years. Although partly due to the Phillips' mechanism and additional government contributions to the social security system, this was mainly a consequence of substantial depreciations in other currencies and thus the continuous appreciation of the guilder. The levelling off of inflation is not shown specifically in Table 6.1, but the present rise in wages is of the order of 7 per cent per annum, while the rise in prices is only about 5 per cent.

Thus, the figures clearly reveal how economic welfare has been built up. There is much less concern now about inflation than there was some years ago and the balance-of-payments current account is not too

*Table 6.1   Macroeconomic indicators for the Netherlands economy, 1950–77*

|  | 1950 | 1959 | 1968 | 1973 | 1977 |
|---|---|---|---|---|---|
|  | (annual percentage changes) | | | | |
| Volume of production[a] | 4.0 | 5.9 | 5.9 | 2.5 | |
| Labour productivity[a] | 3.2 | 4.6 | 5.6 | 3.1 | |
| Employment in man–years[a] | 0.8 | 1.2 | 0.3 | – 0.6 | |
| Investment in fixed assets[a] | 4.6 | 8.1 | 3.3 | 0.9 | |
| World trade (volume)[b] | 6.9 | 8.8 | 10.6 | 4.8 | |
| Real wage costs | 3.4 | 5.4 | 5.9 | 4.0 | |
| Currency appreciation[c] | 0.6 | 0.6 | 1.8 | 4.1 | |
| Wage level | 7.1 | 9.4 | 13.6 | 11.8 | |
| Consumer prices | 3.1 | 3.7 | 7.2 | 9.0 | |
|  | | | (percentages) | | |
| Labour's share of income[d] | 74.3 | 72.8 | 80.3 | 84.8 | 92.5 |
| Share in national income of: | | | | | |
|   Taxes plus social | | | | | |
|     security contributions | 35.6 | 34.1 | 42.7 | 48.6 | 52.0 |
|   Non-tax revenues | 2.1 | 2.6 | 2.6 | 2.9 | 5.2 |
|   Current a/c surplus on | | | | | |
|     balance of payments | – 6.7 | 5.2 | 0.3 | 4.2 | 0.4 |
| Unemployment rate | 2.1 | 1.9 | 1.8 | 2.4 | 4.5 |
| Active/total population | 37.3 | 36.2 | 35.9 | 34.9 | 33.5 |

Source: Calculated from data published by the Central Bureau of Statistics; the 1977
       figures are provisional estimates.
[a] In the whole business sector, public and private.
[b] Weighted according to the geographical distribution of exports.
[c] On export markets.
[d] In all industry except natural gas, public utilities and the leasing of dwellings.
Labour income includes wages and salaries *plus* an imputed income for the self-
employed.

unsatisfactory. From these points of view the economy seems strong.
Essentially weak, however, is the business sector (except for gas), as
a result of past trends and, more recently, of low growth in international trade, currency depreciations and capacity surpluses.
Government policy has provided, and provides, some offset, but it is
understandable that full counterbalancing policies are far from easy,
certainly with the strong upward trend in public expenditure.

*Some econometrics*

It is also of interest to describe the Netherlands economy in model
terms, in order to clarify more concisely how the economy behaves.

Such a model, however, has been fully described in a publication by the Central Planning Bureau [1]. The elements of it worth mentioning in the present context are discussed below.

As already stated, increases in the collective burden were to a large extent passed on in wages. This is derived from the following wage equation based on annual observations over the period 1948–73:

$$\dot{w} = 1.0(\dot{y} - \dot{a}) + 1.0\dot{p}_{c-\frac{1}{4}} - 0.9u + 0.5CB + 2.0$$

where $w$ = nominal wages,

$y - a$ = labour productivity,

$p_c$ = consumer prices,

$u$ = unemployment,

$CB$ = burden of direct taxes plus social contributions,

and dots denote annual percentage changes.

The price of consumption $(p_c)$ includes indirect taxes, which are fully reflected in wages. Similarly, half the increase in the burden of direct taxes and social security contributions appears to be reflected in the increase in wages. In general, therefore, government policies involving higher taxes, etc. have contributed substantially to the wage–price spiral.

While there is no doubt that higher prices lead to higher wages, equally there is no doubt that higher wages are passed on in prices, but only partially so. Experience shows that prices are determined not only by costs but also by competing prices abroad. This can be illustrated by the price equation for merchandise exports:

$$\dot{p}_e = 0.5\dot{k} + 0.5\dot{p}_{ec} + 30\Delta q + 25(q - 0.97) - 1.3$$

where $p_e$ = the price of merchandise exports,

$k$ = total costs (import prices *plus* unit labour costs),

$p_{ec}$ = the price of competing exports,

and $q$ = degree of capacity utilisation.

Similarly, prices of domestic final demand (consumption and investment) are a function not only of costs but also of foreign prices, in this case prices of competing imports.

Such relations for prices and wages reveal, in particular, that a higher collective burden leads to higher wages and lower profit margins, which confirms what was said earlier about the increase in the relative size of the public sector and the weakening of the industrial base in consequence.

Wages and prices also enter the system as determinants of real wage costs. Prices of final demand (and imports) determine the price of (net) production, and real wage costs are defined in terms of nominal wages and production prices.

Real wage costs then play a role as one determinant of capacity production. More generally, a vintage approach is used to arrive at capacity production, the latter being generated by gross investment (in equipment and transport) over the past, with investment subject to technical as well as economic obsolescence. Economic obsolescence is regarded as governed by the quasi-rent of the equipment, which falls to zero in a certain period after installation as a result of increasing real wage costs, which are taken as applying to labour on all vintages – the older more labour-intensive ones as well as the newer ones of lower labour intensity. In other words, if the revenue from a vintage exactly covers its wage costs – implying zero quasi-rent – this vintage is assumed to be still in operation; it is the marginal vintage which is about to become economically obsolete as soon as its wage costs exceed revenue. Therefore, more old equipment will be scrapped the higher the rate of increase in real wage costs. Thus, real wage costs enter the system as a determinant of the total stock of equipment in operation and of the corresponding amount of potential employment. Using the years 1959–73 as observation period, a fair approximation to reality can be obtained with a capital coefficient for all vintages of 1.25 in 1970 prices, and the labour intensity of successive vintages declining at a rate of 5 per cent per annum.

Obviously, potential employment should be distinguished from actual employment. The latter appears to vary with the under-utilisation of capacity, the elasticity being 0.4, when under-utilisation is measured by comparing actual and potential production. The conclusion is that there is no fixed long-term relation between production (capacity) and (potential) employment. Apart from under-utilisation of capacity, labour intensity varies with real wage costs. This holds for industry as a whole, and it is still more pronounced in manufacturing, as will be seen from the next section.

## Trends in Manufacturing Industry

### Manufacturing as a whole

The above analysis revealed considerable changes in overall trends over time; rapid growth was followed by slow growth, increasing employment by a decrease; there were changes in international competitiveness as judged from export performance; the industrial base was strong, but became weak as shown by labour's share in total enterprise income.

Similar changes can be observed in manufacturing industry. This is not surprising: manufacturing accounted on average for about a third of total production and for about 80 per cent of total merchandise exports. And there are inter-industry relations and other complementarities between manufacturing and many service industries which contribute to this similarity.

*Table 6.2   Indicators for Netherlands manufacturing industry, 1950–77*

|  | 1950 | 1959 | 1968 | 1973 | 1977 |
|---|---|---|---|---|---|
|  | (annual percentage changes) | | | | |
| Volume of production[a] |  | 5.9 | 6.3 | 6.7 | 0.8 |
| Labour productivity[a] |  | 4.9 | 5.6 | 7.7 | 3.6 |
| Employment in man–years[a] |  | 0.9 | 0.7 | − 1.0 | − 2.7 |
| Investment in fixed assets (gross)[a] |  | 1.5 | 9.3 | − 0.7 | − 0.9 |
| Merchandise exports (volume) |  | 9.8 | 8.9 | 13.8 | 2.0 |
| Real wage costs[a] |  | 4.6 | 6.9 | 7.9 | 6.6 |
|  | (indices) | | | | |
| Relative unit labour costs[ab] | 100 | 93 | 109 | 115 | 118 |
|  | (percentages) | | | | |
| Labour's share of income[a] | 68 | 66 | 73 | 74 | 86 |
| Home production/ home demand[c] | .. | 74[d] | 67 | 58 | 54 |
| Manufacturing investment/ total business investment[e] | 40 | 31 | 33 | 28 | 26 |

Source: as Table 6.1.
[a] In manufacturing only.
[b] Based on dollar costs.
[c] In current prices.
[d] 1958
[e] In 1970 prices.

Developments in manufacturing can be seen from Table 6.2. Again it appears that the expansion gathered momentum during the 1960s, with production growing at 6.7 per cent per annum in the period 1968–73. In general, growth in manufacturing considerably exceeded growth in total production, but on the whole the difference was decreasing. This is what perhaps may be called a trend towards post-industrialisation, which appears to be more pronounced in value than volume terms; relative prices moved against manufacturing.

In considerable deviation from these long-term trends, the volume growth of manufacturing production was very low indeed after 1973, only 0.8 per cent per annum in comparison with 2.5 per cent for the whole of industry. Partly this can be explained by the low growth of world trade and a poor export performance, in consequence of which the volume of merchandise exports – which is fairly representative of manufacturing exports – has risen by only 2 per cent per annum over the last four years. The bad export performance suggests a deterioration in international competitiveness. When the latter is measured in terms of relative unit labour costs, an improvement can be observed during the 1950s, followed by a deterioration up to the present (Table 6.2).

*Table 6.3   Export performance and relative prices[a] in the Netherlands, 1953–9 to 1973–7 (cumulative percentage changes)*

|  | 1953–9 | 1960–6 | 1967–72 | 1973–7 |
|---|---|---|---|---|
| Share of merchandise exports in volume of world trade | 16.0 | – 4.5 | 17.0 | – 9.0 |
| Export prices relative to those of competitors abroad[b] | – 6.5 | 2.5 | – 5.5 | 9.0 |

Source: as Table 6.1.
[a] Excluding natural gas.
[b] Three-year moving averages, weighted 0.25, 0.50, 0.25.

There is, however, no direct correspondence between unit labour costs and export performance. The latter depends on relative prices, as is clear from Table 6.3, which shows some deterioration in the export position in the early 1960s. This was a consequence of capacity shortages at home; later on the reverse was true, very substantial investment to overcome such shortages led to relatively low export prices and resulted in a larger volume share in international trade. After 1973 the trends were again reversed.

Thus, the availability of capacity played its role in the price mechanism. On average, the price elasticity of exports appears to be about – 2 (a traditional result known as the 'Tinbergen-two'), but since 1973 it seems to have been considerably lower. Probably this is because Dutch exports are relatively energy-intensive, so that, after the rise in oil prices, high export prices exaggerated uncompetitiveness. Equally uncertain is the effect on prices of the increasing capacity surpluses after 1973. The impression is that profit margins on exports have reached their lower limits, which would imply that the export price equation is more complicated than that quoted in the previous section.

Further import penetration contributed to the slow growth of manufacturing production. However, this trend is a long-term one, which became particularly strong in the second half of the 1960s. Undoubtedly, therefore, increased competition from abroad was visible earlier, and more systematically, on the import side than in export performance. The relevant price elasticity is difficult to calculate, since import penetration can be measured (so far) only in current prices (the price elasticity of total merchandise imports is about $-0.6$, a large part of the total consisting of raw materials, where price elasticities are very low, if not zero).

Foreign price competition, together with the rise in relative unit labour costs, led to lower profit margins, profit incomes being severely affected. This is clear from the trend in the share of labour in manufacturing income, which is continuously upward since the early 1960s. It was, however, only rising slowly in the late 1960s because of a very high rate of increase in labour productivity, implying a fall in manufacturing employment. After 1973 it rose very steeply again, in consequence mainly of slow growth, increasing capacity surpluses and only partial adjustment of the actual demand for labour.

The earlier conclusion for the whole of Dutch industry, that its weakening position was clear from the rising trend in labour's share of income up to a very high level at present, is true also for manufacturing industry. Another similarity which can be observed is that there is no constant elasticity between growth rates in production and in labour productivity. Although the well-known 'Verdoorn's law' implies such a constancy, particularly for manufacturing and in conditions of full capacity utilisation, as in the period up to 1973, it appears that there is no simple relation between production and labour productivity, nor – which comes to the same thing – between production and employment. The vintage approach mentioned above accords more closely with actual developments; it can explain, at least partially, the low labour intensity of production in the period 1968–73 from the strong upward trend in real wage costs.

Employment in manufacturing in fact declined from 1965 and slow growth after 1973 accentuated this fall (Table 6.2). When the level of employment in manufacturing is considered (Table 6.4), the results

Table 6.4   Employment in Dutch manufacturing industry, 1950–77

|        | Man–years (millions) | Percentages of total employment |
|--------|--------|--------|
| 1950   | 1.03   | 30.5   |
| 1959   | 1.11   | 30.7   |
| 1965   | 1.23   | 30.8   |
| 1968   | 1.18   | 29.4   |
| 1973   | 1.13   | 27.7   |
| 1977   | 1.01   | 25.4   |

Source: as Table 6.1.

are remarkable. It reached its maximum in 1965 and is at present back to its level in 1950. And this process is continuing, with expectations of a further substantial fall in the short term. In the early 1960s manufacturing employment was above its long-term trend, following the regime of the 1950s with low wages and strong international competitiveness. A fall was therefore to be expected, but not one as dramatic as actually occurred.

At present manufacturing accounts for only 25 per cent of total employment and 27 per cent of total enterprise production. Investment in manufacturing, too, shows a relative decline over a number of years, being now 26 per cent of total investment (Table 6.2). The more general conclusion is that all the tendencies towards de-industrialisation are there, in terms not of labour productivity but of production and employment. Labour's share in total manufacturing income has become very high; investment is comparatively low; import penetration is strong and export performance disappointing.

Certainly, not all these features are peculiar to the Netherlands. This is evident from the slow growth of international trade, as well as from low investment, in consequence, *inter alia*, of capacity surpluses. Outstanding in the Netherlands was the very large expansion of public expenditure and of collective burdens, which accentuated the trend in labour's share of income, both in manufacturing and in industry as a whole, so that they are now very high indeed. Important, too, is the country's wealth in energy, which has contributed to the present high value of the guilder. However, this is not the whole story of de-industrialisation tendencies. Future prospects for the economy have to be taken into account too and this will be done in the concluding section.

## Data on some manufacturing sectors

Apart from trends in total manufacturing, it is interesting to consider the pattern of manufacturing growth. In this section, therefore, that pattern is considered on the basis of data for some industries (Tables 6.5, 6.6 and 6.7). The periods covered are different from those in Tables 6.1 and 6.2, but still representative of the 1950s, the 1960s up to 1973, and the years thereafter.

*Table 6.5    Growth of production in Dutch manufacturing industries, 1953–77 (annual percentage changes)*

|  | 1953–63 | 1963–73 | 1973–7 |
|---|---|---|---|
| Food |  |  |  |
|   Animal products | 5.2 | 4.0 | 0.8 |
|   Other | 3.2 | 3.6 | 1.1 |
| Beverages, tobacco | 6.0 | 7.6 | 5.0 |
| Textiles | 3.2 | 0.8 | − 4.5 |
| Clothing, footwear, leather | 3.0 | − 2.8 | − 9.6 |
| Paper and printing | 8.9 | 4.7 | 2.1 |
| Wood and construction materials | 6.3 | 5.2 | 0.3 |
| Chemicals, plastics, rubber | 9.7 | 12.2 | 2.5 |
| Basic metals | 10.5 | 9.3 | − 2.5 |
| Metal products, precision instruments | 6.2 | 5.7 | 1.5 |
| Electrical equipment | 14.5 | 7.9 | 2.5 |
| Transport equipment | 3.1 | 4.9 | − 1.7 |
| Petroleum refining | 8.0 | 9.0 | − 2.4 |
| *Total manufacturing* | 6.3 | 6.1 | 0.8 |

Source: as Table 6.1.

In so far as production is concerned (Table 6.5), very rapid growth – before 1973 – can be observed in oil refining, chemicals, basic metals and electrical equipment. Food and beverages, paper and printing, wood and construction materials, also metal products, had a reasonable if not full share in the expansion. Textiles and clothing managed to increase their production moderately in the 1950s, but lost considerable ground in the 1960s; import penetration, apparent in nearly all sectors, was particularly strong here.

After 1973 the fast-growing sectors as well as those which had had average growth rates were confronted with low growth; in basic metals and oil refining production even declined. Textiles and clothing suffered a very sharp fall in production and in transport equipment the decline was moderate – a partial reflection only of the difficult situation with which the shipbuilding industry is confronted.

Undoubtedly there were exceptionally large shifts in output between industries in both the 1950s and the 1960s. In the 1960s these were accentuated by still more growth in oil refining and chemicals, and by relatively less growth in other industries generally. After 1973 competition from abroad remained strong – in particular, import penetration continued in nearly all industries, being especially marked in textiles and clothing, where exports also declined. Other industries, particularly basic metals and oil refining, suffered mainly from low growth in overall demand, internally as well as externally.

International comparisons show that manufacturing production in the Netherlands is relatively specialised in food, beverages and tobacco, oil refining and chemicals, and electrical equipment; all other sectors are more or less under-represented. Over time, specialisation has remained constant for food and tobacco, has increased for chemicals, and decreased for oil refining and electrical equipment. In other sectors under-representation increased, with basic metals the most important exception (United Nations, [2]).

Apart, therefore, from general trends in the pattern of manufacturing growth and decline over the long term and the recent past, there is the basic question of whether relative specialisation can be maintained along traditional lines. No precise answer can be given, but the impression is that new specialisations have to be developed to contribute to overall growth.

The trends in labour productivity (Table 6.6) are as striking as those in production. Generally, productivity increases were larger in the 1960s than in the 1950s. Again, there appears to be no close relationship between growth rates in labour productivity and in production, which thus confirms the conclusion drawn from Table 6.2 for total manufacturing.

Under certain circumstances, therefore, Verdoorn's law fails to apply, and these circumstances existed with the acceleration in real wage costs, differing between industries, but generally leading to additional withdrawals of older, relatively labour-intensive equipment. The consequences are clearly shown by the low employment figures in the late 1960s. In fact, employment decreased in many industries, or else increased very moderately, under the combined influence of trends in production and in real wage costs (Table 6.7). In recent years further rises in real wage costs and slow growth of

Table 6.6   Growth of labour productivity in Dutch manufacturing industries, 1953–77 (annual percentage changes)

|  | 1953–63 | 1963–73 | 1973–7 |
|---|---|---|---|
| **Food** | | | |
|   Animal products | 3.6 | 3.2 | 2.8 |
|   Other | 3.3 | 4.9 | 4.7 |
| Beverages, tobacco | 5.6 | 9.5 | 6.0 |
| Textiles | 4.3 | 6.6 | 2.9 |
| Clothing, footwear, leather | 2.1 | 4.1 | 3.5 |
| Paper and printing | 5.6 | 4.2 | 3.4 |
| Wood and construction materials | 5.2 | 6.3 | 3.8 |
| Chemicals, plastics, rubber | 5.6 | 10.7 | 3.2 |
| Basic metals | 3.9 | 6.4 | − 1.1 |
| Metal products, precision instruments | 3.9 | 5.8 | 3.2 |
| Electrical equipment | 8.6 | 6.7 | 4.3 |
| Transport equipment | 3.2 | 3.5 | 0.6 |
| Petroleum refining | 4.5 | 4.2 | − 1.3 |
|   *Total manufacturing* | 4.7 | 6.8 | 3.5 |

Source: as Table 6.1.

Table 6.7   Growth of employment[a] in Dutch manufacturing industries, 1953–77 (annual percentage changes)

|  | 1953–63 | 1963–73 | 1973–7 |
|---|---|---|---|
| **Food** | | | |
|   Animal products | 1.6 | 0.8 | − 1.9 |
|   Other | − 0.1 | − 1.3 | − 3.4 |
| Beverages, tobacco | 0.3 | − 1.7 | − 0.9 |
| Textiles | − 1.0 | − 5.5 | − 7.2 |
| Clothing, footwear, leather | 0.8 | − 6.6 | − 12.7 |
| Paper and printing | 3.1 | 0.5 | − 1.3 |
| Wood and construction materials | 1.0 | − 1.0 | − 3.4 |
| Chemicals, plastics, rubber | 3.9 | 1.4 | − 0.7 |
| Basic metals | 6.4 | 2.7 | − 1.4 |
| Metal products, precision instruments | 2.2 | – | − 1.6 |
| Electrical equipment | 5.3 | 1.2 | − 1.7 |
| Transport equipment | − 0.1 | 1.5 | − 2.3 |
| Petroleum refining | 3.4 | 4.6 | − 1.1 |
|   *Total manufacturing* | 1.6 | − 0.7 | − 2.7 |

Source: as Table 6.1.

[a] In man–years.

production have accentuated the fall in employment. All the sectors distinguished in Table 6.7 became 'labour-releasing' after 1973; on that level of aggregation, no 'labour-absorbing' branch of manufacturing remained.

*Table 6.8   Labour's share of income[a] in Dutch manufacturing industries, 1953–77 (percentages)*

|  | 1953 | 1963 | 1973 | 1977 |
|---|---|---|---|---|
| Food |  |  |  |  |
|   Animal products | 41.3 | 86.2 | 77.5 | 73.2 |
|   Other | 72.5 | 75.3 | 81.8 | 101.2 |
| Beverages, tobacco | 57.4 | 60.6 | 61.3 | 71.0 |
| Textiles | 67.1 | 85.4 | 92.4 | 100.8 |
| Clothing, footwear, leather | 84.0 | 85.5 | 106.5 | 108.7 |
| Paper and printing | 62.7 | 70.9 | 84.5 | 91.1 |
| Wood and construction materials | 75.1 | 75.7 | 75.6 | 83.6 |
| Chemicals, plastics, rubber | 37.2 | 54.6 | 57.5 | 81.7 |
| Basic metals | 52.7 | 53.3 | 61.8 | 90.7 |
| Metal products, precision instruments | 70.2 | 77.9 | 80.0 | 83.6 |
| Electrical equipment | 61.9 | 62.2 | 71.0 | 76.3 |
| Transport equipment | 80.0 | 77.5 | 89.7 | 100.0 |
| Petroleum refining | 75.6 | 82.5 | 31.6 | 95.0 |
| *Total manufacturing* | 65.0 | 72.2 | 74.1 | 86.3 |

Source: as Table 6.1.

[a] Defined as the share of wages and salaries in net value added at factor cost, where wages and salaries include an imputed income for the self-employed.

Characteristic, too, of recent developments is the sharp rise in labour's share of income in nearly all branches of manufacturing. This is evident from Table 6.8, which also shows the movements in labour's share over the period since 1953. Upward trends prevailed from the early 1960s, which is not surprising after what has been said about developments in total manufacturing and industry in general. Increases in unit labour costs which surpass those of foreign competitors and cannot be fully passed on in prices tend to affect profits, particularly in those industries which are most sensitive to foreign price competition, that is, those where exports or competing imports are relatively important. This is, however, only a very partial explanation of the sharp rise in labour's share of income in the recent past. Low growth rates which resulted in capacity surpluses and only partial adjustment of the actual demand for labour were then the main causes.

Table 6.8 reveals that at present labour's share of income is high, if not extremely high, in nearly all branches of manufacturing. This underlines the present difficulties of manufacturing industry, which account for the large amounts the government must spend to support individual industries and firms. The conclusion must also be that relative specialisation (relative to that in other countries) does not guarantee more reasonable profit outcomes; the high level in 1977 of labour's share in the income of the chemical industry is the most obvious illustration of this.

## Concluding Remarks

Thus, over a long period the Netherlands economy has been growing rapidly, with strong trends in manufacturing production and in labour productivity. During this phase, however, some trends were clearly reversed: labour became very scarce, but was less so later; similarly, there were long-run fluctuations in international competitiveness, in labour's share of income and in collective burdens. Over the period of expansion as a whole there were gains in shares of export markets, but import penetration also grew.

During the 1960s there was inevitably a strong upward pressure on wages and prices, reinforced by higher taxes and social security contributions. Profit incomes were increasingly squeezed by high costs and foreign price competition; labour-intensive activities, particularly in manufacturing, lost considerable ground. From 1965 there was a marked fall in manufacturing employment.

The very slow growth of manufacturing production in recent years resulted partly from past trends, partly from low external demand, partly from the exploitation of ample energy resources. Characterising these years were continuous rises in the value of the guilder, reduced inflation, losses of export markets, further import penetration and capacity surpluses. Employment fell substantially in all branches of manufacturing; labour's share of income reached a high level, again in nearly all manufacturing.

The government continued to favour a relative expansion of the public sector, but provided some counterbalance to the undermining of the industrial base. Fiscal encouragement to investment was considerably extended and social security government contributions were substantially increased. Individual industries and firms were and are supported in a number of cases, mainly within manufacturing. These counterbalancing policies are of the utmost importance in present circumstances, particularly the tendency to de-industrialisation; they are even more important when the future is taken into account. There is no doubt that by the early 1980s the balance of payments will be seriously affected by declining exports of natural gas and – more important – additional energy imports. There is equally no doubt that manufacturing industries will have to contribute substantially to economic growth, as well as to maintaining balance-of-payments equilibrium. A strategy of revitalising manufacturing, or more generally the whole industrial sector, is a precondition for attaining such policy goals. Trends must again be reversed, particularly those in labour's share of income.

Fiscal incentives to stimulate investment were and are an important element in such a strategy. Support for industries or individual firms in emergency cases cannot be entirely avoided, but should be replaced as much as possible by support for new activities – those in the energy field being very obvious examples in the context of the longer-run perspectives. Maximum restraint of nominal wages is necessary from the point of view of international competitiveness. Important, too, is restraining the growth of the public sector, in order to avoid further substantial increases in taxes and social security contributions, which tend to frustrate nominal wage restraint. Depreciation of the guilder is no policy option. Apart from its inflationary effects, it tends to be ineffective under the present regime of flexible exchange rates, given the surplus on the current account of the balance of payments.

A strategy of this kind, combined with labour-market policies to reduce unemployment in the short run, has been for some time a subject of considerable discussion in the Netherlands. It remains true, however, that the economy is very sensitive to external conditions. Some concerted international action to stimulate trade and reduce restrictions is necessary for the achievement of a more satisfactory situation.

## References

[1] Central Planning Bureau, *A Medium-term Macro Model for the Dutch Economy*, The Hague, 1977.
[2] United Nations, Economic Commission for Europe, *Structure and Change in European Industry*, Geneva, 1977.

# 7  Price Competitiveness and the Performance of Manufacturing Industry

## by Michael Posner and Andrew Steer

This paper discusses the role of 'price and cost factors' in determining the level of output of British manufacturing industry. It concentrates on the export market. It has less to say about British performance in that small part of the world market which is represented by UK final purchases – partly for reasons of expository ease, partly because we have not looked closely at import price elasticities or import penetration figures. There is also a small point of principle – we believe that it is UK performance in world markets which is important, and that the possibility of price response there is far greater than in the relatively narrow home base.

However, alarm about import penetration figures is widespread and justified. If, for instance, in all countries, world trade grows faster than home industrial production, of course import penetration on average must increase through time. But if one country's domestic growth rate is lower than that of the world average growth of industrial output, and at the same time the excess of trade growth over output growth for all countries taken together is explained by innovation in new products or processes, the supply of which is itself highly correlated with output growth, then the sluggish economy may experience very rapid import penetration, since the 'dynamic imports' are absorbed by the home customer in proportion to the *level* of his total purchases rather than their *rate of growth*. So imports, which we do not discuss, may be very important.

One other major disclaimer is necessary. One of us has long believed that it is non-price factors which are a dominant influence in trade amongst advanced manufacturing countries, and claims to have been one of the first to recognise this (Posner, [29]). Several streams of empirical work have shown the great importance of innovation, of the product cycle, of the operations of international companies, and more mundane factors such as delivery dates and sales effort (NEDO, [25]). To anticipate our conclusions, the basic importance of 'price and cost' competitiveness is limited; it is, however, an influence on trade which might be affected by official policy in the relatively short run; whereas the dynamism, creativeness, and investment behaviour of British manufacturing industry is beyond the short-term influence of the authorities.

It is this notion that cost and price competitiveness may be, however weakly, influenced by official policy that is the justification for this paper. We start by examining the arguments advanced by those who doubt the efficiency of officially induced changes in competitiveness. We then display the different indicators. The third section reports on the main empirical results of those who have estimated elasticities. We then proceed to look at one attempt to quantify the possible effects of changes in competitiveness relative to other trends in the determination of exports. A final section examines policy implications.

## The Theoretical Argument

The orthodox case for believing that changes in the exchange rate can induce suitable changes in price or cost competitiveness is based on Meade, [23], and has been summarised elsewhere (Posner, [30]). Essentially it is the textbook argument about internal and external balance, where an original (expected) disequilibrium in the trade balance leads to a change in the terms of trade sufficient to restore equilibrium. This mechanism, which uses the exchange rate as a way of varying the real wage, relies to an extent which was perhaps not universally understood in the 1950s (but see Henderson, [12] and Balogh, [3]) on the existence of money illusion, particularly among wage-earners. But, for small disturbances, the real wage effect, and therefore the required element of money illusion, is slight; this was implicitly assumed in most discussions until the mid-1960s.

There are at least three other strands to this orthodox doctrine which are relevant. First, it does *not* follow simply that a mere divergence in productivity trends between countries need lead to trade disequilibria; Johnson [15] showed that to make this story stick we had to conceive of the country with low productivity growth producing inferior goods, and this line of thought was afterwards developed into the various dynamic versions of trade theory to which we referred above. But neither for the purposes of this paper nor for policy purposes is it necessary to work out a fully articulated view on this point:

either trade imbalances appear, in which case they must be treated, or if untreated lead to certain consequences; or they do not appear, in which case the problem of cost competitiveness does not arise.

Secondly, traditional specie-flow price-change doctrines can be used very neatly to show how a single burst of technical change in one country leads to a shift in the margin of competitive advantage both in that country and abroad. Given suitable mobility of resources, an innovating firm will acquire labour from one of the previously marginal exporting firms and, in the more backward country, changes in the price level will induce a previously extra-marginal exporter to find some overseas market. That this mechanism might be accompanied by a change in real wages is necessarily true, but the essence of the mechanism is the redistribution of resources, not the change in relative incomes which precipitate that redistribution. We will return to this point below.

Thirdly (see Posner, [31]), it has been argued that the essence of the exchange-rate mechanism is not a redistribution of resources within the trading sector nor a change in factor rewards, but a change in the relative attractiveness of occupations in the traded and non-traded sectors respectively.

All these arguments are about mechanisms of adjustment. They all have the common feature that an original and persisting change in cost or price competitiveness can be induced by a suitable change in the exchange rate. Recent writers (Ball *et al.*, [2]; Odling-Smee and Hartley in Treasury, [35]) have questioned whether any exchange-rate change can influence the competitiveness indicators for long enough to produce the required effect on output and net exports. These arguments suggest that domestic wage or price levels will adjust so quickly as to destroy the profit incentive to exporters before the quantity response has occurred.

The approach of Ball and his colleagues to this issue is to adhere more explicitly to the law of one price. But Kravis and Lipsey ([19] and [20]) illustrate the fact that international differences in prices may be substantial and permanent – for example, they report that the export price of steel from the UK was 22 per cent lower than that from the US during most of the period studied (1953–64). They suggest that 'such disequilibrium situations in which markets have not fully adjusted to changes in competitive advantage may be the norm rather than the exception'. Isard [14] also concludes that 'in reality the law of one price is flagrantly and systematically violated by the empirical data'.

We comment on these results below, but although most recent work by the model builders (see, for example, Flannery and Ormerod, [10] ) show that the exchange-rate effects on cost competitiveness remain substantial for four or five years, many of the estimated response elasticities themselves have long time lags and therefore, once expectations in the industrial community have become adjusted to the recent empirical results of economists, total elasticities may turn out even smaller than those estimated for the past. To that extent even modest claims for the efficacy of the price mechanism in international trade may turn out to be excessive.

There is another strand in the attack on the traditional exchange-rate mechanism. This is the suggestion that changes in cost or price competitiveness delay the true adjustment mechanism, or featherbed inefficiency and old-fashioned producers to the disadvantage of dynamic ones. This argument harps back to the story about changes in the position of the margin of competitive advantage in the specie-flow price-change mechanism to which we referred earlier. A relatively sluggish economy which responds to lost export markets by successive devaluations will give additional advantages to traditional low-wage, low-value-added trades, while competitors will progressively innovate in new high-value-added activities (Johnson, [16]).

The implications are that a country faced with declining traditional markets and insufficient innovatory investment should concentrate on improving its rate of innovation, not on protecting (by lowering international real wages) traditional exporting trades. However, for that benign process to work there has to be a mobility of resources between activities and a responsiveness of innovators to the increased availability of those resources. For these properties it is difficult to find evidence in the British case.

If we choose to operate through exchange-rate-induced changes in competitiveness, we have to assume that existing traditional trades can expand output and will do so even though they recognise that the original price or profit advantage may largely disappear in four or five years time; we have also to assume that this incentive to those trades will not diminish similar incentives to the innovating activities – who after all also gain from the shift in competitiveness. If, on the other hand, we rely on a spot of unemployment in the traditional trades to stimulate innovation elsewhere, then we are relying on easy supply conditions to attract investors. It is understandable that this mechanism appeals to monetarist writers, but it is less easy to understand how it would work in a world where investment outcomes are determined by animal spirits and the prospect of profits.

## Choice of Competitiveness Indicators

This section shows that there is a set of alternative indicators of competitiveness available to us, and that the choice between these indicators will be determined in large part by the economic doctrine to which we adhere. For instance, if it is held that British exporters are for the most part price-takers in the overseas markets, then an index of export price competitiveness will tell us very little, because it will diverge only stochastically from unity. On the other hand, if we believe that British exporters are for the most part able to differentiate their product and choose the price at which they sell in foreign markets, an index of price competitiveness will give us a mixture of two types of information – about the *supply* conditions under which British firms operate, and about the *demand* conditions (or competition from alternative sources) which they face. There is a third possibility, that British manufacturers face foreign markets of a high degree of homogeneity, but only imperfectly competitive, in which they have the choice between selling at a higher or a lower price. In this last case the relative price chosen by the British manufacturer will, in principle, depend largely on his own costs. (This argument is pursued usefully by Enoch [8a], which appeared after the preparation of the present paper.)

This last case of imperfect competition does not lead to the conclusion that a change in the exchange rate will always be allowed to feed through to lower foreign currency prices for home exports. Holmes [13] shows that, if fears of oligopolistic reaction by competitors has led to a form of entry-deterrent pricing, then it will be rational for many firms to maintain their foreign currency prices when the exchange rate falls, unless the foreign elasticity of demand is very high indeed – of the order of six or seven. If the dollar price being charged for Scotch whisky is already a bit below the profit-maximising price, it would be madness to use a sterling devaluation to cut that dollar price; rather the dollar price should be maintained and the increased competitiveness taken out in higher profits.

Corresponding to these differing measures of competitiveness should be different indicators of market response. Thus the familiar 'price elasticities of demand' should apply only in the third case, where prices can be set through arbitrary action of British suppliers. In the other cases what will often be at issue is some sort of elasticity of supply, or elasticity of response to changes in profitability.

We have not, however, been able to differentiate sufficiently between the different coefficients in Table 7.2 below to illustrate the effects of different theoretical approaches. We have indeed presented all the outcomes in terms of demand price elasticity and it seems likely, therefore, as we explain below, that the numbers we report are underestimates of the true volume response to changes in competitiveness.

A foreign importer's demand for UK exports depends on the price of UK exports, the price of equivalent exports from other countries and the price of home-produced alternatives, all measured in the same currency. Thus, in the absence of money illusion, demand for exports is a function of two relative prices (in addition to non-price factors). The supply of exports depends on the absolute profitability of exporting (export prices *minus* unit costs) and on its profitability relative to selling in the home market (export prices *minus* domestic wholesale prices). The enthusiasm with which exports are marketed, as reflected in non-price factors, must depend to an extent on profitability, which must therefore be included as a determinant of international competitiveness.

Some researchers have attempted to explain the supply and demand of exports separately. For example, until recently Whitehall treatment of export behaviour was based on the framework suggested by Hutton and Minford (Treasury, [34]). Prices are assumed to clear the market only in the long run. Short-run export markets may be in disequilibrium, with deliveries determined according to whether constraints occur on the demand or the supply side, and the extent to which stocks and queues are utilised in periods of excess demand and supply. In like vein, Batchelor [4] provides a model which allows for switches between supply-constrained and demand-constrained periods. However, most econometric studies of export behaviour employ single-equation models supplemented by price equations to overcome problems of simultaneity bias (Richardson [32], page 4).

The extent to which exported goods can compete with home-produced goods on the foreign market is, arguably, best measured by relative wholesale prices. This would appear to be preferable to the use of consumer prices, since the latter include the prices of services, which are generally not internationally traded, although Cassel [6] in his original formulation of the doctrine of purchasing power parity is emphatic that the relevant indices are not those that are limited to the measurement of the prices of traded goods and Keynes ([18], pages 244–53) is scathing in his attack on Winston Churchill for the use of relative wholesale prices to justify the 1925 return to the gold standard at the prewar mint parity with the dollar (Moggridge, [24], Chapter 3).

It is now well known that there may exist substantial and sustained divergences between wholesale and export prices (Kravis and Lipsey, [19]) and, since it is, of course, the export price that actually must be paid by importers, a measure of relative export prices or unit values may be regarded as a more appropriate indicator of competiveness. Export prices, however, suffer from several drawbacks. First, they only include those goods which are actually traded, ignoring those marginal goods that might be exported with a slight gain in productivity or reduction in costs. Strictly speaking, any price at which business is actually transmitted is by definition competitive.

Second, export prices may not be at all indicative of the ability of the export sector to produce as efficiently as foreign competitors. In a situation of competitive pricing in the international market and oligopolistic behaviour in the home market, the export price is determined largely by world prices and changes in productivity are reflected in variations in the export profit margin rather than in prices.

A key problem with measures of price competitiveness, therefore, is that price is determined by the interaction of demand and supply factors. For analytic purposes we would need to assume that changing relative prices reflect principally variations in supply-side factors alone; that is, that demand schedules are stable or at least shift in a manner that is easily explained. Without this assumption we cannot expect our measure of competitiveness to help explain changes in quantities traded. For example, if demand for a particular good increases, driving up its price, a country specialising in that good appears to *lose* competitiveness, due to the heavy weight attached to that good's price in its export price index. Kravis and Lipsey [19] partially overcome this problem by constructing an index of relative prices of a bundle of commodities that is the same for all countries, even although many countries do not export many of the goods included. Any increase in the demand for a particular product raises the price of that product relative to the other products in all competing countries, with no resulting change in competitiveness (as long as each country's supply elasticity is the same).

The difficulty involved in disentangling demand from supply

influences is the principal argument in favour of using unit costs rather than prices in measures of relative price competitiveness, since the former, it may be assumed, respond more slowly to shifts in demand. No comprehensive series of relative unit costs has yet been compiled and the best we can do is a measure of relative normal unit labour costs (constructed by the IMF), or various close substitutes for this measure, including the well-known NIESR version. In addition to largely excluding demand-side effects, this measure reflects productivity improvements directly and thus is not affected by whether these improvements are passed on in export prices or profit margins. There is some evidence that the relationship between exports and relative labour costs is more stable over different time periods than that between exports and other measures of competitiveness (Richardson, [32]). Such a measure is then very much a step in the right direction, although labour costs form only a part of total unit costs. This proves a serious drawback, particularly where imported raw materials comprise a substantial part of an industry's input. A depreciation of the exchange rate or a rise in foreign prices affects unit labour costs only gradually through the wage bargaining process, but total unit costs are influenced immediately. Care must be taken therefore in assessing the gains or losses in competitiveness accruing from changes in the exchange rate when this measure is employed.

Most indices of competitiveness are based upon unit values rather than on the prices actually paid. Unit values may vary, however, according to shifts in production from one type of product to another and this effect may cause substantial distortion in measuring competitiveness in manufactured goods.

The most comprehensive attempt to construct indices designed to overcome many of the difficulties discussed above remains that of Kravis and Lipsey [19]. These 'international price indexes' included offer prices as well as traded prices and, to ensure the comparability of products, the respondents to the questionnaires were allowed themselves to define the product when giving price relatives. An important additional feature was the estimation of 'hedonic' indices to overcome the problem of variation in quality. Further empirical work along these lines might well be useful for the UK, to provide policy-makers with guidance in exchange-rate policy and econometricians with important new fodder for their export equations. It would certainly seem preferable that time and money should be devoted to the careful specification and compilation of better indices of competitiveness than to the disputation of the relative merits of a number of highly imperfect measures.

*A priori* it cannot be said whether an ideal price index, adjusted for quality changes, would demonstrate a higher or lower price elasticity of exports than conventional measures. To the extent that price changes reflect variations in quality, we would expect conventional measures to yield downward biased elasticities. However, to the extent that quality changes substitute for price adjustments following changes in unit costs, conventional price measures would yield upward biased elasticity estimates. The Kravis–Lipsey indices indicate that the former influence is dominant, since their estimated elasticities were significantly greater than those of previous studies for similar industries. (A price elasticity of UK exports to the US of −3.4 was reported.)

*Chart 7.1    Recent trends in alternative indices of competitiveness*
*(1970 = 100)*

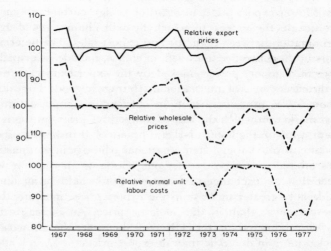

Charts 7.1 and 7.2 illustrate the variability of UK export competitiveness in recent years. The depreciation of sterling in 1975 was insufficient to counteract the greater rate of inflation in this country than abroad, while the continued depreciation in 1976 more than compensated for this. At the end of 1976 the relative export price index was 8.9 per cent lower than at the beginning of that year. UK competitiveness was, by this test, at a historically high level. During the same period relative wholesale prices and unit labour costs fell by

9.8 and 13.3 per cent respectively, while sterling depreciated by 17.2 per cent. Between the fourth quarter of 1976 and the fourth quarter of 1977, however, UK competitiveness in terms of relative export prices deteriorated by 15.2 per cent, and indeed was then worse than at any time since the second quarter of 1972, but the increase in relative unit labour costs was much less than this (6.9 per cent) and by this criterion the UK continued to enjoy a degree of competitiveness that was high by the standards of 1970–5. By the end of April 1978, by all tests, there had been an improvement of around 7 per cent.

It has already been argued that export prices may be poor indicators of underlying trends in costs and productivity, and the pricing behaviour of exporters has become the subject of considerable interest (Magee, [22]; Branson, [5]; Kalter, [17]; Kravis and Lipsey [20]; Batchelor [4]; Flannery and Ormerod [10]; Hague *et al.*, [11]; Holmes, [13]). Following an exchange-rate devaluation an exporter is faced with two related pricing decisions: first, he must decide whether he will lower export prices in terms of foreign currency; second, he must decide the extent to which he will change the degree of discrimination between domestic and export sales. The determining factors in these two decisions will, of course, include principally the degree of oligopoly power enjoyed by the exporter in each market and the effectiveness of international arbitrage in goods. For example, suppose a UK firm operates in an unfriendly oligopolistic international market, in which the fear of competitive price cutting is ever-present, while in the home market it practices 'British' pricing of the familiar cost-plus variety. If international arbitrage in that particular firm's product is discouraged for one reason or another, we would expect that an exchange-rate depreciation would bring about a considerably greater increase in the export price (measured in the home currency) than in the domestic price. An increase in unit costs of production in the UK, on the other hand, would be reflected more in domestic than in export prices.

Chart 7.2, which plots relative export prices and the relative profitability of exporting over selling at home, illustrates these points. For example, following the November 1967 sterling devaluation of 14 per cent, relative export prices fell 9.5 per cent within a quarter, implying that, in terms of sterling, some export prices were increased immediately. Since most UK export prices at that time were denominated in the home currency, the immediate pass-through was greater than it would have been if denomination were in terms of the

Chart 7.2 *Relative profitability of exports and home sales, and relative export prices, 1966–77*

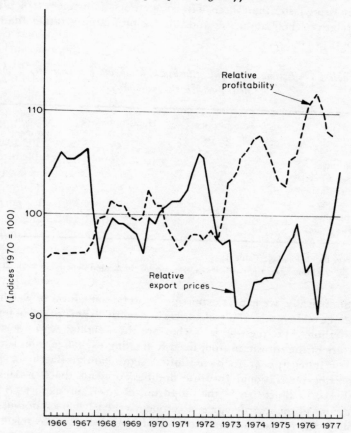

Note: relative profitability defined as export price divided by domestic wholesale price for manufactured goods.

foreign currency, due to the fact that, for administrative reasons, it takes some time for firms to raise prices. Thus, relative profitability continued to rise during the first three quarters of 1968 as export prices rose faster than wholesale prices, so that by the end of that year the relative profitability of exporting was 5 per cent higher than a year earlier. This analysis of the aggregate trends is supported by the microeconomic evidence provided by Rosendale [33]. When, on the other hand, a shift in competitiveness is caused by internal factors, such as in the latter part of 1974 and early 1975, when UK costs were rising faster than those of its competitors, adjustment took place in relative wholesale prices and relative profitability rather than in export prices.

Table 7.1  Estimated weights attached to home and foreign prices in the determination of export prices

| | Foreign price in sterling | Home price | Speed of adjustment[a] |
|---|---|---|---|
| Fixed rates | | | |
| Pre-1967 devaluation | − 0.07 | 1.07 | 0.25 |
| Post-1967 devaluation | 0.61 | 0.39 | 0.55 |
| Floating rates | 0.87 | 0.13 | 0.33 |

Source: Batchelor, [4], Table 6.
[a] Defined as one *minus* the coefficient estimated on the lagged dependent variable.

Statistically, we expect export prices to be some form of weighted average of domestic wholesale prices and world export prices in terms of sterling. The question is – what are the weights? An important feature of the transition from fixed to floating exchange rates is that the weights appear to have shifted significantly. Batchelor [4], reporting on National Institute findings, presents the estimates in Table 7.1. Since 1973 the importance given in export-pricing decisions to the maintenance of competitiveness has been dominant, while in the 1960s prices were fixed to a far greater extent by reference to domestic costs and prices. (This latter proposition is supported by the findings of Artus [1] and Flannery and Omerod [10], but not by those of Dornbusch and Krugman [8].) The reason for this shift appears to be that, since the profitability of exporting has increased since the days of the overvalued exchange rate in the early 1960s, greater care is taken in setting competitive prices, as the importance of maintaining market shares has become the prime concern of many firms. In addition, there has been a shift towards foreign-currency invoicing on the part of exporters during the period of realignment of exchange rates, resulting in an increase in the speed of adjustment of export prices to world prices. However, a large proportion of UK exports continue to be invoiced in sterling – 81 per cent according to a *Banker* survey in May 1976 – and there is even evidence to suggest a move away from foreign-currency invoicing since 1972 (Page, [28]); however, the recent CBI enquiry (Oppenheimer *et al.*, [27]) and Holmes' work [13] both report a strong shift towards foreign-currency invoicing.

*Table 7.2*   *The effect of devaluation[a] on competitiveness (percentage change in measures of competitiveness as a proportion of percentage change in the exchange rate)*

| | Constant output[b] | | | Variable output | | |
|---|---|---|---|---|---|---|
| Effect after: | 1 yr | 2 yrs | 6 yrs | 1 yr | 2 yrs | 6 yrs |
| Relative export prices[c] | | | | | | |
| Treasury | 0.28 | 0.24 | 0.14 | 0.28 | 0.24 | 0.08 |
| LBS | 0.39 | 0.22 | 0.01 | 0.38 | 0.27 | – |
| Relative profitability export/home sales[d] | | | | | | |
| Treasury | 0.40 | 0.36 | 0.20 | 0.40 | 0.34 | 0.12 |
| LBS | 0.19 | 0.16 | 0.09 | 0.19 | 0.16 | 0.06 |
| Relative normal unit labour costs | | | | | | |
| Treasury | 0.96 | 0.86 | 0.52 | 0.96 | 0.82 | 0.26 |
| Relative consumer prices[c] | | | | | | |
| Treasury | .. | .. | .. | 0.84 | 0.76 | 0.16 |
| LBS | .. | .. | .. | 0.60 | 0.44 | 0.28 |
| NIESR | .. | .. | .. | 0.80 | 0.70 | 0.44 |
| Terms of trade[e] | | | | | | |
| LBS | 0.60 | 0.39 | 0.16 | 0.59 | 0.46 | 0.06 |

Sources: Compiled from the simulation results reported in Treasury, *Economic Progress Report*, March 1978; Ball, Burns and Laury, [2], pp. 26–7; Laury, Lewis and Ormerod, [21].

[a] Treasury and NIESR models simulate a 5 per cent devaluation; the LBS model simulates a 20 per cent one. The new exchange rate assumed to be held for the entire six years.

[b] Government expenditure assumed to be adjusted to prevent an expansion of activity.

[c] Foreign prices in foreign currency assumed constant throughout.

[d] Defined as export price *minus* domestic sales price, or in LBS results as implicit deflator for exports *minus* implicit for consumers' expenditure.

[e] Implicit deflator for exports divided by implicit deflator for imports.

It is clear, therefore, that great care must be taken in interpreting the extent to which price competitiveness can be manipulated through exchange-rate adjustments. Table 7.2 derived from the reported results from simulations of the Treasury, London Business School and National Institute econometric models. The results illustrate the effect of devaluation on different measures of competitiveness and the speed with which such gains fade away according the strength of arbitrage in goods, oligopolistic price setting, and the wage bargaining process. An optimist may conclude that in terms of costs 95 per cent of the initial gain from a devaluation remains after a year and, depending on the extent to which the government supplements its exchange-rate policy with expenditure-reducing policies, between 26 per cent and 52 per cent of the initial gain remains after six years. A pessimist, on the other hand, notes that in terms of relative export prices only about 30 per cent of the initial gain lasts for a year and, even if the authorities show no wish to use a gain in exports to increase home employment, there will remain no more than between 1 and 14 per cent (depending on which model he believes) of the gain after six years. Devaluation as a means of shifting the real factoral terms of trade requires a highly effective incomes policy (Posner, [30]).

## Price Sensitivities: the Empirical Estimates

This section reports the results of other people's investigations – chiefly the elasticity terms which appear in the main British macroeconomic models. The starting point is Table 7.2, which displays the attrition of an original exchange-rate change as it works through to various competitiveness indicators – what we might call 'static attrition' – and also the dynamic attrition which takes place through time. The static attrition is least for the unit labour cost statistic, but the rate of dynamic attrition seems to vary more between the underlying models than between the tests of competitiveness. The story then continues in Table 7.3; we have converted on our own responsibility the CEPG elasticity, which is estimated on the unit cost index of competitiveness, into an 'export price' elasticity. The main results of this table support what one of the authors calls 'the first law of econometrics', which states that all macro elasticities lie in the range $-1$ to $-2\frac{1}{2}$ (the second law states that all micro elasticities lie in the range $-0.2$ to $-0.4$, a result well-proven in such diverse fields as energy economics, transport economics and telecommunications). The table also shows the rate at which this elasticity builds up through time – in all the models not more than two thirds of the final effect appears by the end of two years (Winters, [37]). The special feature of the CEPG results are that, despite their position on the probable inadequacy of exchange-rate manipulation, the assumptions they build into their model seem to lean towards giving price competitiveness the benefit of the doubt: their elasticity estimate is above that of their fellow estimators and it comes through at least as fast as in the other models. This seems to be evidence of very fair scientific dealing.

*Table 7.3   Relative export price elasticities for UK manufactured exports implied in major macroeconomic models*

| | Period of estimation | 1 year | 2 years | Long-run[a] |
|---|---|---|---|---|
| LBS | 1951 I–1976 IV | − 0.37 | − 0.39 | − 1.00 |
| CEPG[b] | 1960–76 | − 0.35 | − 1.23 | − 2.36 |
| NIESR | 1967 II–1975 IV | − 0.46 | − 1.11 | − 1.61 |
| Treasury[c] | 1966 I–1976 IV | − 0.26 | − 0.65 | − 1.30 |
| CPG[d] | | | | |
| Own price | | − 0.37 | − 0.90 | − 1.34 |
| Importer's domestic price | 1954–73 | 0.16 | 0.29 | 0.37 |
| Competitor's price | | 0.18 | 0.52 | 0.97 |

Sources: LBS Econometric Forecasting Unit, 'The quarterly econometric model of the UK economy – relationships in the basic model', p. 17; Fetherston, [9], pp. 25–6; NIESR, [26], p. 25; Richardson, [32]; Winters [37].

[a] In LBS and NIESR models effect assumed complete after 15 quarters, in Treasury model after 18 quarters and in CPG model after 20 quarters. CEPG model has a geometrically decaying lag structure.

[b] The CEPG model emphasises the use of relative costs rather than export prices as preferable indicators of competitiveness. For ease of comparison the export elasticity with respect to the latter is included here, this is derived from the relative cost elasticities and the elasticity of export prices with respect to costs, which the CEPG report as 0.5.

[c] The chosen equation in the Treasury model is based on relative unit labour costs yielding an elasticity of − 0.93, which implies, on the assumption of a scaling factor of 1.4, a long-run elasticity of 1.3. The export elasticities with respect to export prices and relative export profitability were constrained to be equal.

[d] Aggregate elasticities reported are obtained by the trade-weighted averaging of the elasticities estimated from 16 separate commodity groups. The sum of the three price elasticities were constrained equal to one (i.e. no money illusion) in the long run.

*Table 7.4    Estimated long-run relative price elasticities of exports for selected countries*

|  | No. of estimates | Range | 'Best point' estimate |
|---|---|---|---|
| United Kingdom[a] |  |  |  |
| Manufactures | 3 | − 1.00 to − 3.00 | − 2.00 |
| All exports | 9 | − 0.24 to − 1.94 | − 0.48 |
| France |  |  |  |
| All exports | 6 | − 1.06 to − 2.27 | − 1.31 |
| Germany |  |  |  |
| All exports | 6 | − 0.65 to − 1.80 | − 1.11 |
| Japan |  |  |  |
| Manufactures | 12 | − 0.35 to − 2.62 | − 1.24 |
| All exports | 7 | − 0.71 to − 2.38 | − 1.25 |
| United States |  |  |  |
| Manufactures | 10 | − 0.56 to − 2.62 | − 1.24 |
| All exports | 14 | − 0.56 to − 2.53 | − 1.41 |

Source: R. M. Stern, J. Francis and B. Schumacher, *Price Elasticities in International Trade*, London, Macmillan, 1976, Table 2.1, pp. 15–20.

[a] These estimates are from earlier studies than those reported in Table 7.3.

Table 7.4 compares the UK estimates with those for other countries. If anything, the UK estimates seem to lie on the high side for manufactures.

Summarising the evidence on elasticities, we may say the following. The impact effect of an exchange-rate devaluation must be to improve factor rewards at home or to lower prices to foreign customers. The coefficients for year one in Table 7.2 merely exhibit the results of different pricing choices by exporters and the results of the high import content of British exports. Through time, the total effect of the devaluation is diminished by the internal inflation of prices and incomes, and the distribution of the gain between profits and wages at home and prices to the overseas customers changes – although again in Table 7.2 the speeds of attrition attributed to the Treasury are very similar one to the other, implying that the redistribution of effects through time is not great.

While the advantage from devaluation lasts, there is an effect on export performance. In Table 7.3 we display that effect in terms of conventional price elasticities. However, implicit in the method of calculation and the underlying studies which are drawn upon is ample support for the proposition that there is an effect 'on the supply-side' through increased profitability.

These effects are whittled away through time, and unless there are benign dynamic consequences (higher profits leading to high investment leading to higher rates of innovation, etc.) there is nothing in these tables to question the general assumption that one original disequilibrium might need successive doses of devaluation.

What effect might changes in competitiveness have on the volume of manufactured output? It seems to us that the steps which lead to an answer can be specified as follows:

(1) Assume a change in competitiveness, using any chosen indicator and any assumed time path.
(2) Calculate the change in net exports, after taking into account the import content of the goods exported. (Go through the same steps for the effect of competitiveness changes on import substitution in the home market, which we have chosen not to discuss in this paper, but which remains of course an important part of the total story.)
(3) Assume that the whole of this increase in net exports is 'used up' by an expansion of home demand, of a size determined by the marginal propensity to import.
(4) Then the total effect on manufactured output is equal to step (2) *plus* step (3).

Ideally, of course, model simulations should be used, since the direct effect on manufactured output is only one part of the total effect. But it is possible to approximate model simulations by assuming suitable values for the 'marginal propensity to import' and for the share of UK manufactured output in the final increment in demand satisfied by home output in total.

The Appendix reports details of this calculation. We can claim no precision or robustness for our simple sums, but the commonsense suggestion that an $X$ per cent increase in one or other of the indices of competitiveness might lead to an increase of $2X$ per cent in manufactured output, for a year or two, after a time lag of around three years, is at least not denied by our calculations.

## The Relative Importance of 'Price' and 'Non-price' Competitiveness

There are a number of different approaches to the question of the relative importance of price and non-price competitiveness. In the international empirical literature on the relative importance of different causes of trade, attempts have been made to separate the contributions of factor endowment, economies of scale, 'product-cycle' causes, and other causes (see, for instance, Vernon [36]). This literature has not been conclusive, largely because the various factors interact in a way which *systematically* destroys any naive attributions.

Again, there is much impressionistic evidence (most readily available in Kravis and Lipsey, [19] and NEDO, [25]) about the importance of non-price factors. For instance, Kravis and Lipsey reported in their study of German–American trade by the questionnaire method that only 28 per cent of US exporters attributed success to lower prices, while 37 per cent suggested that the critical factor was product superiority; 12 per cent gave weight to after-sales service and 10 per cent to product uniqueness. Of German importers, only 7 per cent went shopping in America because of lower prices, and 'non-availability' of products at home accounted for 63 per cent of imports. Part of this study concludes with the words 'it seems probable that there is a widespread product inferiority both in objective characteristics and in marketing and salesmanship'.

The contribution of price competitiveness to these sad stories can be either positive or negative, according to the theoretical approach adopted. Thus Batchelor [4] presents results which are consistent with an increase in competitiveness providing a stimulus, and, through increased profits, a means, for improved non-price performance. Stout (NEDO, [25]) backs the alternative horse, suggesting that declining unit values (masquerading as improved price competitiveness) are more likely to indicate that UK industry is moving down-market and that any devaluation would merely exacerbate that trend, making UK entrepreneurs more comfortable in their apathy.

Stout's pessimistic interpretation is quite consistent with other impressionistic surveys (Oppenheimer, [27]; Holmes, [13]) which show price competitiveness as contributing some help to some entrepreneurs in some circumstances. The pessimists need not deny that such assistance to export performance genuinely helps in the short run, because they would stress the adverse long-run consequences of encouraging down-market production: inferior products eventually disappear from the scene. But to this pessimism there is as usual an optimistic counter-argument: manufacturers in a multi-product enterprise may well use windfall profits from one dying 'inferior' product to finance innovation elsewhere. This, after all, was the traditional interpretation of Japanese success.

Some additional evidence is provided by the results of an investigation of a slightly different question – the CEPG's calculation of the declining UK share of world exports in manufactures over the years since 1960. The argument goes as follows: between 1960 and 1976 the UK share of manufactured exports fell from 15.3 per cent to 8.3 per cent, while simultaneously UK competitiveness (on a cost basis) improved by 11.4 per cent. Regressing export shares on price competitiveness and cyclical factors alone leads to the suggestion that the UK export share should have risen; 104 per cent of the relative decline of the UK in world trade remains unexplained, or to be explained by non-price factors. However one might try to chisel away at particular facets of this rock, its massive gloom is impossible to disguise. There does seem to be a steady divergence between the rate of increase of UK imports of manufactures and of her exports which is hard to attribute to any simple once-and-for-all relaxation of trade barriers or catching up with individual new products from overseas.

We are, it is true, sceptical about the validity of extrapolating into the future divergent rates of increase of exports and imports of manufactured goods for the UK economy. Whether the divergence arises because of the 'time trends' so despised of econometricians, or because of high 'income propensities to import', or because of the 'low income propensity of foreigners to buy UK exports', our basic scepticism is about the essentially unidentified nature of the effect on which reliance is placed. It is a black box whose basic laws are not well understood.

Our impression of the relationship between price and non-price influences may be summarised as follows. Historically there is no doubt that non-price influences have dominated – the proportion of the total change which they 'explain' is an order of magnitude greater than the explanatory power of price competitiveness. Even when price competitiveness works, it may have 'featherbedding' effects. Nevertheless, *if* price competitiveness could be improved it would have a modest but significant effect on the scale of manufacturing output. In the days when effects of the order of 5 or 10 per cent were all that was sought, this would be a relatively good conclusion for price or cost competitiveness. Now that we are contemplating far bigger gaps to fill, it is hard to avoid the conclusion that the role of price and cost competitiveness has to be rather small.

## Policy Implications

The first policy implication is that, looking ahead over a ten-year period, what happens to non-price factors must be more important than any gains that can be got from increases in price competitiveness. The second implication is that it is not clear from the evidence how far gains in price competitiveness should be regarded as complementary to or competitive with improvements in non-price factors. It is certainly true that in some cases profits earned from export sales have encouraged innovation and investment. It is even more certainly true that in many cases exporters who have been denied good export profits have failed to innovate successfully – although whether the relationship here is one of cause and effect is difficult to discern. It has been suggested to us that the competitive advantage secured by the large devaluation of 1967 provides evidence for a third, malign, relationship between good profits from exports and appropriate patterns of investment and development at home – the motor car industry and the steel corporation might have come to grips with their problems in the late 1960s instead of a decade later if their profit margins in the international market had been squeezed earlier, and that adjustment might have been easier in the conditions of 1968–73 than now.

Our conclusion is indecisive. One of the present authors (MVP) feels strongly that a profits squeeze is the last thing that British industry needs at the present, and therefore that the balance of the argument must be in favour of buying some more price (or in this case cost) competitiveness, even if in some firms the consequences will be too prolonged a period of cosy sleep.

Those who wish to argue that in present circumstances British exporters at the margin of profitability should be denied temporary artificial props for their operations, must, we suggest, pay regard to the degree and speed of flexibility in adjustment and redistribution of resources from one line of production to another. To increase the scale of an already successful operation is one thing; to abandon it and search for another intra-marginal activity is a larger and more time-consuming job. This implies support for increased price competitiveness over the next few years, on the grounds that the middle of the recession is not a good occasion to risk adding significantly to 'transitional' unemployment. But it is also fair to add that the middle of a world recession is not a good time to seek price advantages in an oligopolistic world market.

Thirdly, it is quite clear that, for at least a short period of years, the Marshall–Lerner conditions, as suitably adjusted to take account of different ways in which price competitiveness is manifested, are satisfied on the export side alone. Improvements in competitiveness do give increased volumes of employment and output, even though eventually this gain may be whittled away and even though there may be some permanent adverse effects on the price level. For those who are in favour of some form of 'tuning' of the economy, the exchange rate is an instrument whose attractions cannot be ignored.

Fourthly, the present climate of opinion gives great weight to the argument that expectations tend to be rationally formulated in the market. While we remain somewhat sceptical of this proposition, it should be noted from the CBI enquiry (Oppenheimer *et al.*, [27]) that most businessmen who actually export recognise the advantages which accrue to them from a relatively low exchange rate. If they recognise these advantages, and perceive that the authorities are doing their best to achieve a continuing degree of extra price competitiveness, there is some reason to suppose that, wholly rationally, the business community will take advantage of the favourable export climate thus promised. So circumstances are perhaps more propitious than those of the past (in 1967 the CBI strongly opposed devaluation) for the use of the exchange-rate weapon, and this provides some offset to that progressive abandonment of money illusion which is often pointed to as a reason for increased scepticism about the value of this instrument.

If we may float for a last half page free of the constraints of our empirical investigations, our main concern remains that the middle of the worst postwar slump is not a good occasion to seek by financial manipulation of one sort or another to gain an advantage over our competitors, and thus push back to them some of the unemployment they have caused us to import. There is a very real sense in which the shadow wage of a lot of manufacturing labour is extremely low at the moment and may, on some projections, continue to be low for a long time in the future. Anecdotal evidence about the performance of the Japanese economy suggests that perhaps some countries are better at running an 'overhead economy' than we are: if all labour costs are a fixed overhead, then the marginal social cost of production need not even cover material costs if these materials themselves (for example, steel) are made at home. Perhaps a high exchange rate together with a very aggressive and discriminatory marketing policy is a better device for grabbing and retaining markets than a low exchange rate and non-discriminatory pricing.

But that sort of arrangement would run counter to all sorts of other trends in our economy, notably the extremely important steps towards rationalisation and cost reduction in the public sector, which management and unions alike notably failed to obtain in the 30 postwar years of extraordinarily high employment. If commercial pricing is going to dominate, and companies (with the memory of 1975 still very close in their minds) are constantly awake to the possibility of insolvency, general financial manipulation through the exchange rate may have better prospects of success than a network of complex, negotiable, and necessarily arbitrary, interventions.

But we prefer to end with the firm statement that, while it is true that, both for economic analysts and for policy-makers, it is non-price factors which deserve most long-run attention, for those who remain necessarily concerned with day-to-day macro management, the exchange rate remains an eligible weapon in the armoury. We should be able to raise one and a half weak British cheers for the exchange rate, and perhaps therefore (taking proper account of the import content in the total costs of our exports) one cheer for price competitiveness.

## Appendix

This Appendix is built on an Odling-Smee and Hartley type of analysis, according to which the gain in competitiveness fades away. The present authors are not wholehearted in their endorsement of that model, but they believe it is useful expositionally at least.

An improvement in price competitiveness provides some slack in the balance-of-payments constraint on the expansion of national income, as a temporary trade surplus is induced. Here we provide a rough-and-ready answer to the critical question – how much additional expansion of home manufactures are we allowed before the constraint is once again taut?

The increase in manufactured output in this model is temporary. We consider the second year after a devaluation and assume a 10 per cent improvement in export price competitiveness (which from Table 7.2 would require a 40 per cent devaluation). The following relative price elasticities are postulated:

For exports, $-1.5$ (a rough average derived from Tables 7.3 and 7.4)

For imports, $-0.2$ (about an average of the CEPG value of $-1.15$ and the NIESR range of $-0.26$ to $-0.3$).

This implies an improvement in the balance of trade (all other accounts are assumed to be in balance throughout) of approximately 17 per cent. If all the increase in exports and import substitutes is in the form of manufactured goods and if 50 per cent of manufactures are exported, the increase in total output of manufactured goods is of the order of 8.5 per cent.

The economy may expand, assuming excess capacity, up to that point at which the trade account is again balanced; that is, imports may rise by 17 per cent. Some of that expansion is of course already generated through the foreign trade multiplier. The government is assumed to induce the additional expansion through, say, a reduction in income tax. The potential for the increase in manufactures depends, of course, on the elasticities of expenditure on imports, home-produced services and home-produced manufactured goods with respect to total expenditure. Considering the two scenarios in Table 7.5, the true elasticities probably lie between those postulated in A and B. The NIESR model includes a short-run import elasticity of 1.0 (1.46 in the long run) (NIESR [26]). The elasticities in B are chosen roughly to correspond with a CEPG import elasticity of 2.7 (Fetherston, [9]).

*Table 7.5   Possible combinations of expenditure elasticities*

|  | Imports | Services | Domestic manufactures |
|---|---|---|---|
| *Scenario A* |  |  |  |
| Marginal propensity to spend on: | 0.33 | 0.33 | 0.33 |
| Average propensity to spend on: | 0.33 | 0.33 | 0.33 |
| Elasticity = marginal/average | 1.00 | 1.00 | 1.00 |
| *Scenario B* |  |  |  |
| Marginal propensity to spend on: | 0.82 | 0.10 | 0.08 |
| Average propensity to spend on: | 0.33 | 0.33 | 0.33 |
| Elasticity = marginal/average | 2.48 | 0.30 | 0.24 |

In case A total manufactured output may be increased by 17 per cent, and so the total allowable expansion is $17 + 8.5 = 25.5$ per cent from the initial gain in competitiveness of 10 per cent (40 per cent devaluation). In case B total expenditure may only be expanded by 6.8 per cent, resulting in an increase in manufactured output of 1.6 per cent. When added to the initial increase of 8.5 per cent, the total expansion of manufactures is 10.1 per cent, brought about by a 10 per cent gain in export price competitiveness. These results are illustrative of the rough magnitude of the gains from devaluation, although of course we do not claim them to be definitive. Their purpose is to stimulate discussion.

It is worth pointing out finally that, although it might appear that results more favourable to devaluation would have emerged had we looked at the gain in competitiveness in terms of relative unit labour costs, which from Table 7.2 appears to fade very much more slowly than that in terms of relative export prices, the export elasticity postulated would then have had to be very much lower and the end-result would have been roughly the same.

*References*

[1] Artus, J. R., 'The behaviour of export prices in manufactures', *IMF Staff Papers*, November 1974.

[2] Ball, R. J., Burns, T. and Laury, J. S. E., 'The role of exchange rate changes in balance of payments adjustment: the UK case', *Economic Journal*, March 1977.

[3] Balogh, T., *Unequal Partners*, Oxford, Blackwell, 1963.

[4] Batchelor, R. A., 'The stability of export demand and pricing under alternative exchange rate regimes' (paper presented at the University of Warwick, September 1977).

[5] Branson, W., 'The trade effects of the 1971 currency realignments', *Brookings Papers in Economic Activity*, no. 1, 1972.

[6] Cassel, G., *Post-War Monetary Stabilization*, New York, Columbia University Press, 1928.

[7] CEPG, *Economic Policy Review*, no. 4, 1978.

[8] Dornbusch, R. and Krugman, P., 'Flexible exchange rates in the short run', *Brookings Papers in Economic Activity*, no. 3, 1976.

[8a] Enoch, C. A., 'Measures of competitiveness in international trade', *Bank of England Quarterly Bulletin*, June 1978.

[9] Fetherston, M. J., 'Technical manual on the CEPG model', Department of Applied Economics, Cambridge, 1977.

[10] Flannery, P. and Ormerod, P. A., 'Manufactured export prices in the UK and the "law of one price"' (unpublished NIESR working paper), 1978.

[11] Hague, D. C., Oakshott, E. and Strain, A., *Devaluation and Pricing Decisions*, London, Allen & Unwin, 1974.

[12] Henderson, H. D., 'The function of exchange rates', *Oxford Economic Papers*, January 1949.

[13] Holmes, P. M., 'Industrial pricing and devaluation: a case study approach' (PhD dissertation, Cambridge), 1978.

[14] Isard, P. 'How far can we push the law of one price?', *American Economic Review*, September 1977.

[15] Johnson, H. G., *International Trade and Economic Growth*, London, Allen & Unwin, 1958.

[16] Johnson, H. G., *Comparative Cost and Commercial Policy Theory for a Developing World Economy*, Stockholm, Almquist & Wiksell, 1968.

[17] Kalter, E. R. J., 'The effect of exchange rate changes on the price of traded goods' (PhD dissertation, University of Pennsylvania), 1977.

[18] Keynes, J. M., *Essays in Persuasion*, London, Macmillan, 1931.

[19] Kravis, I. and Lipsey, R. E., *Price Competitiveness in World Trade*, New York, Columbia University Press, 1971.

[20] Kravis, I. and Lipsey, R. E., 'Export prices and the transmission of inflation', *American Economic Association Proceedings*, May 1977.

[21] Laury, J. S. E., Lewis, G. R. and Ormerod, P. A., 'Properties of macroeconomic models of the UK economy: a comparative study', *National Institute Economic Review*, February 1978.

[22] Magee, S. P., 'Prices, incomes and foreign trade' in P. Kenen (ed.), *International Trade and Finance*, Cambridge University Press, 1975.

[23] Meade, J. E., *Theory of International Economic Policy*, vol. 1: *The Balance of Payments*, London, Oxford University Press, 1951.

[24] Moggridge, D. E., *British Monetary Policy, 1924–31: the Norman Conquest of $4.86*, Cambridge University Press, 1972.

[25] NEDO, *International Price Competitiveness, Non-price Factors and Export Performance* by D. K. Stout, London, 1977.

[26] NIESR, 'A listing of National Institute model 3' (NIESR Discussion Paper), London, 1977.

[27] Oppenheimer, P. M. *et al.*, *Business Views on Exchange Rate Policy*, London, Confederation of British Industry, 1978.

[28] Page, S. A. B., 'Currency of invoicing in merchandise trade', *National Institute Economic Review*, August 1977.

[29] Posner, M. V., 'International trade and technical change', *Oxford Economic Papers*, October 1961.

[30] Posner, M. V., 'Wages, prices and the exchange rate' in M. J. Artis (ed.), *Current Economic Problems*, Oxford, Blackwell, 1978.

[31] Posner, M. V., 'The search for common ground' in M. V. Posner (ed.), *Demand Management*, London, Heinemann, 1978.

[32] Richardson, P. W., 'Aspects of official research on UK exports of manufactures models' (paper presented at the University of Warwick, September 1977).

[33] Rosendale, P. B., 'The short-run pricing policies of some British engineering exporters', *National Institute Economic Review*, August 1973.

[34] Treasury, *A Model of UK Manufacturing Export Prices* by J. P. Hutton and P. Minford, London, HMSO, 1975.

[35] Treasury, 'Some effects of exchange rate changes' by J. Odling-Smee and N. Hartley (Government Economic Service working paper), 1978.

[36] Vernon, R., *The Technology Factor in International Trade*, New York, Columbia University Press, 1970.

[37] Winters, L. A. 'Lagged responses to prices: the case of UK visible exports' (paper presented at the University of Warwick, September 1977).

# Comment

## by Francis Cripps

The paper by Posner and Steer about the export performance of UK industry covers wider ground than the title suggests, making many important observations about the effects of various exogenous changes on the price and quality (in the broadest sense) of manufactures offered for export, and hence on the volume and value of export sales actually achieved. The paper emphasises devaluation as the principal policy instrument acting on the export environment.

Throughout the paper the authors stress that quality is at least as important as price in determining export demand, and recognise that, since neither factor nor product markets are perfect, the 'volume' of available factor supplies and product demand may be aspects of the environment which are just as important as factor costs and product market prices. The paper also accepts from the outset that devaluation, apart from cutting the foreign currency equivalent of home costs and home market prices in the short run, will also affect the availability of factors to different establishments (for example, by deferring plant closures) and may in the long-run raise home costs in domestic currency so as to eliminate the advantage more or less completely.

Whether and under what circumstances devaluation will be offset in the long run by additional inflation of home costs is a crucial policy issue, as also are the side-effects of devaluation on other aspects of the performance of the economy. These are, however, questions about the functioning of the economy as a whole, not just about the performance of manufacturing industry. For example, Posner and Steer make it clear that the CEPG's views about the direct effects of devaluation on exports are more optimistic than most. Yet their assessment of devaluation as a policy instrument is rather negative because of indirect effects which depend on properties of the economy as a whole and have to be considered in the light of the whole range of objectives of policy.

Their method of estimating the effects of a sustained improvement in competitiveness on the volume of manufacturing output (on which their paper particularly suggests I should comment) involves an implicit policy assumption that the government chooses (and is able) to absorb a rise in export revenues by expanding domestic demand so as to generate an equal addition to imports; it leaves out of account the policy actions needed to achieve and maintain the given improvement in competitiveness as well as the consequences of such policies for all other aspects of economic performance. It is important to note that the calculation does *not* tell us about the effects of a change in the exchange rate on the volume of manufacturing output.

Although policy cannot very usefully be discussed within the framework of the paper, it does raise many interesting issues of applied theory. My remaining comments will be confined to three themes: first, how the empirical evidence on price and volume responses to devaluation should be interpreted; second, effects of devaluation on 'quality' and productivity; third, the choice of measures of 'competitiveness'.

## Interpreting the Empirical Evidence

Posner and Steer's general conclusion from the evidence is that non-price factors are very important, but that changes in relative costs or prices also have significant and reasonably systematic effects on the volume of exports. The stylised facts are that a devaluation causes export prices to rise in home currency and fall in foreign currency by roughly equal amounts (abstracting from the effect of subsequent increases in home costs) and that the volume of exports rises with an elasticity of more than unity with respect to the fall in export prices in foreign currency.

The significance of these facts becomes clearer if one take account of the abundant evidence that marginal costs of production of manufactures are generally constant or falling, and that average costs certainly fall with an increase in output. Given this, the pronounced rise in export prices in home currency (relative to costs and home prices) which occurs after a devaluation cannot be explained by a low 'supply elasticity' unless exporting industries are working at full capacity. The rise in export prices must therefore tell us something important about demand. The implications can be clarified with the aid of a simple formal model.

Suppose the volume of exports, $q$, is determined by a demand function $q = f(rp)$, where $r$ is the exchange rate and $p$ the export price in terms of home currency, while profits, $\pi$, are given by $\pi = (p - c)q - F$, where $c$ is the level of marginal cost (assumed constant) and $F$ is fixed costs. Profit maximisation requires:

$$\frac{p}{c} = \frac{e_1}{1 + e_1} \tag{1}$$

where $e_1$ is the price elasticity of demand. If the price elasticity of demand were constant, there would be no reason for the export mark-up to change after devaluation. Export prices would rise in home currency only to the extent that input prices rose and pushed up marginal costs. If the model is a valid approximation and the export mark-up does in fact rise after devaluation, it follows that the price elasticity of demand is not constant, or in other words that the demand function is 'kinked'. Abstracting from any change in input costs, it can be shown that the change in export prices in home currency which maximises profits after a small devaluation is given by

$$\frac{r}{p} \cdot \frac{dp}{dr} = \frac{e_2}{1 + e_1 - e_2} \tag{2}$$

where $e_2$ is the elasticity of $e_1$ with respect to a change in foreign currency prices. Assuming a price elasticity, $(e_1)$, of less than $-1$, export prices will rise by a proportion less than unity with respect to a fall in the exchange rate if (and only if) the elasticity of the elasticity $(e_2)$ is positive. A positive value for $e_2$ indicates oligopolistic behaviour, in which competitors do not mind if a firm chooses to price itself out of the market, but are prepared to retaliate by cutting their own prices if it sets its price too low. For example, if the price elasticity $e_1$ is $-2$ and export prices in home currency rise by half the amount of any devaluation (both measured relative to marginal costs), the elasticity of the elasticity can be inferred from (2) above to be unity (if prices in home currency rise more, the elasticity of the elasticity must be greater than unity). The evidence therefore suggests that the 'law of one price' is an oligopolistic law, not a reflection of atomistic competition.

**Effects of Devaluation on Quality and Productivity**

Posner and Steer raise the important question whether devaluation (or other forms of protection) has an adverse effect on product quality or productivity, either by inhibiting the transfer of labour to more efficient and innovative firms or by reducing the imperative for internal reorganisation. So far as the reallocation of labour is concerned, there is plenty of evidence that in modern circumstances this is made far more difficult when industry suffers from low demand and intense competition than in a boom, because redeployment of labour is more easily achieved when it is voluntary than when it is resisted.

The ideal circumstances for industrial innovation and reorganisation are almost certainly the combination of high and fast growing demand with a fast trend increase in wage costs relative to prices such that firms have both the opportunity and necessity to improve quality and productivity without needing to attempt involuntary redeployment of labour. Devaluation (if it raises exports) improves the volume of demand but alleviates the pressure of costs relative to prices in open sectors. In addition to the well-known evidence that growth of demand is favourable to growth of productivity, a cross-country study of several industries (Cripps and Tarling, [1]) suggested that growth of home-market sales has a strong beneficial effect on export performance (itself agreed to be due mainly to non-price factors). The negative effects of 'featherbedding' in the cost–price sense do not, so far as I know, show up in econometric evidence. It would therefore be very surprising if the favourable effects of devaluation on quality and productivity arising from a higher level of demand could be shown to be dominated by unfavourable featherbedding effects.

## Measures of Competitiveness

Posner and Steer discuss alternative statistical measures of competitiveness without specifying clearly the purpose of the measurement. If the purpose is to provide the most appropriate equations for representing the response of manufactured export prices and volumes to other variables in a macroeconomic model, it is important to choose equations which give 'quality' as well as price factors a chance to operate, even though the former cannot be measured explicitly. On this basis the most appropriate indicator would seem to be a measure of relative costs, since the advantage afforded by a cost reduction may be taken up either by a price reduction or by intensification of non-price competition.

The measurement of costs in the UK is not difficult because ample statistics are published on prices of material inputs as well as on wages and productivity. It would however be a major exercise to quantify all relevant costs for a large number of other countries. Nor is the use of comparisons of labour costs alone satisfactory, especially for the last few years when costs of energy and raw materials have varied dramatically and far from uniformly across countries.

The procedure adopted by the CEPG has been to compare a comprehensive index of UK costs with an index of 'world' export prices on the hypothesis that the latter provides the best available measure of average costs in competitor countries. We experience little difficulty in interpreting the actual response of export volumes to changes in cost competitiveness measured in this way, and can trace the predicted influence of a change in *any* component of UK costs (including subsidies, taxes, fuel prices and prices of imported inputs as well as labour costs). UK export prices can be interpreted quite naturally as a weighted geometric average of UK costs and world market prices, with the weight of world market prices depending on the 'kinkiness' of the demand curve discussed above.

The main problem in analysing export performance is not that of measuring changes in cost competitiveness and their effects, nor one of establishing that non-price factors are important, but rather that of determining how different environmental circumstances influence non-price competitiveness in the long run. After two decades at least of government attempts to improve the non-price competitiveness of UK exports, none of the policy instruments tried so far seems to have had any measurable effect.

# 8 De-industrialisation and Industrial Policy

by D. K. Stout

## Introduction

In most advanced industrial societies in the last two decades the share of manufacturing in total employment has fallen. The UN Economic Commission for Europe (United Nations, [10]) has observed that this tends to happen in economies whenever the share of agricultural employment has fallen below a threshold of somewhere around 10 per cent. In most European economies the share of manufacturing in total *output* (at constant prices) was none the less maintained through the 1960s; the fall in the share of total employment was due largely to faster productivity growth, and partly to changes in industrial structure away from labour-intensive industrial branches (like textiles, clothing and footwear) and towards more capital-intensive branches (like chemicals, petroleum products and electrical engineering), where growth has been comparatively fast.

Table 8.1   *Ratio of net trade balance to the sum of exports and imports in manufacturing*

|  | 1963 | 1976 | 1976/1963 |
|---|---|---|---|
|  | ($ values) | | (%) |
| UK | 0.389 | 0.118 | 30 |
| France | 0.177 | 0.065 | 37 |
| Germany | 0.397 | 0.303 | 76 |

Source: NEDO calculations.

However, British manufacturing industry has registered a recent decline in importance measured by real output. This has not been a consequence of the changing demands of a rich community in a

Chart 8.1   *Growth of imports volume and of industrial production (annual percentage growth rates, 4½-year averages ending year shown)*

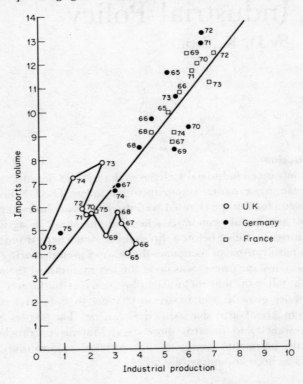

successful economy. It has reflected, instead, the widespread weakness of our industrial performance on almost every comparative measure. The UK's falling share in world exports of manufactures, and rising import penetration of the home market for manufactures, has been amply documented elsewhere in this book. Two points are added here: on the import side, Chart 8.1 shows how the movement of import growth in relation to industrial production has been quite different in the UK from that in Germany and France – the UK has combined declining production growth and increasing import dependence. Bringing exports into the assessment, the ratio of the net trade balance in manufactures to the sum of exports and imports had fallen by 1976 to less than a third of its 1963 level in dollar terms – a greater fall than in France and a much greater fall than in Germany (Table 8.1). The deterioration in trade performance was widespread: it can be observed between 1970 and 1977 in nine out of twelve branches of manufacturing. The reasons for these failures do not appear to be uniform and obvious; correspondingly, industrial policies to try to stop the rot are not easily generalised.

## The Unsatisfactory Nature of General Explanations

Past attempts to find a salient reason for Britain's industrial decline have mostly been unconvincing and over-ambitious. Explanations of this sort have often broken into one of a number of chains of cause and effect, highlighting some feature or stage of a circular process which is as much a symptom as it is a cause.

One popular over-simplification of what is a quite intricate and qualified argument in Bacon and Eltis [1] is that the expansion of the public sector has eroded the industrial base by taking a lien on scarce resources of skilled labour and investible funds required for industrial growth. That shortages of skilled labour or finance occasionally prevent expansion is well established. But they do not appear, on the evidence of the CBI's survey of factors likely to limit output, to support the view that it is inadequate capacity and not inadequate demand which limits growth.

In a subtler version of the same explanation, the financing of non-market sector growth through increases in taxation, whose effect on consumption is neutralised by compensating wage increases, reduces the flow of retained profits available for industrial investment unless companies are willing and able to increase their gearing. There is little sign that capacity expansion has been forestalled recently by the cost or availability of finance. Historically low real rates of return on corporate assets and low expected marginal efficiency of investment have inhibited expansion. But that is an observation which does not take us very far towards an explanation, for low corporate rates of return *before* tax have themselves been the result of growing market disadvantages which have had deeper causes. The paucity of market sector investment and the weakness of the balance of payments on current account is regarded by Bacon and Eltis as the inevitable concomitant of an increasingly high share of marketable output taken by public and private consumption and public sector investment. They employ an identity to search out a cause, which is not very helpful. One would have to be able to demonstrate that no way existed to raise net exports (contributing to total marketable output) without commensurately increasing the claims upon this output before a case could be made that the low growth of industrial output was due to an increase in non-market sector activity.

Many general explanations are unconvincing because they do not distinguish Britain from other more successful industrial countries, or they do not hold for the whole period of relative decline in industrial output. When blaming cyclical instability for our poor performance many commentators fail to recognise that stop–go policies have been a short-run response to long-run balance-of-payments weaknesses. They may have exacerbated industrial decline by discouraging long-term investment planning, but such policies have not been a cause independent of industrial performance. Furthermore, they often over-look the fact that fluctuations of demand and employment have been more pronounced in other much more fast-growing economies (NEDO, [4]). Other observers who lay the blame on the alleged disincentive effects of high personal income tax rates have to accommodate the evidence of tax structures that are in some senses more progressive in other economies, and to acknowledge that the experience of failure in industrial markets was as prevalent when the UK top rate of income tax was no more than 7 per cent (Phelps Brown, [8]).

The confusion between cause and effect in accounts which lay the blame on the growth of the (non-industrial) public sector is highlighted by the fact that quite contrary policy conclusions can be drawn from it depending upon which of the schools of macroeconomic thought the critic espouses. In the Bacon and Eltis account, elasticity pessimism and a high natural rate of unemployment limit total supply in the short run. Within that limit the growth of public expenditure could be made consistent with a strong market sector only if personal taxes could be increased effectively (without correspondingly inflating money wages). The problem is seen by them, for the most part, as one of making room for employment of resources by the market sector; it is the practical and political difficulty of squeezing consumption that leads them to advocate cutting back on the growth of the public sector. Others, approaching the question from the side of industrial investment incentives and the determinants of innovative effort, argue that it is because the growth of the public sector has to be financed by tax increases that it cannot be accommodated even at high levels of unemployment. They concentrate upon the alleged disincentive effects (still not well-established empirically though often asserted) of high marginal rates of personal taxation.

Many quite general structural explanations of industrial decline are unsatisfactory because, while they account for (or at least describe in revealing terms) a low *level* of productivity or trade performance, they are not carried far enough to make it clear why that low level should not make relatively rapid *growth* thereafter easier if anything rather than more difficult. For example, if a given set of industrial relations problems was characterised by a given degree of over-manning, this could no more explain a growing productivity gap than would working a 35-hour week on average instead of a 40-hour one. The same stricture applies to greater X-inefficiency as an explanation, or to a lower level of capital per man, or indeed a lower investment–output ratio unless technical progress is capital-biased.

To argue from a given disadvantage to a cumulative relative contraction (as Singh does for instance), one has to find reasons why the existence of a gap like a technology gap, or a design gap reflected in product irrelevance, creates conditions which prevent its closure, or even cause it to widen further. One reason that turns out to be important in some industries is the presence of important *dynamic* economies of scale. Trouble is created for the laggard producers not by the existence of a given historical productivity gap (which would, by itself, simply cause the share of the laggard in a growing market to be smaller, but not a decline in unit cost); it is caused by the opening of a new productivity gap that was not there before, by the action of a competitor moving ever closer to the technical horizon, for example, or relatively improving the design and other selling features of his product. In either case, the shift of share towards the competitor adds to his experience and his ability to take further such steps, and correspondingly weakens the ability of the backward producer to follow suit.

The implications of this view for economic policy are radical. It is not so much the features which are associated with the existence of low productivity or a large share of manufactured imports which matter, but the institutional and structural reasons for the closing of the gap by successful economies. Thus, the correction of the (static) competitive disadvantage of an overvalued currency is not by itself sufficient to lead to the transformation of industry, orientating it towards the design and successful marketing of products for which the income elasticity of demand is high, and eliminating the various non-price competitive disadvantages which lead to a cumulative decline of market share and a slow growth of the unit value of both exports and import substitutes.

On a dynamic view, to emulate successful industrial economies it is necessary to establish conditions for a fast rate of innovation and for the inauguration of an extended episode of unusual growth – a closer approach to the moving horizon of technique and design – rather than continued growth at the rate of technical progress set by the 'leader' economy. Favourable macroeconomic conditions, including the expectation of a competitive exchange rate (to justify intangible investment in the improvement of non-price competitiveness) are necessary but by no means sufficient to bring about such a 'take-off'. Detailed diagnosis at product level, and policies tailor-made progressively to improve product design and marketing and to assist in the transfer and diffusion of technology at industry and company level are required.

*Table 8.2    Analysis of aggregate labour productivity change in the UK and West German manufacturing industry, 1954–76 (percentages)*

| | United Kingdom | | | West Germany | | |
| | | Attributable to: | | | Attributable to: | |
| | Total change in labour productivity | Inter-sectoral employment shifts | Increased productivity | Total change in labour productivity | Inter-sectoral employment shifts | Increased productivity |
|---|---|---|---|---|---|---|
| 1954–9 | 11.7 | 1.1 | 10.5 | 19.2 | – | 19.2 |
| 1959–63 | 8.3 | 0.4 | 7.9 | 18.6 | 0.1 | 18.5 |
| 1963–8 | 22.7 | 0.2 | 22.5 | 32.5 | 0.7 | 31.6 |
| 1968–72 | 12.9 | 0.3 | 12.6 | 19.2 | – 0.2 | 19.4 |
| 1972–6 | 16.1 | – 0.1 | 16.2 | 21.0 | – | 21.0 |

Sources: NEDO [5]; NEDO calculations.

A good deal of statistical work in recent years has established that relative industrial decline in Britain is not explained by differences in industrial structure at Order level. Bringing up to date some earlier work, Table 8.2 shows the unimportance of inter-sectoral shifts of employment in explaining the growth of productivity in both the UK and Germany up to 1976. Over a period of widely different industrial performance from 1954 to 1976, Table 8.3 shows that the inter-industry distribution of employment and of capital stock, as well as the pattern of capital intensity and capital productivity, have moved closer together.

For ten European economies, the Economic Commission for Europe has recently demonstrated an increasingly similar broad industrial structure through the 1960s, with convergence in twelve out of

*Table 8.3    Comparison of the distribution of employment and capital, and the pattern of labour productivity, capital productivity and capital intensity in UK and West German manufacturing*
*(rank correlation coefficients)*

|  | 1954 | 1976 |
|---|---|---|
| Employment | 0.69 | 0.74 |
| Capital stock | 0.83 | 0.95 |
| Capital per man | 0.79 | 0.92 |
| Labour productivity | 0.87 | 0.75 |
| Capital productivity | 0.60 | 0.70 |

Source: NEDO calculations.

eighteen branches (United Nations, [10]) in spite of quite rapid changes in the distribution of output and employment between industrial branches. This similarity was little affected by somewhat further industrial disaggregation; furthermore, no overall relation was found between national growth rates and the amount of shift in broad industrial structure.

*Table 8.4    The distribution of exports between fast-growing and slow-growing categories in world trade (percentages of value)*

|  | UK | | France | | Germany | | Japan | |
|---|---|---|---|---|---|---|---|---|
|  | 1955 | 1973 | 1955 | 1973 | 1955 | 1973 | 1955 | 1973 |
| The faster-growing product groups | 52 | 68 | 37 | 60 | 57 | 68 | 25 | 64 |
| The slower-growing product groups | 48 | 32 | 63 | 40 | 43 | 32 | 75 | 36 |

Source: NEDO, [7].

The structure of trade by growth-classes of industries points in the same general direction (Table 8.4). For the UK, Germany, France and Japan there was the same sort of increase in the share by value between 1955 and 1973 of exports in the faster-growing products in world trade, though the structural shift in Japan was predictably larger. The UK disadvantage has not lain in the broad product structure of her exports.

## Conditions for an Extended Episode of Unusual Industrial Growth

The similarity between the structure of industry in Britain and Germany and the fact that over a long period the rate of growth of industrial productivity in Britain has been close to that of the technological leader, the US, suggests that British industrial performance may have been overtaken not because it has dropped progressively further behind best-practice techniques but because equivalent industries in rival economies have taken advantage of the existence of a technological gap to grow unusually fast in the process of narrowing it. In the course of realising some of this potential they have moved around a well-known virtuous circle, where success removes some of the obstacles to further advance.

The two main differences in performance between individual industries in Britain and their counterparts in Germany are the difference in the speed with which it has proved possible in German plants to improve techniques (and raise direct labour productivity for any given scale of production) and their continuing success in designing and selling within most product groups increasingly expensive products, the demand for which tends to increase more sharply over time than does the demand for cheaper alternatives.

There are two ways of locating the unrealised potential for unusually fast productivity growth in an individual industry. One is to make comparisons between plants of similar size and vintage in different countries as Pratten [9] has done for multinational corporations. He found direct labour productivity levels typically about a third higher in Germany. Other scattered evidence that NEDO has collected suggests the existence of even wider (and of course widening) differences. If one regards levels of productivity in North American plants as providing a target theoretically achievable over twenty years, about 60 per cent above the present UK level and increasing at about 3 per cent a year, then joining the group of fast-growing 'catchers-up' might imply productivity growth rates twice as high as before, leaving aside increased economies of scale.

The second statistical approach to productivity potential is to look at Census of Production data for establishments at minimum list heading (MLH) level rearranged by productivity class. The scope for unusual growth depends on the dispersion of productivity, the weights attached to the various productivity classes, the room for the movement of resources between productivity classes and the extent to which productivity-spread depends upon the variety of products in each

MLH industry rather than upon inevitable features of the process of production.

Some idea of the local potential for unusual growth of productivity on top of normal trend growth in different industries can be derived from a measure of the effect on overall productivity of reduced dispersion. If one picks out the twenty out of the 144 MLH sectors in which the productivity gain would be greatest if the lowest decile of establishments were able to match within a period of ten years the productivity level of the top decile, the consequent increase in productivity growth in manufacturing as a whole would be 0.25 per cent a year. If instead the twenty largest sectors were to achieve such a miracle of transformation the gain would be more than 0.5 per cent a year.

The contribution that Census data can make alone, either to the explanation of relatively slow productivity growth or to policies directed to the achievement of 'unusual' growth, is very limited. When the results on productivity dispersion and changes in dispersion between Censuses are combined with other inter-industry variables, like measures of capital intensity, trade performance and concentration, some more pertinent questions can be directed to those actively engaged in the industries concerned.

Other results are suggested by inter-industry investigation of the other Census characteristics of high- and low-productivity establishments, especially of differences in ratios of investment to output, and gross to net output (as a proxy for specialisation), and of the gross profit-share of value-added.

Among the earliest results were that high-productivity dispersion goes with high 'specialisation', and with high profit per head and a low share of wages in net output; also, that increases in dispersion between Censuses accompanies increases in the gross profit-share and is found in industries where the initial dispersion is high. No relation across industries has been found between high growth of productivity and reduced dispersion, so that if we take dispersion to be a crude measure of the potential for unusual productivity growth, it is plain that this potential is not going to be released without help.

A system of sector working parties formed out of those engaged in particular industries may provide a means for deciding whether productivity potential is not apparent but real and, if real, what actions (for example, the sharing of technical information, changes in industrial concentration, product standardisation or the redesign of products) are relevant. The 39 sector committees which are at work in

NEDO have not so far looked at performance in this way. As they begin to look more carefully at the level and rate of growth of productivity, structural indicators of theoretical potential may turn out to be one useful starting-point.

Among the main matters for investigation at the individual industry level are the mechanisms by which some of the factors which explain a low average level of productivity can also inhibit the growth of productivity. There is no necessary connection between low productivity levels (and correspondingly high theoretical potential for 'catch-up') and continuing low growth. The benefits from the closing of a technology gap, from increases in scale and from improvements in product design are all likely to be greater in an industry the further average practice has fallen behind. But the improvement may be made much more difficult because of low relative growth in the past, and it is the business of industrial policy to help to start a process of recovery at rates of growth well above the steady-state level.

The experience of low growth in the past, and low current levels of industrial productivity, are inhibiting because of the resistance generated among employees to changes in technique which, following the slow past changes, carry the prospect of very large reductions in labour requirements without, over a comparable period, compensating increases in output. The re-equipment that is needed when an industry has fallen a long way behind is on a dauntingly large scale and lack of confidence in the degree of its utilisation, low current profitability and perhaps financial constraints can all lead to the putting-off of all re-equipment – even that which would be undertaken by a company at the optimum distance behind best-practice techniques.

It is, of course, a mistake to think of productivity growth as entailing an increase in the physical output of a homogeneous product per unit of labour or capital employed. Productivity growth in that sense may be resisted in the belief that price reductions would be matched without much benefit to output and that, therefore, the productivity gain would accrue to profits and cost jobs. If productivity growth takes the form, in the first instance, of an increase in the *quality* of the product with unchanged inputs, then, because imitation lags are longer when competition takes this form and because of increasing preference for advanced and high unit value products in world trade, it is likely that unusual manufacturing productivity growth which takes this form will face less resistance and be more effective in the longer run – both in creating opportunities for scale economies and further rounds of productivity gain, on the one hand, and increasing (rather than decreasing) employment opportunities, on the other.

The second important respect in which British manufacturing performance has been indifferent is in just those terms of the up-to-dateness, technical specification and design of the particular products on which British manufacturers have specialised, as well as their reputation for reliability, delivery and after-sales service – in short, their non-price competitiveness. The connection with productivity growth runs three ways: first an improvement in physical productivity – like devaluation but without its untoward effects upon inflation – creates a surplus over wage costs which can be devoted to product improvement and complementary investment in marketing. Secondly, an improvement in non-price competitiveness tends to increase market share and to present opportunities to raise physical productivity without creating large-scale redundancy. Thirdly, product improvement with unchanged inputs is directly an important expression of productivity gain and one to which international demand is clearly sensitive.

Given that, over a long period and using a variety of indicators of price competitiveness, exchange-rate changes have broadly compensated for the relative rise in sterling costs of production, and given that (as earlier shown) the broad product composition of British exports and domestic output of manufactures is very similar to that of Germany and not very different from that of France, the differences between the British and the German or French income elasticities of demand for manufactured imports, as well as the differences in the elasticity of foreign demand for exports support the now quite widespread evidence that non-price competitive disadvantages underlie Britain's industrial decline (NEDO, [6]).

Chart 8.2 plots a regression of moving-average growth rates of the volume of exports against the growth of world trade for UK, Germany and France between the periods 1960 II–1965 and 1970 II–1975. The fit is not very good, particularly for the UK, but it suggests that the UK tends to lose share at any growth rate of world trade, and to lose it more rapidly when the world economy is growing faster.

Chart 8.3 plots the growth rates of the volume of manufactured imports against the growth rate of GDP in the same way, from 1968 to 1976. The slopes of the French and German lines are practically identical. The UK line is steeper and to the left. Unless policies can be found which permanently shift the UK's imports line to the right, or shift and steepen its export line, then the prospects for faster economic

Chart 8.2   *Growth of exports volume and of world trade*
(*annual percentage growth rates, 4½-year averages ending year shown*)

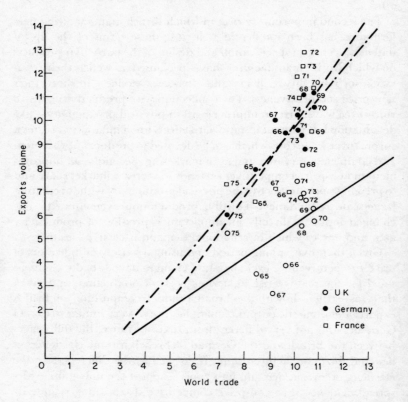

growth in the UK, close to French and German rates, will be limited by ability to increase invisible earnings faster than in the past. With fixed exchange rates and a medium-term world trade growth rate of manufactures of (say) 10 per cent, the domestic growth rates at which the annual increase in manufactured imports and exports are in balance are just under 4 per cent for France, 3¼ per cent for Germany and just under 1½ per cent for the UK. The disparity between Germany and the UK is considerably widened if one takes account of Deutschmark revaluations and sterling devaluations of these ten years.

The differences in the price per unit of British, German and French exports in almost every manufactured product group are striking. They have been calculated for those Standard International Trade Classifications (SITCs) which correspond with sectors represented in

Chart 8.3  Relative growth of GDP and of imports of manufactures,
UK, France and Germany (percentage growth rates year-on-year based on
$4\frac{1}{2}$-year moving averages ending year shown)

Note: based on the following regression equations:
> UK:      MI = $- 3.5 + 5.615$ GDP (R = 0.92)
> France:   MI = $- 3.5 + 3.075$ GDP (R = 0.80)
> Germany: MI = $- 1.1 + 2.979$ GDP (R = 0.93)

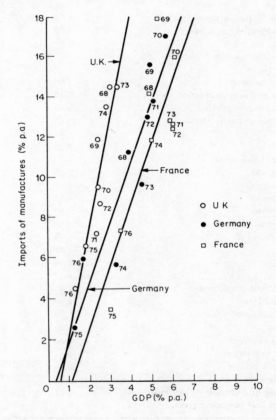

the government's industrial strategy and are set out in Table 8.5.
For a group of five SITCs representing mechanical engineering, it
was possible to trace the movement of unit values of German, French
and British exports from 1963 (when they were closely similar) to 1975.
Chart 8.4 shows the extent of the qualitive change in the composition
of exports for these categories, particularly over the last four years.

Table 8.5   Ratio of unit values of German and French exports to
UK exports by sector, 1974

| | Germany/UK | France/UK |
|---|---|---|
| Construction equipment/mining machinery | 2.76 | 2.44 |
| Office machinery | 2.25 | .. |
| Telecommunications | 2.22 | 1.67 |
| Machine tools | 1.99 | 1.53 |
| Food and drink packaging equipment | 1.92 | 1.23 |
| Mechanical handling equipment | 1.88 | 1.21 |
| Pharmaceuticals | 1.80 | 1.00 |
| Heavy electrical machinery/industrial equipment | 1.76 | 1.23 |
| Pumps and valves | 1.70 | 1.08 |
| Brewing and malting | 1.68 | 1.09 |
| Automation and instrumentation | 1.47 | 1.52 |
| Electronic consumer goods | 1.46 | 1.33 |
| Petrochemicals/speciality chemicals | 1.45 | 1.25 |
| Biscuits | 1.42 | 1.02 |
| Bearings | 1.39 | 1.10 |
| Process plant fabrications | 1.39 | 0.92 |
| Industrial trucks | 1.38 | 0.98 |
| Industrial engines | 1.34 | 1.20 |
| Textile machinery | 1.34 | 1.01 |
| Man-made fibres | 1.30 | 1.27 |
| Meat and meat products | 1.30 | 0.94 |
| Constructional steel | 1.26 | 1.14 |
| Clothing | 1.22 | 1.27 |
| Iron and steel | 1.22 | 1.09 |
| Rubber | 1.17 | 1.06 |
| Domestic electrical equipment | 1.10 | 1.17 |
| Printing machinery | 1.10 | 0.92 |
| Ferrous foundries/drop forgings | 1.08 | 0.70 |
| Wool textiles | 1.03 | 0.86 |
| Hosiery and knitwear | 1.00 | 1.43 |
| Electronic components | 0.92 | 0.96 |
| Milk and milk products | 0.89 | 1.12 |
| Paper and board | 0.84 | 0.82 |
| Space heating and ventilating machinery | 0.72 | 0.63 |
| Radio, radar and electronic goods | 0.43 | 0.87 |

Source: NEDO, [6], p. 28; NEDO calculations.

*Note:* The product coverage used for this analysis corresponds broadly to the principal
products of the sector working parties indicated, but is limited to some extent
by the availability of comparable international data. The unit values from
which the ratios were derived, originally expressed in terms of metric tons per $,
were calculated using average exchange rates.

Chart 8.4 *Comparative export performance of UK, French and German mechanical engineering industries,[a] 1963–75*

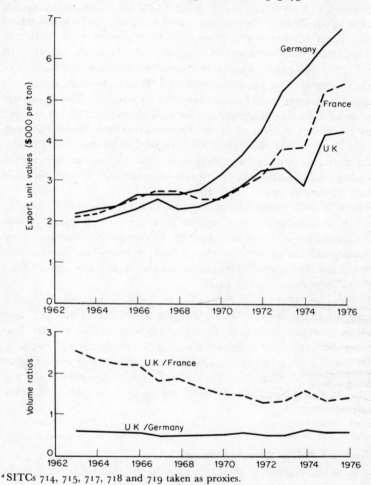

[a] SITCs 714, 715, 717, 718 and 719 taken as proxies.

Inflation and increasing sophistication have raised the price per ton of exports for all three, but a one-ton 'basket' of German mechanical engineering exports was by 1976 worth about 60 per cent more than a representative ton of British exports, not the 12 per cent more they were worth in 1963, while the rate of tonnages exported remained almost unchanged. A French 'basket' from being 6 per cent dearer had become almost 30 per cent dearer than a British 'basket', while the ratio of French to British tonnages had fairly steadily increased.

These results, it can be argued, are strongly affected by sterling devaluation. However, on the evidence of the volume ratios, the decline in the sterling–Deutschmark exchange rate, with its attendant effects upon relative unit values, can be regarded as an offset to increasing uncompetitiveness in terms of product quality, as well as in many other non-price respects. In spite of devaluation, the balance of trade in engineering products worsened. It may be that, as an unwanted consequence of devaluation, the structure of British exports was impelled further down-market because of generally higher relative price elasticities of demand at the down-market end. Had it not been for devaluation, the absence of a determined campaign and a heavy investment in stopping the growth of non-price disadvantages would have led to a catastrophic fall in employment and output over this period, especially in the years 1972–6.

There is little compensation in the long run from a favourable (low) UK–German ratio of import unit values in producer goods sectors, since this will tend to impose on the user industries an imported technological backwardness. (A number of important engineering sectors have this uneasy combination of low export unit value ratios and low import unit value ratios.)

In the course of 1977 a number of sector working parties have drawn special attention to the relation between the design of products and trade performance both in exporting and in supplanting imports. Discussions of investment requirements and of the paradox of capacity constraints in the midst of apparent excess capacity at the particular industry level often turn out to refer indirectly to the problem of the partial irrelevance of the existing product-mix to world market requirements.

## Industrial Policy Considerations

The guiding principle of policy to prevent the perpetuation of long-term industrial decline is that it should attack the process at the points of origin and not try to treat the symptoms allopathically. There are no completely independent origins, of course, and detailed causes vary from one industrial sector to another.

Chart 8.5 sets out schematically some of the dynamic dependencies which appear to hold, fairly generally, in manufacturing industries. Each box denotes an increase ( + ) or decrease ( − ) in a variable. The two preferred points of entry for industrial policy into this tableau are

Chart 8.5    *Dynamic dependencies in manufacturing industries*

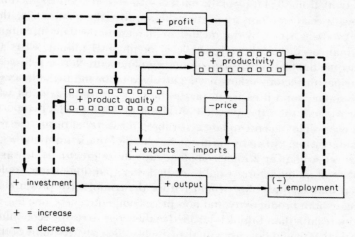

+ = increase
− = decrease

productivity growth and the improvement of product quality – that is, its up-to-dateness and sophistication and competitiveness in non-price respects. Connections by dashed lines (for example, from investment to product quality) are intended to show only that investment may make possible an increase in non-price competitiveness, not that capacity-creating investment, generated by an increase in output, for example, will necessarily do so. Likewise, to increase gross profit is not automatically to increase expenditure on product improvement, though it provides the means to do so.

On this view, policy intervention directly on the trade balance (for example, by protection) need not generate a continuous process of improvement in trade performance and output, because it will not necessarily lead to improvements in either productivity or non-price competitiveness and product relevance, which are the routes into improved trade performance. Indeed it may operate perversely to reduce the improvement in product quality that would otherwise have occurred. The same holds true of general investment incentives as distinct from the transfer of technology or investment in the development of new products and processes.

The connection between product 'quality', productivity and employment is important. At high levels of industrial unemployment and employment-insecurity, schemes for increasing industrial sales and output by reducing accumulated over-manning in an industry run into difficulties because the immediate effects on jobs are more obvious than the second-round beneficial effects through a higher general level of activity from the lifting of the balance-of-payments constraint. This throws special emphasis upon efforts to improve the quality of tradeable products, since, by this means, an increase in the value of output per man occurs at the original level of physical output, with no consequential first-round reduction in employment. Not surprisingly, the tripartite sector working parties involved in the industrial strategy have so far found it easier to tackle the issue of product design and improvement than the question of raising physical productivity.

It is possible to contemplate generalised measures of protection for manufacturing, either by tariffs or by share-of-market quotas, with floors set so that at a higher consequent rate of growth of demand imports of manufactures would not be lower than under free trade. Given that such a policy would reduce the competitive pressure to increase both productivity and non-price competitiveness, one has to rest more faith than I think is justified in the scope to realise economies of scale that would flow from increased self-sufficiency. In many of the industries where comparisons have been possible between plants here and in Germany, for example, large shortfalls of UK productivity are associated with the lack of specialisation of output, with under-utilisation of capital and labour as a whole because of chronic skill or component shortages, or because the optimum scale of plant is lower here for industrial relations reasons.

There are protagonists for a 'market' policy, whereby competition policy would be strengthened, taxation and government expenditure in support of industry reduced and, presumably, reliance placed on the absence of any alternatives to re-equipment, product improvement and the elimination of over-manning as a means of survival. It appears from the recommendations of many of the sector working parties that a non-interventionist policy, which takes no account of the reasons for past failure and the effect of that failure on industrial attitudes at plant level, would tend to speed up industrial decline without a commensurately rapid release of under-employed resources.

Cooperative policies that go further than they have so far seem to be necessary to increase the mobility of factors of production from declining products and unproductive uses to products earlier in their life cycle and to establishments where productivity is high, as well as to help languishing companies to re-equip by means of selective investment assistance.

One other non-selective but radical policy that has support both from Bacon and Eltis [1] (and implicitly from F. E. Jones [2]) is to make room, by the reduction of public and private consumption, for very large-scale increases in market sector investment. There is, presumably, some price of capital low enough to ensure that the investment is undertaken.

The familiar relation between growth and the investment ratio is improved when export growth is added as a second explanatory variable. Kern, in a seventeen-country comparison of growth of GNP from 1953 to 1976, gets an excellent fit for an equation which relates GNP growth to investment as a proportion of GNP and export growth (Kern, [3] ). However, there still appears no reason from the statistical evidence to suppose that sustained GNP growth, with export growth as a consequence, can be investment-led. In his comparison of Japanese and UK accounting data, Jones finds that, although Japanese asset values per man employed in manufacturing are four times as high as in the UK and value-added per man only 2.4 times as high, taxes and wages per man are sufficiently much stickier than value-added for gross profits as a ratio of asset values to be higher in Japan than in the UK. It is difficult to be confident that the £100,000 million of additional investment required to raise assets per man from £7500 to £30,000 in the UK would have the same effect on gross profitability here. Nor is it clear how such capitalisation could be engineered as the *seed* rather than the *fruit* of success.

## The Industrial Strategy

The 'supply-side' approach to industrial policy which the government initiated in November 1975 is based on four main considerations: that the main deficiencies of comparative performance in the private sector exist within manufacturing, on which Britain will have to continue to rely for the exports needed to support full employment; that relatively low growth of value-added per man in manufacturing runs across almost all product groups and is not the result of an unfavourable distribution of factors of production between industries broadly defined; that several decades of experience show that neither demand-led national economic planning 'from the top down' nor the reliance solely upon a benign macroeconomic economic suffice to match the 'unusual' growth – growth rates above the rate of technical progress – which many industrial competitor countries have managed; that in a mixed economy with a history of conflicts of interest between the two sides of industry regeneration is a responsibility of government, but one which cannot be realised by imposed solutions – the detail of the industrial deficiencies is intricate and the necessity for cooperative solutions paramount, so that policies have to be discovered and agreed upon by those actively engaged in each industry.

About 40 per cent of manufacturing is covered by tripartite sector working parties working within the framework of NEDO and to a steering brief agreed by the NEDC. These groups provide the main focus of the industrial strategy which in fact extends much more widely, so that almost all branches of government now take into account the compatibility of policy with the industrial objectives.

There is no room here fully to describe this policy. It is reflected in the detailed reports of the sector working parties and in the response of government to the sectors' recommendations. The effects will depend ultimately upon the success of the participants in translating the sectors' self-referring recommendations into collaborative decisions within (and between) individual companies: decisions about product design, the installation and use of new plant and equipment, export development, communication with customers and suppliers, training and manpower planning, specialisation and restructuring.

The objective of each of the sectors involved in the industrial strategy is to improve upon the trend changes in share of world exports and import penetration. Quantitative objectives for sales by 1980 were set early in 1977. So far as exports are concerned. these targets have come to look increasingly ambitious as the expected growth of world trade has declined. Directly assessing progress towards these targets will therefore be difficult. Success is best measured by the progress in changing the trend in share rather than in reaching the target for export sales. So far as imports are concerned, the measurement of improvement on what would have happened in the absence of the industrial strategy is complicated by the rapid development of competition from the newly industrialising countries in many product areas, as well as by the rate of growth of home demand. The lower and right hand columns of Table 8.6 show some industries where the recent increase in competition from Japan and newly industrialising countries is so important that even to slow down the recent fall in the index of UK trade performance could be counted as a success. Objectives were set without full knowledge of these recent pressures.

One advantage of a working party setting itself an export objective is that there is really no way in which the improvements in product, marketing and efficiency in production, on which long-term industrial competitiveness must depend, can be short-circuited by measures which temporarily achieve the target. Such is not the case with import substitution targets, where it would be theoretically possible to confuse cause and effect and regard the strategy as having been successful if imports were simply restricted. (This is not to deny that the limitation of 'downpour' imports may be a necessary condition for the improvement of industrial performance, nor that the conditional selective and temporary limitation of imports may sometimes provide an umbrella

*Table 8.6    The UK's changing trade performance and the level of import penetration for some manufacturing industries, 1970–6 (MLH numbers)*

| | Long-term trade performance | | | | | |
|---|---|---|---|---|---|---|
| | Up | | Little change | | Down | |
| | IP low | IP high | IP low | IP high | IP low | IP high |
| **Short-term trade performance** | | | | | | |
| Up | 272 | 336 | 484 | 335 | | 364 |
| | 271 | | 362 | | | 366 |
| | 341 | | 461 | | | |
| | 333 | | 275 | | | |
| | 337 | | 274 | | | |
| | 367 | | 464 | | | |
| | 491 | | 277 | | | |
| | 361 | | | | | |
| | 339 | | | | | |
| | 349 | | | | | |
| Little change | 279 | | 496 | | 311 | |
| | | | 276 | | | |
| | | | 495 | | | |
| | | | 353 | | | |
| | | | 391 | | | |
| | | | 354 | | | |
| | | | 462 | | | |
| Down | 380 | 351 | 494 | 352 | 365 | |
| | 334 | | 312 | | 368 | |
| | | | 331 | | | |

Sources: Calculations by FCO; J. D. Wells and J. C. Imber, 'Home and export performance of UK industries', *Economic Trends*, August 1977.

*Notes:*   (i)  Trade performance defined as exports *minus* imports as a percentage of manufacturers' sales *plus* exports. Long-term, it is 'up' if the average annual increase 1963–73 was at least 0.16 per cent, 'down' if the average decrease 1963–73 was at least 0.16 per cent. Short-term, it is 'up' if there was *any* increase 1970–6, 'down' if there was a loss of more than 8 per cent over the six years.

   (ii)  IP = import penetration, defined as imports in 1976 as a percentage of home demand. It is 'low' if less than 50 per cent.

(iii) The following are the MLHs shown:

271  general chemicals
272  pharmaceuticals
274  paint
275  soaps and detergents
276  synthetic resins, plastic materials
277  dyestuffs and pigments
279  miscellaneous chemicals
311  iron and steel (general)
312  steel tubes
331  agricultural machinery
333  pumps and valves
334  industrial engines
335  textile machinery
336  construction equipment
337  mechanical handling equipment
339  other machinery
341  industrial plant and steelwork
349  other mechanical engineering
351  photographic, etc., equipment
352  watches and clocks
353  surgical instruments
354  scientific instruments
361  electrical machinery
362  insulated wires and cables
364  radio, radar and electronic components
365  broadcast receiving and sound reproducing equipment
366  electronic computers
367  radio, radar and electronic capital goods
368  domestic electric appliances
380  tractors
391  hand tools
461  bricks, fireclay and refractory goods
462  pottery
464  cement
484  other paper and board
491  rubber
494  toys, games and sports equipment
495  miscellaneous stationary
496  other plastic products

for the investment and restructuring needed to increase long-run competitiveness. Such measures have to be used very circumspectly, however, since a temporary shelter can easily become a permanent retreat from competitive pressures.) Import substitution targets can also be ambiguous, since if trade performance in a product group (measured by the growth of the net trade balance to home sales *plus* exports, for example) is improving partly as a result of increased specialisation, increased import penetration cannot be reasonably regarded as a sign of failure. Between 1962 and 1972, for example, in the mechanical engineering group of industries as a whole, the volume and, *a fortiori*, the value of output increased much more rapidly in Germany than the UK – as did productivity – and its share of world exports (by value) rose at about the pace that the UK share fell. Meanwhile the share of imports in UK domestic demand rose by 18.5 per cent, but by 28 per cent in Germany. Export share targets lead fairly unambiguously towards the twin points of entry into improved performance set out in Chart 8.5 – productivity and non-price competitiveness. There are no short cuts.

A microeconomic, self-regarding approach to the development of industrial policies can be vitiated if macroeconomic policies are not broadly benign. While international industrial competitiveness cannot be created by a dash for growth or by exchange-rate manipulation, the government has taken the view that detailed recuperative action would be discouraged by unfavourable overall policies – particularly those which create doubts either about the long-run profitability of determined export-marketing investment, market-oriented R and D, the recruitment and training of scarce skills and increases in capital intensity, or about the long-run employment prospects of those who collaborate in changes in the organisation and techniques of production. It is impossible for the government to guarantee a particular growth rate of GNP without knowing in advance how successful the industry strategy will be, what is the likely growth of world demand, and what are the balance-of-payments policies of major competitors. Some overall commitments can be given in support of industrial recovery: that the tax structure will not further squeeze undistributed profits; that exchange-rate policy will be directed at maintaining, so far as possible, a stable real exchange rate (corrected for differences in the movement of relative unit costs); that all branches of economic, social and educational policy will be broadly helpful; that government spending on industrial infrastructure and selective investment assistance will be kept up.

The work of the sector working parties, with their self-imposed trade objectives, has so far been mostly in directions where controversy and conflict is small, and where quite a lot of improvement has been possible through analysis and the exchange of information. Export market opportunities have been investigated and reported on; opportunities for the transfer of new technology, the financing of R and D and future technical change have been considered; the reasons for import penetration are now well understood and a start has been made in bringing makers and users together so that the requirements of large users can be met in good time; standards and specifications are being agreed upon which can enable producers to satisfy both home and overseas customers at once. Progress has been slower in the investigation of ways of emulating the productivity of efficient producers both within Britain and abroad, but in several sectors international comparisons of production methods have revived a long tradition of self-analysis, and NEDO's own work on the dispersion of productivity at establishment level has revealed something of the very large potential scope for productivity improvement.

Progress has also been predictably slow in reaching agreement about the rationalisation of output and its redistribution between companies, which ought not to have to wait upon the wastes and redundancies of eventual bankruptcies. These last two important fields of action are like the others in the sense that, on a long view and considering the painfulness of the alternatives, a net collective benefit to those engaged in the industry exists, but its distribution is so uneven or its delay so great that agreement on action is difficult. In these cases some form of bargain may have to be struck as the price of agreement. A sector working party rarely represents enough of the producers and workers concerned – and not at the level where changes have to be negotiated – for such bargains to be worked out.

The critical problem, once the relevance to the trade objective of some action has been established (like specialisation or automation or the abandonment of one product and the development of another) is to communicate the recommendation to individual companies.

The reason why the contemplation of industry-wide objectives inside a sector working party can result in any trades unionist or any industrialist acting differently from the way he would act otherwise is that the stage is thereby set for a cooperative strategy. What was an $n$-person low-sum game can, in principle, be transformed into a two-person higher positive-sum game, with side-payments, where one player is the collection of UK producers and the other is the foreign competition. The theory of collusive oligopoly applies. Some of the possible contacts and of the resulting contingent decisions may be difficult to make because they may seem to fall foul of competition policy. Others are difficult to organise because they presuppose an understanding of the options and considerable trust at every level inside the place of work. Others again (like maker–user understandings or the polling of information on potential manpower bottlenecks) reach across a number of sectors and need to be discussed at more widely representative industrial meetings.

Understanding has increased most quickly, within the individual sectors, between the industrial members and the government itself. As a result, a string of helpful intitiatives have been taken on behalf of particular sectors and in response to recommendations by several sectors at once. Most of these relate, fairly directly, to increases in value productivity (through assistance with re-equipment and the diffusion of new technology) or to increases in product relevance to export markets, to non-price competitive strength and to longer-term investment in overseas marketing. Sectoral industry schemes, asked for by individual working parties, have run their course in six sectors and are working in eight others (including paper and board, electronic components, wool textiles, non-ferrous foundries, instrumentation and automation, and footwear). There is also a selective investment scheme, with a high (10 to 1) financial leverage, intended to improve economic performance. Under this scheme, projects involving a total outlay of £250 million have already been supported. Those under consideration involve outlays of a further £1750 million. As the result of recommendations by several working parties about the risks of innovation facing smaller companies, a product and process development scheme was introduced last year, contributing to development costs in various ways. An export market entry guarantee scheme now exists to underwrite some of the risks faced by small firms entering a new overseas market.

For all this catalogue of selective measures (which is by no means complete), the main criticism is that it is hard to see how the speed of improvement in productivity and non-price competitiveness (and hence in trade performance) which can be brought about in this way can be fast enough to counteract protectionist pressures. It may be that we shall not be prepared to work for perhaps a generation to see the end of a decline which has gone on for four.

The present approach to industrial policy is limited in its coverage and voluntary and responsive, rather than *dirigiste*. Its success depends very much upon the rate of recovery of the world economy. There is a large 'catch up' potential for unusual growth through changes in work practices, modernisation of capital stock and the redesign of products. But these depend on cooperative agreement at plant level, which will be difficult to achieve unless overall employment prospects improve and unless some means is found to overcome the suspicion and conflict between the industrial parties that has led to such sluggish adaptation to changing competitive conditions in the past. The government's keener perception of detailed industrial problems has helped a great deal. Translating the industrial strategy into ways and means inside each company will also help. But, as Sir Henry Phelps Brown has recently suggested [8], we may still stand in the end in need of something more.

## References

[1] Bacon, R. W. and Eltis, W. A., *Britain's Economic Problem: too few producers*, London, Macmillan, 1976.

[2] Jones, F. E., 'Our manufacturing industry – the missing £100,000 million', *National Westminster Bank Quarterly Review*, May 1978.

[3] Kern, D., 'An international comparison of major economic trends', *National Westminster Bank Quarterly Review*, May 1978.

[4] NEDO, *Cyclical Fluctuations in the United Kingdom Economy*, London, 1976.

[5] NEDO, *The United Kingdom and West German Manufacturing Industry, 1954–72*, London, 1976.

[6] NEDO, *International Price Competitiveness, Non-price Factors and Export Performance* by D. K. Stout, London, 1977.

[7] NEDO, *Product Changes in Industrial Countries' Trade, 1955–73* by M. Panić and A. H. Rajan, London (forthcoming).

[8] Phelps Brown, Sir Henry, 'What is the British predicament?', *Three Banks Review*, December 1977.

[9] Pratten C. F., *Labour Productivity Differentials in International Companies*, Cambridge University Press, 1976.

[10] United Nations, Economic Commission for Europe, *Structure and Change in European Industry*, Geneva, 1977.

# Comment

## by Thomas Balogh

Stout's essay dismisses most general explanations of the steady relative decline of British industry. He tests statistically – mainly for the period 1954–76 – various hypotheses and disposes of most of them.

His task was not easy – one of the great difficulties in the way of success in deriving causal connections in this field is the rapid structural change which renders most statistical relationships highly unstable. The statistics themselves are complicated aggregates which show startling variations according to which years are taken as the base and final date. This explains some of the surprising discrepancies in the results between explanatory schemata even of scholarly standard. In the end he focuses attention, in my opinion rightly, on the growing import penetration in manufactures, the loss in our share of export markets and, (partly) consequentially, the seeming incompatibility between full(ish) employment and a favourable balance on the current account of international payments.

He is convincingly sceptical about suggestions that the expansion of the public sector is *the* cause of the British doldrums. He does not believe that the frequent alternation of 'stops and goes' were responsible for it – more successful countries had sharper fluctuations. He rejects the explanation beloved by the conventional, and finding rapid acceptance by politicians and journalists of all political loyalties, that the decline is due to high (personal and corporate) taxation, by pointing out that it lacks rigorous proof. The relative decline embraces periods when taxation was non- (or hardly) existent. Nor did it show any slowing down after the drastic cuts in taxes such as those administered in the period following 1951. He points out that relatively low *level* of productivity should enhance rather than impede the possibility of taking remedial action. The victorious over-running by Japan and Germany of our markets, while their unit export prices seems to have risen even faster than ours, leads him to conclude that non-price factors, quality, delivery dates, servicing, design and advanced technology played a decisive role in our eclipse, which excluded us from the markets for high technology and for more effective, more sought-after products. Differences in manufacturing structure, however, do not seem to have affected the outcome (though he does not deal with the impact of shifts from agriculture to manufacture which might well have been a powerful stimulus to the 'dynamic economies of scale' he rightly stresses). His hopes, consequentially, turn towards a period of extra rapid growth so as to make use of the possible dynamic advantages of full employment and large-scale production. So far as the critique of the British performance is concerned I largely accept his results. It is his remedial measures which I find insufficient, though necessary.

No doubt we have been suffering from a severe and probably self-stimulating gap in education, training, technology, design, marketing and, above all, manpower management. This result, however, must be supplemented with enquiry as to what caused these gaps before we can remedy them. For a long time conventional economists, given stout support by *The Times* and the *Economist*, had held the view (mostly as the result of a gross misinterpretation of the lessons of the 1925 up-valuation and the 1931 depreciation of sterling) that a change of parity, indeed the 'floating' of the currency, was the panacea for all ills. While devaluation and depreciation might have kept sterling prices momentarily competitive, it should have been obvious to any sensible observer that devaluation or depreciation can do so effectively only if *unexpected* and so long as some sort of money illusion remains; that is, that the 'Chicago School' of monetarists is not merely wrong but preaches the opposite of the truth. Once the public get suspicious, as a result of a repeated use of these sharp weapons, they will anticipate further similar changes and will try to protect themselves, thus accelerating the ill through income claims not corresponding to the increase in productivity (Balogh, [1], vol. I, section 3). Devaluation, moreover, cut real wages and permitted the country to retain for a long time the old industrial structure, when important changes were required if the standard of life of the workers was to be protected because of the long-run menace of the growing disparity in the increase in productivity.

Quite comprehensibly Stout was reticent to go further than an analysis of impersonal aggregates in outlining his conclusions for industrial policy in the face of the threat of de-industrialisation. It is, however, essential to go beyond and behind them. I shall shortly and very tentatively try to indicate the general preconditions and policy-means needed if success is to be achieved.

The first and most important fact is that the process of decline of Britain's relative industrial and economic (as against financial) weight is not a postwar phenomenon, as is, for instance, suggested by implication by the curious conclusion of the so-called 'Clare' group of economists (*Midland Bank Review*, [2]) blaming mainly government interference for our ills. The decline has been all but continuous since at least 1873. The relative growth of Britain before the first world war, that is in a period of total dominance of the free trade and *laissez-faire* doctrines, was appreciably inferior to post-1949. Indeed most of the new industries were established and developed in periods when British industry enjoyed protection, either by the disappearance of foreign competition as a result of the U-boat blockade, or by securing preferences and introducing and extending tariffs. Since and including the last quarter of the nineteenth century, British expansion only caught up with that of other countries in the periods when some type of protection was in force. This fact was obfuscated and veiled by an immense foreign income, the result of investment initiated in a more dynamic age and the existence up to 1931 of a *de facto* (after 1932 a *de jure*) Imperial Preference in the even-wider territories Britain ruled.

The very fact that the decline has gone on for so long suggests backwardness in education and a social system where the choice of the élite is mismanaged – 'knowing not what but whom' and being a 'good' member of committees and boards, that is non-cantankerous and lacking in original conceptions. This is a heavy handicap and will not be eliminated easily. It certainly is resistant to impersonal general economic policies: one of the odd ideas of most economic explanations of our troubles is the avidity with which high income elasticity of supply of management skill and of entrepreneurial verve are assumed in the case of societies which have performed sluggishly for a very long time despite all their initial advantages (Argentina is a good example!).

It follows that risk-taking is more restrained (contrariwise the adventurous – as we have seen in 1972–4 – get more rope) than in less stodgy countries. The fear of excess capacity, the dread of investing in new plant when the old would do is notable. This means that the limits of expansion are reached in this country before they press on our foreign competitors. Thus, our improvement is interrupted at an increasingly early stage of the upswing.

Disregarding, or worse still in total ignorance of, this weakness, the Foreign Office, the Treasury and the Bank of England, despite the evidence of boringly repetitive crises were set irrevocably on a path of liberalisation. Hardly had we managed to survive – through Marshall Aid – the crisis caused by the insufficiency of the means provided in Bretton Woods relative to the rigours of the rules of the game it had imposed, when we plunged back into liberalisation. We gleefully joined the GATT and tried to organise a free trade area, thus effectively compressing our field of economic manoeuvre. We disregarded the lessons of the considerable success of the reconstruction period, when comprehensive and discriminating controls were at our disposal, and plunged into a rearmament programme far beyond our capacity, while abolishing controls. The 1951, 1955, 1961 and 1964 crises and the forced devaluation of 1967 followed, but the intrepid adherence to the doctrine was not shaken. We then had 1973, 1974 and 1976, despite the appearance of the oil slick on the angry economic seas. The policy continued to embarrass and continues to embarrass us without much hope of altering it. The entry into the EEC further and violently restricted our capacity to deal with the basic problem of the country.

The resulting insufficiency both of the volume and the quality of capital investment throughout this period limited the possibility of a satisfactory increase in real wages. The growing concentration of economic power on the sides of both labour and the employers increasingly constituted a bilateral monopoly, in which the bargaining advantage varied according to a number of often non-quantifiable, social, sociological, psychological and political, as well as economic, factors. Obversely, the degree of oligopolistic control of the commodity markets, especially in manufactures, permits the manipulation of prices. Consequently it is possible to shift higher money wages to the consumer (to a large extent wage-earners). The insufficient economic progress results in strikes to obtain higher real incomes than warranted; this leads to a cost-induced inflation and, finally, to indirect monetary and fiscal restraint and unemployment.

In my opinion a successful industrial policy requires:

(a) a permanent incomes policy;
(b) an acceleration of growth and increase in productivity without which no government can obtain compliance with that policy;
(c) a social compact over a large field, by which the workforce can be integrated into policy-making, including the sort of cooperation which Stout advocates.

I cannot deal with the wider aspects of such a broad package, but I doubt whether a narrower one could successfully be made acceptable, especially so long as anti-inflationary policies are pursued which increase unemployment or the fear of unemployment.

On the narrower economic field, we need a drastic increase in investment to accelerate growth. This is difficult for the private sector to undertake at a time when there is a large amount of idle, if obsolescent, plant. To achieve it, some measures are needed to create a vacuum in markets, inevitably in that segment which has been supplied by imports. Alternatively imports must be limited while national production and money income are allowed to rise. Either would help to reduce costs, as unit fixed outlays are cut and profits rise, and this might create the basic preconditions for modernisation and a virtuous circle. Without such a protective system we seem likely to once more be stifled by imports at an early stage of recovery.

In view of the proven incapacity of management to provide for an up-to-date renewal of plant and to organise adequate design and marketing, it would be essential to make protection dependent on industry discussing agreements detailing their plans with the unions and the government. The fulfilment would have to be monitored by the NEDC. The creation of sector working parties is a step in the right direction. It is unlikely, however, that self-criticism and non-supervised action will suddenly do the trick. Protection then aids inefficiency.

These considerations suggest that the present policy – means reliance on the money supply or on other monetary indicators as policy determinants – are likely to perpetuate our malaise. Much more direct and discriminating policies and means are needed. Unfortunately it is difficult to hope for an automatic boost for our industry by a sufficiently rapid and sufficiently extensive world and economic recovery so long as the persistent creditor countries stubbornly adhere to the restrictive policies which are appropriate to persistent debtors and thereby stultify efforts at readjustment.

I do not claim that such an approach would necessarily 'work'. I do claim however that present policies, which represent a relapse into thinking from before the 'Great Depression', are doomed to failure and I doubt whether Stout's working parties based on self-criticism and self-help would be powerful enough to accomplish the remedy of the century-old defect.

## References

[1] Balogh, T., *Unequal Partners*, Oxford, Blackwell, 1963.
[2] *Midland Bank Review*, Autumn 1977.

# 9 North Sea Oil and the Reconstruction of UK Industry

## by A. Singh*

## Introduction

As a people we have been given the chance to harness our talents and energies to a programme of National Recovery that will rebuild Britain's prosperity and greatness. It is in that spirit that the Government invites the nation to use the decade of opportunity presented by North Sea oil. (Department of Energy, *The Challenge of North Sea Oil*, Cmnd 7143, London, HMSO, 1978, hereafter referred to as the North Sea White Paper.)

My brief in this paper is to discuss 'the specific problem of using the North Sea oil period in some way to strengthen the UK's manufacturing base'. The implication that the UK's industrial base does need strengthening is obvious and uncontroversial. But this statement also implies that the decade or more of substantial benefits to output, the balance of payments, etc., which the country will be obtaining from North Sea offshore oil and gas should be used, at least partly, for the explicit purpose of industrial regeneration, rather than, say, entirely for consumption, or foreign investment, or repayment of foreign loans. The recently published North Sea White Paper makes it clear that this is certainly the intention of the present government.

Even if there were agreement about objectives, the subject of industrial regeneration in relation to North Sea oil raises a whole range of analytical and policy issues. In this paper I shall confine myself to outlining a particular way of examining the problem which I hope is useful, and to discussing the policy choices which follow from it and from a study of the experience of other countries. The question of the exact amount of direct benefits which are

*I am grateful to P. E. Atkinson, T. S. Barker, J. M. P. Bradley, T. F. Cripps, J. L. Eatwell, M. J. Fetherston, A. Hughes, R. R. Neild, A. W. A. Peterson, W. B. Reddaway and L. A. Winters for helpful discussions or comments. I alone am responsible for any errors.

likely to flow from the North Sea, and their duration, is in itself a major one, but it must remain outside the scope of the present paper. The calculations of these benefits are, of course, dependent upon assumptions about the size of oil reserves, the future relative price of oil, the state of the economy, the exchange rate, etc. However, for the purpose of the following discussion only rough orders of magnitude are relevant, and we shall therefore adopt the broad estimates presented in the North Sea White Paper (see also CEPG, [7] and [8]; Page, [26]; Treasury, [30]).

These estimates suggest that the UK will become self-sufficient in oil by 1980; by then North Sea oil production is likely to contribute £4.5 billion (at 1977 prices) to GNP, amounting to about 3 per cent of current GNP. The contribution will rise to £6 billion by the middle 1980s, and will then begin to decline, with the UK eventually becoming a net importer of oil again in the 1990s. Assuming unchanged levels of activity and a constant exchange rate, the direct positive impact of oil on the balance of payments is expected to amount to £5.5 billion in 1980 (at 1977 prices) and about £8–£9 billion in the middle 1980s. To put these figures in perspective, the direct gains on the external account are roughly equivalent to a 'windfall' increase in the country's normal export earnings of about 15–18 per cent a year during the 1980s. As for the contribution to government revenues, these will build up over time; by the middle 1980s, the oil and gas operations are expected to yield £4 billion (again at 1977 prices), which amounts to about 5–6 per cent of government revenues. Thus the likely benefits from the North Sea for the UK economy are not particularly large; they are for instance relatively much smaller than those which countries like Holland (OECD, [25]) and Norway will obtain, let alone those accruing from the oil bounty to many countries in the Middle East. But it is important not to underestimate the significance of North Sea oil for the UK economy; this is due to the current position of the economy and the international economic situation, and to the availability of these resources at a time when energy prices have risen sharply and several of the competing industrial countries will for many years have great difficulty in balancing their external accounts because of their energy needs (Feinstein and Reddaway [11]).

In the next section, I shall outline the basic analytic approach to the problem of using the oil revenues, in part or in whole, for the purpose of industrial regeneration. In particular, a conception of long-term industrial efficiency in the context of the historical structure of the

UK economy will be presented and the notion of long-term structural disequilibrium discussed. In the third section, I shall provide some tentative estimates, on the basis of *existing* trends in the economy, of the magnitude of the task involved in making manufacturing industry efficient in the long run. The experience of Norway and Holland, which have been beneficiaries of North Sea oil and gas over a some-what longer period than the UK, will be briefly examined in the fourth section, as will the case of Japan – a country where industrial policy since the war has been conspicuously successful. Finally, I shall outline the broad policy choices open to the UK for industrial reconstruction, paying particular attention to the role of industrial policy.

## The Basic Analytic Approach

The evolution of the structure of the UK economy over the last century has rendered it a net importer of food and raw materials, which have to be paid for largely by exports of manufactures. As I have argued in Singh [28], given this historical evolution, an efficient manufacturing sector for the UK economy may be defined as one which, given the normal levels of other components of the balance of payments, yields sufficient net exports (both currently, but more importantly, potenti-ally) to pay for import requirements at socially acceptable levels of output, employment and the exchange rate. The latter restrictions are extremely important, since at low enough levels of output and employ-ment, or more arguably at a sufficiently low exchange rate, almost any manufacturing sector may be able to meet this criterion of efficiency. (The exchange rate should be regarded here as an indicator of acceptable levels of inflation and inequality of income distribution.) To be efficient, the manufacturing sector must be able to fulfil the above requirements not merely currently, but also in the long run. For instance, a windfall gain to the balance of payments (for example from North Sea oil) may put it temporarily into surplus (at desired levels of output and employment) although manufacturing industry may be incapable of ensuring this when 'normal' conditions return. (Similarly, this definition of efficiency also implies that if North Sea oil revenues were expected to last for ever, then even a shrinking or a very small manufacturing sector might be regarded as efficient. This anomaly can be avoided to some degree by including an additional restriction concerning the desired rate of growth of the economy. Then a dynamic manufacturing sector of a particular size will most likely be essential for 'efficiency' on the argument, *à la* Kaldor, that manufacturing is inherently characterised by higher productivity growth than other activities.) Thus, the objective of 'industrial regeneration' during the North Sea oil period must be to attempt to transform UK industry in such a way that in the 1990s, when the oil revenues begin to run out, the country is able to balance its external account on a sustained basis, at full employment and at a 'reasonable' exchange rate for sterling.

Having thus specified the final aim, we now turn to a character-isation of the initial conditions. The story of the UK's relative industrial decline during the last two decades is well known (Singh, [29]; Ray, [27]) and is extensively documented elsewhere in this book. The only apparently bright spot in the UK's generally unsatis-factory performance is the growth of productivity. Between 1955 and 1973 there was a trend increase in manufacturing productivity; begin-ning in the late 1960s there was also a significant reduction in the gap between the rate of growth of productivity in the UK and in the advanced European countries. However, during the last four years, manufacturing productivity in the UK appears to have stagnated, a phenomenon which cannot be explained in purely cyclical terms (CEPG, [8]). Moreover, as a consequence of the much greater productivity growth achieved by the competitor countries in the past, productivity in manufacturing industry in the UK in 1974 was nearly 40 per cent lower than that of West Germany or France, whereas twenty years earlier it had been much the same in the three countries (Jones, [15]).

Further, there is evidence not only that UK manufacturing industry is 'inefficient' in the specific sense discussed earlier – characterised by long-term disequilibrium – but that this disequilibrium has been growing worse over time (see Singh, [28] and [29] for a full discussion.) The essential point is that, mainly because of the decline in the per-formance of UK industry in the world economy, there has been, until the recent arrival of North Sea oil in significant amounts, a trend deterioration in the UK's current balance at full employment despite improved cost and price competitiveness (brought about by currency depreciations). This has increasingly prevented the economy from working at its full potential during the last decade. Thus, for example, in 1965–6 the UK was able to achieve a rough balance on its current account although there was near full employment (unemployment of 1.5 per cent). In 1970–1 the current account was in surplus to the tune of £1500 million (at 1975 prices), but unemployment was 3 per cent. Yet in 1975, although nearly 4 per cent of the labour force was unemployed, there was a current account deficit of £1700 million. Part of this was, indeed, due to the effects of the rise in oil prices since 1973. However, as the Cambridge Economic Policy Group model (CEPG, [6]) shows, even assuming that the terms of trade had remained constant at the pre-1972 level, there would have been a current account deficit of £2000 million at full employment in that year; the corresponding figure for 1977 is estimated by Martin Fetherston to be about £6000 million.

This experience suggests that, unless there is a major change in the performance of UK manufacturing industry – and a reversal of the current trends – the country will have even greater difficulty in sustaining a balance of external account at reasonable levels of activity and the exchange rate when North Sea oil runs out than it has until recently.

The main reason for this disequilibrium is the growing deficit on the UK's trade in finished manufactures with other advanced industrial countries. This phenomenon is seen to arise from (or, if one prefers, to be reflected in) a structural imbalance, whereby the UK's income elasticity of demand for finished manufactures is not only greater than that observed for other industrial countries, but is also considerably larger than the world income elasticity of demand for UK exports (Houthakker and Magee, [13]). The latter has in turn a lower value than that estimated for other advanced economies. As a consequence of these unfavourable elasticities, the UK economy is able to maintain an external balance by growing only very slowly. In terms of Myrdal's theory of cumulative and circular causation, a slow rate of growth of output and employment over a long period, relative to that of competing countries, would *ceteris paribus* tend to make the underlying disequilibrium more acute than before (see below).

There are many plausible hypotheses, on both the demand and the supply side, which can be put forward to account for the UK's relatively high income elasticity of demand for imports and the low world income elasticity of demand for UK exports (or more simply for the unfavourable time-trend terms in the regression models of imports and exports of finished manufactures – for those who do not approve of the specification of the problem in terms of income elasticities). For example, with respect to imports, the most important of these on the demand-side are:

(a) peculiarities in the structure of UK demand;
(b) too rapid a rate of change in the level and pattern of demand in this country;

(c) a low initial average propensity to import relative to that in other countries;

(d) too high a level of aggregate demand (and hence pressure on resources) in the UK compared with elsewhere.

However, available studies lend little empirical support to these theories.

The balance of the evidence suggests that it is weaknesses on the supply side which account for the UK's high income elasticity with respect to manufactured imports. The domestic productive system is clearly unable to respond adequately to changes in demand brought about by growth in consumer incomes. However, it is also found that such inadequacies cannot be traced to an unfavourable structure of UK industry, as conventionally understood, that is to the industrial distribution of inputs and outputs. Nor are they reflected in a rise in relative costs or prices, compared with other countries. The reverse is the case, at least since the early 1960s.

A number of studies have stressed the importance of non-price factors in international competition. In particular, empirical research on the relative competitiveness of UK and foreign products shows that the former are weak in terms of factors such as delivery dates, quality, design and performance (NEDO, [20]). These non-price characteristics take us a long way towards an explanation both of the UK's high income elasticity of demand for imports and of its obverse – the low world elasticity of demand for UK exports. (How far a reduction in price might compensate for non-price factors is discussed in CEPG, [7] and by Posner in Chapter 7.) They suggest a lack of dynamism in the productive system, which must in turn be related to the slow growth of manufacturing production in this country. Economies which grow quickly are thereby enabled to achieve faster technical progress, more product innovation and improvements in other important non-price spheres of competition. In addition, the take-home pay of workers in a faster growing economy will generally also be growing more quickly. Other things being equal, this is likely to lead to better relations between workers and managers, with consequent benefits to productivity and performance. Because of its slow growth, UK industry has suffered on both these counts. The result has been a vicious circle of causation, by which industry is increasingly unable to hold its own in either overseas or home markets.

Several economists have recommended that the economy should grow at a faster rate so as to reduce unemployment or to slow down inflation (CEPG, [7] and [8]; Feinstein and Reddaway, [11]). However, the main burden of the basic approach adopted here is to argue that a transition to a higher long-term expansion path is also necessary in order eventually to establish an efficient manufacturing sector, that is, one which will be (and remain) competitive in the world economy. A faster rate of industrial growth will require a much larger volume of investment than has been achieved in the last few years, *as well as* its more effective utilisation. However, an increase in the rate of investment is not only required from a long-term point of view, but may also be necessary during the period of transition, since otherwise reflation of the economy may lead to a vast increase in imports due to shortage of capacity. From the point of view of economic policy during the North Sea oil period, the central question is to discover the mix of policy instruments (micro as well as macro) which will lead to both a trend increase in manufacturing investment and its more productive use.

### The Size of the Adjustments Required

To provide an idea of the magnitude of the economic adjustments involved in raising the growth rate of the economy and of industry (so as to correct the long-term industrial disequilibrium), I shall report briefly in this section on some estimates of the effects of the various macroeconomic policy instruments which the government may use for this purpose. These estimates are based on existing trends and relationships between economic variables and derived from the two large macroeconomic models (the Cambridge Economic Policy Group (CEPG) model and the Cambridge Growth Project (CGP) model). Of course the purpose of economic policy must be to change these relationships over time; nevertheless, they necessarily provide the starting point for any realistic policy discussion.

The CEPG model (CEPG, [8]) considers three policy instruments: existing government policy, devaluation and import controls. The requirements and effects of these policies are examined up to 1990 on the basis of a common set of assumptions and of targets to be achieved. The model does not deal explicitly with the problem of correcting long-term industrial disequilibrium in the sense discussed above, but the information provided by it has an important bearing on the subject. Moreover, the members of the CEPG have also been kind enough to allow simulations of the model which directly treat some of the issues connected with industrial disequilibrium.

Current government policy is assumed to consist of a 'cautious' fiscal policy, together with an incomes policy and an 'industrial strategy'. Devaluation comprises sterling depreciation to an extent which permits a continuous improvement of 4 per cent a year in *real* terms in the cost competitiveness of UK producers relative to those in other industrial countries. The policy of import controls involves the restriction of manufactured imports, as well as additional manufacturing investment to the extent necessary to reduce unemployment to one million in 1985 and half a million in 1990. The underlying assumptions of the model are growth of world trade during the next decade at the rate of 6 per cent a year, constant non-oil terms of trade and a gradual improvement of 50 per cent in terms of trade between oil and manufactures during the 1980s. The set of constraints or targets assumed to be common to all three policies consists of the following: that money wage-settlements should be reduced to 5 per cent a year after 1980 (enforced by wage control if necessary), that there should be a small current account surplus so as to repay at least some part of foreign debt, and that UK costs do not rise relative to those of competitors denominated in a common currency (except that under devaluation cost competitiveness is allowed to improve).

*Table 9.1   CEPG model: actual and forecast performance: orthodox policies*

| | Actual | | Forecasts | | |
|---|---|---|---|---|---|
| | 1973 | 1977 | 1980 | 1985 | 1990 |
| GDP[a] (1973 = 100) | 100 | 100 | 108 | 116 | 116 |
| Fixed investment[a] (1973 = 100) | 100 | 91.4 | 100 | 111.9 | 122.8 |
| Current balance (1975 £m) | + 88[b] | + 45 | 864 | 580 | 224 |
| North Sea contribution to current balance (1975 £m) | − 30[b] | + 890 | 3040 | 5780 | 7530 |
| Unemployment (millions) | 0.6 | 1.4 | 1.8 | 2.9 | 4.6 |
| Consumer prices (% increase p.a.) | 5.9[c] | 15.7 | 10.6 | 5.3[d] | 5.8[e] |
| Weighted exchange rate (US $)[f] | 3.06[b] | 1.83 | 1.60 | 1.49 | 1.5 |

Source: CEPG, [8].

[a] Constant 1975 prices.
[b] Average for 1964–73.
[c] 1964–73.
[d] 1980–5.
[e] 1985–90.
[f] The weighted average rate for sterling in terms of other currencies converted into dollars at the end-1977 rate for the dollar in terms of other currencies.

The results for the three policy choices are reported in Tables 9.1 to 9.3. Table 9.1 shows that under existing government (or orthodox) policies, GDP can grow only at less than 3 per cent a year up to 1980, at about 2 per cent a year up to 1985 and that it will not grow at all between 1985 and 1990, with serious consequences for unemployment. The main reason for this is the balance-of-payments constraint, which in turn derives from industrial disequilibrium. The disequilibrium is so acute that, despite a large contribution to the balance of payments from North Sea oil throughout the period under study, growth of GDP and hence of industrial output is held back. Even if it is assumed that the volume of trade increases by 10 per cent a year over the next decade, the rate of growth of GDP under orthodox policies will still be below 2 per cent a year during the 1980s.

Table 9.2    CEPG model: forecast performance to 1990: devaluation

| 1980 | 1977 | 1980 | 1985 | 1990 |
|---|---|---|---|---|
| GDP[a] (1973 = 100) | 100 | 111 | 133 | 154 |
| Fixed investment[a] (1973 = 100) | 91.4 | 103.3 | 131.4 | 166.7 |
| Current balance (1975 £m) | 45 | 629 | 2712 | 3506 |
| North Sea contribution to current balance (1975 £m) | 890 | 3040 | 5780 | 7530 |
| Unemployment (millions) | 1.4 | 1.5 | 1.5 | 1.4 |
| Consumer prices (% increase p.a.) | 15.7 | 11.7 | 6.8[d] | 8.1[e] |
| Weighted exchange rate (US$)[f] | 1.83 | 1.42 | 1.00 | 0.65 |

Source: CEPG, [8].
*Notes:* see Table 9.1.

The policy of *continuous* devaluation does produce more favourable results (Table 9.2). (Instead of an extremely large depreciation at one stroke, the model assumes that the authorities can achieve this in steps.) Although it still implies a level of unemployment of 1.5 million throughout the 1980s, it yields a growth rate of GDP of about 3.5 per cent, which in turn suggests a manufacturing growth rate of about 4 per cent. However, a policy which implies a *real* reduction in UK relative costs of more than 50 per cent over a ten-year period can only be of academic interest. Between 1965 and 1976 the UK's relative costs fell only by 15 per cent in real terms, despite a huge nominal depreciation of sterling and its effects on inflation. To achieve a reduction three times as large at a time when North Sea oil is making a substantial contribution to the balance of payments must be regarded as impractical; but, if by some chance the authorities do succeed in doing so, it will lead to an enormous increase in domestic inflation. The latter possibility is excluded in the simulation in Table 9.2 by the assumption of a successful incomes policy in operation throughout the period. With incomes policy, devaluation would produce a major reduction in the share of wages in national income.

*Table 9.3*    *CEPG model: forecast performance to 1990: import controls and increased investment*

|  | 1977 | 1980 | 1985 | 1990 |
|---|---|---|---|---|
| GDP$^a$ (1973 = 100) | 100 | 114 | 139 | 167 |
| Fixed investment$^a$ (1973 = 100) | 91.4 | 108.5 | 136.7 | 164.8 |
| Current balance (1975 £m) | 45 | 966 | 637 | 153 |
| North Sea contribution to current balance (1975 £m) | 890 | 3040 | 5780 | 7530 |
| Unemployment (millions) | 1.4 | 1.3 | 1.0 | 0.5 |
| Consumer prices (% increase p.a.) | 15.7 | 10.6 | 3.8$^d$ | 3.7$^e$ |
| Weighted exchange rate (US$)$^f$ | 1.83 | 1.61 | 1.60 | 1.59 |

Source: CEPG, [8].
*Notes:* see Table 9.1

The imposition of import controls on manufactured goods leads to a relaxation of the balance-of-payments constraint sufficient to permit a very respectable rate of growth of the UK economy of about 4.5 per cent a year until 1990. At one level this is a very cheering result, since the implied restrictions on imports are not severe: they amount to restricting the *rate of growth* of manufactured imports to 8 per cent a year (which it is assumed does not lead to retaliation). However, to achieve the results reported in Table 9.3, there would also need to be a large increase in manufacturing investment, building up to £3 billion a year at 1978 prices from 1982 onwards, over and above that predicted by historical trends. Further, the model incorporates what many would regard as a very favourable assumption about the effects of this extra investment: each £150 of investment is postulated to lead to an increase in productive capacity of £100 two years later; £50 of this larger capacity results in cumulative substitution of manufactured imports and increases in manufactured exports.

Leaving aside the ideological aspects of import controls, the important economic question in the present context is whether they would eventually lead to an 'efficient' manufacturing sector (in our sense) which can function in the world economy without such restrictions. The results obtained from computer simulations suggest that, under a set of rather optimistic assumptions about the level and impact of extra investment, import controls could be completely eliminated soon after 1990. However, under more realistic hypotheses it appears that they may be necessary for a relatively long time.

The results of the other large Cambridge model (the CGP model) are, if anything, even more pessimistic about the possibility of increasing the rate of industrial growth. This is a more disaggregated and much bigger model than the CEPG one; its main features are described in Barker, [1] and CGP, [9]. Recent simulations of the model (Barker, Peterson and Winter, [2]) suggest that, given the existing economic relationship, a policy of 'no change' (a constant sterling exchange rate, government expenditure levels as stated in the latest White Paper, all taxes indexed in line with inflation) will lead to a rate of growth of manufacturing output of only 0.4 per cent a year in 1977–85, taking into account the large North Sea oil contribution to the balance of payments. The traditional policy of reflation (which is assumed to bring the standard rate of income tax down to 25 per cent by 1981, to double personal allowances by 1985, etc.) leads to only 0.9 per cent annual growth in manufacturing output until 1985. As in the CEPG model, the reason why industry is projected to grow at such a slow rate is the balance-of-payments constraint; given the existing trade propensities, this constraint becomes binding at a very low rate of growth of demand. For example, the policy of reflation produces only a 2.4 per cent annual growth in total demand for manufactures, but the growth of manufacturing output is even smaller, since the forecast growth of imports is 8.8 per cent a year.

The CGP model does not consider depreciation of the exchange rate as a policy instrument because of the difficulties of achieving it during the period of oil revenues, and because of its projected impact on domestic inflation. However, it does examine policies of selective import controls and massive subsidies to two currently 'collapsing' industries: electrical engineering and motor vehicles. The results indicate that the latter policy, together with reflation, would help to raise the growth rate of GDP from 1.3 per cent (on a policy of no change) to 2.3 per cent a year. It also enables the selected industries to avoid collapse. However, partly because of the investment equations embodied in the CGP model (based on past behaviour), import controls and subsidies to the two industries up to 1985 do not help them to become competitive in the world economy at the end of this period. The growth rates forecast by the CGP model for a selection of industries under the three alternative policies are given in Table 9.4.

Table 9.4   *CGP model: actual and forecast growth rates for selected industries (percentages per annum)*

|  | Actual 1973–7 | Forecasts 1977–85 with policy options[a] | | |
|---|---|---|---|---|
|  |  | No change | Reflation | Reflation *plus* subsidy |
| *Declining markets* |  |  |  |  |
| Tobacco manufacture | − 4.4 | − 7.2 | − 7.2 | − 7.2 |
| Iron and steel | − 1.5 | − 2.6 | − 2.3 | − 2.1 |
| Non-ferrous metals | − 0.1 | − 1.1 | − 0.9 | − 0.5 |
| Textiles | 1.7 | 1.1 | — | 0.2 |
| *Stationary output* |  |  |  |  |
| Mechanical engineering | 2.1 | 0.3 | 0.1 | 0.6 |
| Metal goods n.e.s. | 1.0 | − 0.9 | − 0.3 | 0.1 |
| Textile fibres | 2.8 | − 0.9 | − 0.7 | − 0.6 |
| Paper and board | 2.9 | − 0.9 | − 0.7 | − 0.5 |
| *Growth industries* |  |  |  |  |
| Drink | 2.8 | 5.1 | 6.1 | 6.2 |
| Chemicals, etc. | 5.0 | 4.3 | 4.6 | 4.7 |
| Manufactures n.e.s. | 5.4 | 3.9 | 4.3 | 4.7 |
| *Collapsing industries* |  |  |  |  |
| Electrical engineering | — | − 1.8 | − 1.9 | − 0.3 |
| Shipbuilding | − 5.1 | − 9.5 | − 9.5 | − 9.1 |
| Motor vehicles | − 1.1 | − 7.1 | − 6.9 | − 5.1 |
| Aero-space | − 3.5 | − 9.1 | − 9.0 | − 8.7 |

Sources: Barker, Peterson and Winters [2]; and T. Barker, to whom I am grateful for permission to quote these results.

[a] For explanation, see text.

The results of the two models above are not directly comparable, since they consider the effects of different policy strategies. The CGP model does not examine the possibility of comprehensive import controls of the kind envisaged in the CEPG model; the latter, on the other hand, being an aggregate model, is unable to consider the implications of selective import controls. Nevertheless, what the above results bring out clearly is that if past trends and economic relationships continue in the future, UK industry is destined to a very slow rate of growth even with the maximum contribution to the balance of payments from North Sea oil. In general, in terms of the models considered in this section, faster industrial growth can be achieved only by a major change in the country's international economic policy, involving import controls, and a large trend increase in manufacturing investment and/or its productivity.

There are two important qualifications to the above conclusion: it it based on past relationships and, by and large, it considers only macroeconomic policy instruments. (In the CEPG model, 'industrial policy' is assumed to have little effect on the relevant economic variables.) In relation to the former, it is however important to stress that, both the models being dynamic ones, they do embody the various feedback effects of investment on productivity, international competitiveness, etc. Nevertheless, it could be argued that with the help of an 'offensive' industrial policy (Lindbeck, [18]) and microeconomic instruments of intervention, it may be possible to change the established economic relationships. These issues will be taken up in the final section. In the next section, we shall examine briefly the experience of Norway and Holland with their North Sea resources, as well as that of Japan, which has pursued an aggressive industrial policy to promote and to maintain the efficiency of its manufacturing industry in a changing world economy.

## Experience in Holland and Norway

Holland and Norway are greater beneficiaries from North Sea oil and gas than the UK; they have also been enjoying direct benefits from these resources for a somewhat longer period (since the early 1970s). Yet both economies have in recent years run into serious difficulties, which some economists have traced to their North Sea riches (Ellman, [10]). The purpose here is merely to interpret the general experience of the two countries in terms of the analytic approach adopted above, with a view to drawing possible policy conclusions for the UK.

The first important point is that both Norway and the Netherlands were in a much stronger initial position than the UK when oil or gas started to make an important contribution to their respective economies (OECD, [24] and [25]). Unlike the UK at present, in the early 1970s neither of them could have been regarded as being in 'long-run disequilibrium' with respect to their balance-of-payments current accounts. The international position of industry in both countries was satisfactory. For example, throughout the 1960s and up to 1973 the Netherlands share of export markets had been increasing at the average annual rate of 1 per cent a year. Given the stronger starting base and larger potential oil and gas resources, the two countries, therefore, had more options with respect to the possible uses of these revenues than does the UK (that is, they could use more for consumption or foreign investment, or exercise wider choice with respect to depletion). As they also had full employment at the time, the problem they faced was that of bringing about a change in the structure of the balance of payments without causing undesirable changes in their real economies.

However, during the last four years there has been a serious deterioration in the non-oil current account in both countries. For instance, in 1977, Norway recorded a deficit on current account amounting to more than 14 per cent of its GDP; this is the largest deficit ever sustained by Norway or any other OECD country. It could be explained partly by specifically oil-related factors – a shortfall in the production of oil and gas and unexpectedly large imports of ships and oil-sector equipment – and partly by world recession. But it was also largely due to the worsening trade deficit of 'mainland Norway', which must, at least to some extent, be due to the cumulative deterioration in the competitive position of industry in recent years. Because of a trend increase in unit labour costs in manufacturing in terms of domestic currency, as well as an appreciation of the krone, relative unit labour costs of Norwegian industry increased by 35 per cent between the first quarters of 1974 and 1977. Similarly in the Netherlands, the non-gas current account in 1977 was in deficit to the extent of 4.5 billion guilders, as compared with annual surpluses of 4 billion guilders in 1972 and 1973. Again, the 6 per cent loss in the Netherlands export market share in 1977 was probably due to exceptional circumstances; but there have been small market share losses ever since 1973, in contrast with the gains normally recorded in the earlier period. Although Dutch unit labour costs in terms of domestic currency have not risen faster than elsewhere, they have increased more quickly in terms of dollars, because of the appreciation of the guilder. This has not been reflected in export prices, and may consequently have reduced profitability in export industries (OECD, [25]).

Thus there is evidence that, although at the beginning of the substantial oil and gas period in the two countries, industry was not in disequilibrium, it may by now be entering such a phase, which will not necessarily be self-correcting (Singh, [28]). The second point to note is that both the Netherlands and Norway have since 1974 followed relatively strong expansionary demand management policies. In the former, the volume of final domestic demand grew by 9.5 per cent between 1974 and 1977, as compared with a growth of 5.5 per cent for the four major European economies. (In Belgium, whose economic structure and degree of openness are similar to that of the Netherlands, final domestic demand grew by 5 per cent between 1974 and 1977.) The increase in domestic demand in Norway has been much faster; it rose by 26.5 per cent between 1973 and 1977, compared with the OECD average of 6.5 per cent. In both countries, increases in public expenditure and social security payments have been the main vehicle for demand expansion. The results of the policy, particularly in Norway, have been very satisfactory from a short-term point of view. For example, Norwegian unemployment throughout the years 1974–7 was only about 1 per cent, a remarkable achievement given the international economic situation. From a longer term point of view, however, the consequences are less desirable. A fast increase in domestic demand has been predictably accompanied by greatly increased import penetration, but also by the growth of sheltered sectors at the expense of industries exposed to international competition. For instance, between 1976 and 1977 Norwegian GDP grew by a respectable 3.5 per cent; however, this was associated with a 5 per cent growth in the output of trade, transport and other service sectors, but no increase at all in that of manufacturing or traditional mining. Thus, unless the government adopts reconstruction measures in the interim, so as to strengthen exposed industries, or starts new industries which will be able to generate the necessary export earnings in the future, the 're-entry' problem will be clearly extremely difficult when the oil runs out.

In order partly to reduce the pressure on the guilder, the Dutch have in recent years been encouraging the outflow of capital. Until 1971 the Netherlands was a net importer of long-term foreign capital. But since 1974 there has been a massive outflow, with the result that the Dutch are now ahead of the UK and Canada, as the largest direct foreign investors in the United States. This build-up of foreign assets will certainly help when the gas reserves are depleted; but if in the meantime trading industries are allowed to decline, investment income may not prove sufficient to meet the country's full-employment import requirements in the long run. The history of the UK economy between 1870 and 1914 is instructive in this respect (Lewis, [17]).

## Japan

I shall now examine briefly the case of Japan – a country which at the end of world war II perceived itself to be in long-term industrial disequilibrium as defined in this paper, and used an aggressive industrial policy to correct it. It is paradoxical that at one level the Japanese government has very little direct control over output compared with that of other capitalist economies. Nationalised industries account for a far larger proportion of total production in Italy, Sweden, France and the UK, than they do in Japan (Nino [21]; Friedmann, [12]). However in Japan the government has played a far more fundamental role in the postwar reconstruction of industry than in any of the other advanced industrial economies. The cornerstone of the country's industrial policy is the so-called structural policy aimed at adaptation and technological development of certain specific industries thought to be vital to the economy at various stages. The role of the government in developing these industries and hence bringing about Japanese economic success had been so crucial that, as Nino, [21] remarks, 'whereas [the] USA is said to be a country of [the] military industrial complex ... in this sense, Japan may be called a country of the Government industrial complex'.

At the end of world war II, the bulk of Japanese exports consisted of textiles and light manufactured goods (labour-intensive products). In the view of the Ministry of International Trade and Industry, although such an economic structure may have conformed to the theory of comparative advantage (Japan being a labour-surplus economy at the time), it was not viable in the long run. It is worth quoting in full Vice-Minister Ojimi's rationale for the Ministry's industrial policy (OECD, [23]):

> The MITI decided to establish in Japan industries which require intensive employment of capital and technology, industries that in consideration of comparative cost of production should be the most inappropriate for Japan, industries such as steel, oil-refining, petro-chemicals, automobiles, aircraft, industrial machinery of all sorts, and electronics, including electronic computers. From a short-run, static viewpoint, encouragement of such industries would seem to conflict with economic rationalism. But, from a long-range viewpoint, these are precisely the industries where income elasticity of demand is high, technological progress is rapid, and labour productivity rises fast. It was clear that without these industries it would be difficult to employ a population of 100 million and raise their standard of living to that of Europe and America with light industries alone; whether right or wrong, Japan had to have these heavy and chemical industries. According to Napoleon and Clausewitz, the secret of a successful strategy is the concentration of fighting

power on the main battle grounds; fortunately, owing to good luck and wisdom spawned by necessity, Japan has been able to concentrate its scant capital in strategic industries.

The government has used a wide variety of instruments to bring about this structural transformation. The most important of these have been bank finance, import controls and protection, control over foreign exchange and importation of foreign technology (Caves and Uekusa, [5]; Boltho, [4]; Nino, [22]; OECD, [23]). To give an example of the last kind, the Ministry used its powers to ensure that only large-scale plants were built for ethylene production. It simply refused to authorise any contract importing technology for plants with a capacity of less than 300,000 tons.

It is important to note that, although in the 1950s and early 1960s the structural policy could be justified in orthodox infant industry terms, this policy has continued ever since. The more recent thinking about the appropriate long-term industrial structure for Japan in the present context envisages a shift in the 1980s towards 'knowledge-intensive' industries such as electronic computers, electric cars, new synthetics, communications equipment, the more sophisticated products of heavy and chemical industries and software (Kojima, [16]). It is also proposed that further increases in productive capacity in intermediate goods (such as steel and basic chemicals) should take place abroad.

The above account raises two important issues for economic policy in the UK. First, is a highly interventionist industrial policy of the Japanese type desirable, or perhaps more to the point, feasible in this country? The second main issue is whether it is useful for the government to encourage a concentration of resources on specific industries, and if so how such industries should be chosen.

## Policy Options

The strands of the previous analysis may now be drawn together, and economic policy during the North Sea oil period considered with a view to correcting the worsening long-term disequilibrium characterising UK industry. As has been argued above, the correction of disequilibrium and the eventual establishment of an efficient industrial economy requires a large trend increase in the rate of growth of industrial output, so as to change the unfavourable underlying economic relationships. I shall outline below the broad policy options which are technically possible in the context of North Sea resources and briefly examine their implications. Whether or not they are feasible depends on the balance of political forces; their relative desirability is, of course, a matter of political perspective.

First we consider the policy which takes as given the present institutional framework of the economy. The most important elements of this framework are:

(i) the current international economic arrangements, consisting essentially of free trade and free convertibility of currency;
(ii) a powerful trade union movement, with a major influence on wages and related economic decisions.

The present policies of the government, as enumerated for example in the North Sea White Paper, are restricted by these institutional boundaries. Basically, they comprise reflation and an incomes policy on the demand side, and the 'industrial strategy' on the supply side. Such policies are similar to those practised during the last two decades by governments of both political Parties; they are based on the belief that as long as macroeconomic policies can ensure an adequate growth of demand, 'supply' will respond automatically (Blackaby, [3]). However, there is now more recognition of the 'supply' problems and in its public statements the government has put a great deal of emphasis on the 'industrial strategy'.

As both the CEPG and CGP models have demonstrated, government policies, at least on the demand side, are very far from being able to increase the rate of industrial growth sufficiently, eventually to restore equilibrium. The experience of Norway and the Netherlands – countries whose industry was in a much stronger initial competitive position than that of the UK – with demand management policies in recent years confirms this view. But it could be argued that this conclusion is too pessimistic since the government's 'industrial strategy' will act directly on investment functions, import propensities, etc., and help to modify them favourably.

The past evidence of similar policies and the present state of the economy do not lend support to this view. It is difficult to believe that the sector working parties will succeed in bringing about the major change which their predecessors, the little Neddies, failed to achieve. It is often said that the latter produced disappointing results partly because the overall rate of economic growth in the event turned out to be very low; however, despite North Sea oil, the growth rate will still be severely constrained by the balance of payments. Further, the funds envisaged for bodies such as the National Enterprise Board to help raise the level of productive investment seem to be much too small compared with the economic adjustments required – which involve, according to the CEPG model, for example, a 50 per cent increase in manufacturing investment, over and above its trend rate, for at least a decade. Therefore, the conclusion must be that, given the kind of policies envisaged at present for the North Sea oil period, at best industrial disequilibrium may not become worse over the next few years; (this is partly because industrial growth in competitor countries is also likely to be lower over this period); however, after the middle 1980s, when oil revenues begin to decline, the prospects are of previous trends reasserting themselves, leading to a continuing deterioration in the competitive position of industry.

The second set of policy options are predicated on the relaxation of the institutional constraints mentioned earlier. There are two alternatives here, involving respectively a weakening of the power of the unions and the imposition of import controls. The latter in turn can be used in conjunction with either an interventionist or a non-interventionist industrial policy.

First, if the power of workers and trade unions is sufficiently reduced, a policy of continuous real depreciation of the kind discussed earlier could be adopted. If such a policy were carried out for a sufficiently long time and were coupled with complementary measures (for example, cuts in tax rates for the better off), it could in principle lead to an efficient industrial economy. The diminished power of the workers would bring about a change in the wage–price equation, making it possible for UK relative costs and prices to fall, as a consequence of currency depreciation, without leading to a high degree of inflation. Further, in this more favourable environment, private industry might be expected to increase the trend rate of investment appreciably and to ensure its more productive utilisation, leading eventually to equilibrium. However, such a policy requires a fundamental shift in the balance of political forces in society; it may also prove extremely difficult to implement on the exchange markets at a time when North Sea oil resources are making a large contribution to the balance of payments.

Secondly, the policy of import controls raises interesting possibilities which are worth examining. For the purpose of the following discussion it will be assumed that they are of the kind proposed by CEPG – quantitative restrictions on manufactured imports limiting their rate of growth to 8 per cent a year. Such a policy clearly does not imply a siege economy; by permitting imports to grow at this high rate, it should limit the possibilities of retaliation. It has been suggested that selective import controls are preferable to comprehensive ones. However, even if the former were more than just a euphemism for controls only against the products of third world countries, and possibly Japan, they are unlikely to be as helpful as comprehensive controls, given the general weakness of UK industry. The NEDO study of UK and West German manufacturing industry over the period 1954–72 showed that the former had performed worse in most of the individual industrial groups examined and not just in a few specific industries (NEDO, [19]). Further, the CGP model, which simulated the effects of selected import controls and subsidies for two major industries (vehicles and electrical engineering), has shown that, although they help with these particular industries, they lead to increased imports of other products such as steel.

Contrary to popular belief, import controls do not necessarily mean greatly increased state intervention in other sectors of the economy. It would not be illogical, or economically irrational, for a Conservative government, for example, to introduce import controls of the kind recommended by CEPG and at the same time reduce the existing degree of state intervention in the economy. Those who believe in the beneficial influence of competition on economic activity could simply institute a stringent antitrust policy on the supply side instead of the existing plethora of direct controls, many of which were in fact brought in by a previous Conservative administration.

Import controls would enable the economy to grow more quickly, and it could be argued that, if they were coupled with an aggressive competition policy at home, this would lead to a virtuous circle of industrial improvement. The present problems of the British economy cannot be said to be due to *lack* of competition (in fact, quite the contrary, in view of international competition). There is therefore little case at present for a greatly strengthened competition policy to promote industrial efficiency (Singh, [29]; Hughes, [14]). However, with a reduction in international competition as a result of import controls, a far more stringent antitrust policy would in any case be necessary. Such a policy would have to go much further than suggested in the recent government Green Paper; for instance, it would probably be necessary to adopt a 'per se' policy with respect to horizontal mergers above a particular size, and greatly to strengthen the powers of the Monopolies Commission and the Price Commission to deal with co-ordinated activities by leading firms which fell short of registrable restrictive practices.

A policy of import restrictions combined with a tough anti-monopoly policy is in principle a viable alternative, and one which has a much greater chance of success than existing government policies. Whether or not it would eventually succeed in making British industry efficient would depend on the investment response of entrepreneurs and the effects of increased competition between domestic firms.

A policy of import controls could also be used in conjunction with an active industrial policy of the Japanese (or the French) type. The broad aim of such a policy would be to promote an appreciable trend increase in industrial investment, and systematically to raise the productivity and technical levels of UK industry to world standards so that it became internationally competitive. In principle, the government could also adopt a 'structural' policy of the kind used in Japan (and in socialist countries), which would attempt to transform the industrial structure according to a preconceived long-term plan.

Formally this is a relatively straightforward optimisation problem; a list could be produced of industries with characteristics such as those favoured by the Japanese in their industrial structure – with 'a high income elasticity of demand, rapid technical progress and fast growth of labour productivity'. In practice, given the uncertainty about the future state of the world economy and of international economic relations, and more importantly the present state of UK industry, such an exercise may not be operationally very useful. The UK already has a diversified industrial economy, which, as suggested above, is afflicted by a general malaise. Therefore, in practical terms, apart from singling out priority areas, such as energy industries, where there is a long gestation lag and there will clearly be an increasing long-term demand, the government's efforts should be directed at raising the general technological level of UK industry.

Such a programme would involve a strengthening and greatly increased use of existing policy instruments, such as planning agreements, and a far larger allocation of investment funds to the National Enterprise Board. An important reason why measures such as planning agreements work in Japan and not in the UK is that the government in this country has relatively little power to reward or to punish individual large firms as in Japan. It must, however, be recognised that, given the history of the relationship between industry and the government in this country and the strength of the trade unions, an interventionist industrial programme of this kind (although perfectly acceptable in Japan) might be resisted by the business community. If this led to reduced private investment or capital exports or both, the government might have to undertake investment activity directly, impose stringent exchange controls and ultimately perhaps even nationalise the foreign multinationals operating in this country (Ellman, [10]).

In conclusion, in order for the country to make the best use of the North Sea oil period to strengthen its manufacturing base, it would be necessary to institute a relatively long period of import controls against finished manufactures. Without such controls (or a continuing effective depreciation of the currency), the long-run prospects for UK industry are not at all encouraging – a situation which, in turn, has very serious implications for future employment and living standards when the oil revenues begin to decline. Import controls are a necessary, but not a sufficient, condition for starting a successful reconstruction of industry; they would have to be supplemented by supply policies, whose character and effectiveness would depend on the balance of political forces. However, given the existing framework of electoral politics, the years in which the North Sea is making substantial contributions to the economy seem to be those least likely to bring about the kind of major policy change which such controls would entail.

*References*

[1] Barker, T. S., 'Towards strategic paths in economic planning' in W. Peterson and R. Stone (eds.), *Econometric Contributions to Policy* (forthcoming).

[2] Barker, T. S., Peterson, W. and Winters, A., 'Britain's three economic options', *Business Observer*, London, 15 January 1978.

[3] Blackaby, F. T., 'British economic policy 1960 – 74: a general appraisal', *National Institute Economic Review*, May 1977.

[4] Boltho, A., *Japan: an economic survey 1953–73*, London, Oxford University Press, 1975.

[5] Caves, R. and Uekusa, M., *Industrial Organisation in Japan*, Washington (DC), Brookings Institution, 1976.

[6] CEPG, *Economic Policy Review*, no. 2, 1976.

[7] CEPG, *Economic Policy Review*, no. 3, 1977.

[8] CEPG, *Economic Policy Review*, no. 4, 1978.

[9] CGP, 'A model for an industrial strategy', Cambridge, Department of Applied Economics, 1978.

[10] Ellman, M., 'Report from Holland: the economics of North Sea hydrocarbons' *Cambridge Journal of Economics*, September 1977.

[11] Feinstein, C. H. and Reddaway, W. B., 'OPEC surpluses, the world recession and the UK economy', *Midland Bank Review*, Spring 1978.

[12] Friedmann, W. (ed.), *Public and Private Enterprise in Mixed Economies*, London, Stevens and Son, 1974.

[13] Houthakker, H. S. and Magee, S. P., 'Income and price elasticities in world trade', *Review of Economics and Statistics*, May 1969.

[14] Hughes, A., 'Competition policy and industrial policy (mimeo.), 1978.

[15] Jones, D. T., 'Output, employment and labour productivity in Europe since 1955', *National Institute Economic Review*, August 1976.

[16] Kojima, K., *Japan and a New World Economic Order*, London, Groom Helm, 1977.

[17] Lewis, W. A., 'The deceleration of British growth 1873–1913' (mimeo.), 1967.

[18] Lindbeck, A., 'Research in internal adjustment to external disturbances: a European view' in C. F. Bergsten (ed.), *The Future of the International Economic Order: an agenda for research*, Lexington (Mass.), D. C. Heath, 1973.

[19] NEDO, *The UK and West German Manufacturing Industry, 1954–72*, London, 1975.

[20] NEDO, *International Price Competitiveness, Non-price Factors and Export Performance*, by D. K. Stout, London, 1977.

[21] Nino, K., 'On efficiency and equity problems in the industrial policy – with special relation to the Japanese experience', *Kobe University Economic Review*, no. 19, 1973.

[22] Nino, K., 'Dilemmas of anti-monopoly policy in Japan', *Kobe University Economic Review*, no. 21, 1975.

[23] OECD, *The Industrial Policy of Japan*, Paris, 1972.

[24] OECD, *Economic Surveys: Norway*, Paris, 1974.

[25] OECD, *Economic Surveys: Netherlands*, Paris, 1978.

[26] Page, S. A. B., 'The value and distribution of the benefits of North Sea oil and gas', *National Institute Economic Review*, November 1977.

[27] Ray, G. F., 'Labour costs in OECD countries, 1964–75', *National Institute Economic Review*, November 1976.

[28] Singh, A., 'UK industry, and the world economy; a case of de-industrialisation?', *Cambridge Journal of Economics*, June 1977.

[29] Singh, A., 'The structural transformation of British industry: an alternative view', Cambridge, Department of Applied Economics (mimeo.) (forthcoming in G. Yarrow (ed.)).

[30] Treasury, 'The North Sea and the UK economy, *Economic Progress Report*, no. 89, August 1977.

# Comment

## by Walter Eltis*

Have the structural weaknesses of the British economy indeed become so great that the correct use of North Sea oil will only suffice for their correction if import restrictions are used in addition to contain excessive import growth? The extremely pessimistic conclusions of Singh's paper derive from the recent published work of the CEPG (in particular, Cripps *et al.*, [2]; Fetherston, *et al.*, [3]; Moore *et al.*, [4]) and such reservations as I have about his analysis stem from the belief that some of the basic interrelationships may not have been correctly specified by 'New Cambridge'.

The CEPG's fundamental propositions that a continuation of past trends will lead to unacceptable unemployment in another decade, and that the reversal of past trends must involve a reversal of the rate of job-loss in industry are surely correct. In the eight years 1966–74 immediately prior to the world recession, 1,335,000 industrial jobs were lost, and if a further 2,670,000 are lost in the sixteen years 1974–1990 (and 640,000 *were* lost in 1974–6) horrific consequences will certainly follow in view of the large projected increase in the British labour force on which all are agreed. On the basis of past trends, between two and a half and three million industrial jobs will be lost in 1974–90, while two million or more additional jobs will be needed in total. These combine to produce a job shortage of between four and a half and five million, on which the service sector will not conceivably make much impact. Private services (which include most of the self-employed) created few additional jobs in 1966–74, a period of reasonable prosperity, and the non-market public service sector cannot create large numbers of extra jobs while industrial employment is falling without increases in taxation to rates which few will consider acceptable. The reversal of the adverse trend in industry must therefore be the key to any policy of medium-term job-creation. Much of Dr Singh's analysis, and that of the CEPG which lies behind it, is therefore extremely plausible and indeed inescapable. Reservations centre on the particular formulation of certain functional relationships which lead to the conclusion that a reversal of the adverse industrial employ-

* I am grateful to Robert Bacon for helpful comments and assistance with the statistical work.

ment trend is impossible without import restrictions. It is arguable that 'New Cambridge' has been unduly pessimistic about the relationship between output growth and the rate of growth of industrial imports, unduly pessimistic about the improvement in cost competitiveness which is needed to maintain export growth, and unduly optimistic about the rate of growth of productivity in British industry which is to be expected on the basis of the continuation of past trends, with the result that they have exaggerated the rate of growth of industrial output which is now needed to maintain employment. These possibilities will be considered in turn.

## An Exaggerated Assessment of Import Penetration

According to the CEPG, 'the share of domestic manufactures in the home market' has fallen from 87 per cent in 1960 to 59 per cent (Moore *et al.*, [4], page 29). Table 9.5 shows the growth of import

*Table 9.5   Industrial import penetration of the UK home market, 1961–75*

|  | Exports | Home sales | Imports | Import content of exports | Imports/home sales | |
|---|---|---|---|---|---|---|
|  |  |  |  |  | Remaining imports[a] | Total imports |
|  | (£ million, current prices) | | | | (%) | (%) |
| 1961 | 3,084 | 12,606 | 1,404 | 210 | 9.5 | 11.1 |
| 1962 | 3,156 | 13,045 | 1,440 | 215 | 9.4 | 11.0 |
| 1963 | 3,372 | 13,839 | 1,572 | 229 | 9.7 | 11.4 |
| 1964 | 3,768 | 15,798 | 2,160 | 286 | 11.9 | 13.7 |
| 1965 | 4,092 | 17,227 | 2,256 | 340 | 11.1 | 13.1 |
| 1966 | 4,392 | 18,138 | 2,472 | 395 | 11.5 | 13.6 |
| 1967 | 4,380 | 19,201 | 2,796 | 420 | 12.4 | 14.6 |
| 1968 | 5,412 | 21,068 | 3,624 | 563 | 14.5 | 17.2 |
| 1969 | 6,252 | 22,543 | 3,948 | 694 | 14.4 | 17.5 |
| 1970 | 6,804 | 25,314 | 4,560 | 810 | 14.8 | 18.0 |
| 1971 | 7,825 | 27,129 | 5,002 | 861 | 15.3 | 18.4 |
| 1972 | 8,257 | 29,454 | 6,093 | 793 | 18.0 | 20.7 |
| 1973 | 10,455 | 35,309 | 8,909 | 1,004 | 22.4 | 25.2 |
| 1974 | 13,685 | 38,643 | 11,928 | 1,314 | 27.5 | 30.9 |
| 1975 | 16,464 | 45,220 | 12,805 | 1,580 | 24.8 | 28.3 |

Sources: Derived as explained in R. W. Bacon and W. A. Eltis, *Britain's Economic Problem: too few producers*, London, Macmillan, 2nd edn, 1978, pp.217–31.
[a] After deducting import content of exports.

penetration for industrial products (excluding oil products and food, drink and tobacco manufactures), a wider category than manufacturing alone. These statistics are derived from input–output tables for the United Kingdom economy, which is necessary because statistics for industrial (or manufacturing) output are published on a value-added basis, so that they merely show the value-added by United Kingdom industry and not the sales value of the goods produced at home. Such statistics omit the raw material and some of the semi-finished material element in the sale price of home-produced manufactures. Import and export statistics include this element, with the result that, if full allowance for the raw material content in home-produced industrial output is not made, the import ratio and the export ratio will both be exaggerated. A further problem involved in the measurement of import penetration of the 'home market' is that some imports go directly into exports, so that rapid expansion in these – and British exports have grown fast in some periods – will lead to an apparent increase in import penetration. In Table 9.5 a preliminary attempt is made to correct for this (work is continuing on these measurement problems and a paper Bacon and Eltis, [1], will be available shortly). The final column, however, shows the gross import penetration ratio without correction.

It will be evident from Table 9.5 that import penetration has risen massively from 9.5 per cent in 1961 to 24.8 per cent in 1975, but what is especially interesting and important is that it only advanced sharply in years when it is plausible that the economy encountered extensive supply bottlenecks; that is in years of rapid industrial growth, 1963–4, 1967–8 and 1972–3, and in 1971–2 and 1973–4, when there were lengthy coal strikes with significant effects on the availability of goods for the home market.

The detailed interrelationship between the rising import penetration ratio and the rate of industrial growth is set out in Table 9.6. The principal conclusion which emerges from this table is that the rate of import penetration rose very sharply in the periods where industrial production rose faster than capacity; that is, in 1963–4, when the industrial production growth rate was 8.3 per cent, in 1967–8, when it was 5.2 per cent, in 1971–3 when there was an industrial production growth rate of 7.2 per cent in 1972–3 and strike-induced supply bottlenecks in 1971–2. In 1973–4, when the import ratio again rose sharply, there were supply bottlenecks as a result of the three-day week. It would obviously be advantageous to have quarterly data, so that the various periods could be distinguished more precisely, but only annual

Table 9.6   Growth rates of output and of industrial imports, 1961-75
(percentages per annum)

| | Industrial production | GDP | Increase in import penetration[a] | |
| --- | --- | --- | --- | --- |
| | | | Adjusted[b] | Unadjusted |
| 1961-3 | 2.2 | 2.5 | 1.0 | 1.3 |
| 1963-4 | 8.3 | 5.7 | 22.7 | 20.2 |
| 1964-7 | 1.7 | 2.1 | 1.4 | 2.1 |
| 1967-8 | 5.2 | 3.6 | 16.9 | 17.8 |
| 1968-71 | 1.4 | 2.0 | 1.8 | 2.3 |
| 1971-3 | 4.9 | 4.0 | 21.0 | 17.0 |
| 1973-5 | -4.4 | -2.7 | 5.2 | 6.0 |

Sources: as Table 9.5; CSO, *Economic Trends*.
[a] The annual percentage increase in figures for import penetration given in Table 9.5.
[b] By deducting import content of exports.

data are available. In the four years, 1963-4, 1967-8 and 1971-3, GDP increased by 17.6 per cent altogether, and the import penetration ratio rose by 81.6 per cent, so 1 per cent growth in GDP was associated with an approximately 4.5 per cent increase in the import penetration ratio, and this proportion rose only slightly between 1963-1964 (when it was 4.0) and 1971-3 (when it was 5.25). Anyone attributing higher imports to higher incomes alone would measure the income elasticity of demand for industrial imports at between 5 and 6.25 in these expansion and capacity bottleneck years. In the slow expansion years, in contrast, the import penetration ratio rose far more slowly: in 1961-3 each 1 per cent of output growth was associated with an increase in import penetration of only 0.4 per cent, in 1964-7 it was associated with a 0.7 per cent increase, and in 1968-71 with a 0.9 per cent increase. These figures would imply that in recession the income elasticity of demand for industrial imports rose from perhaps 1.4 in 1961-3 to about 1.9 in 1968-71. There has thus been some tendency for the import penetration ratio in recession to accelerate, but the ratio was still well below that experienced in the years of rapid expansion and supply bottlenecks. The figures in the last column of Table 9.6, where no correction is attempted for the import content of exports, tell the same story, but a little less sharply. It can perhaps be concluded that until 1971 at any rate the basic income elasticity of demand for industrial imports was as low as 2. However, in expansion, the increase in industrial imports for each 1 per cent increase in

GDP was greater (implying an income elasticity of 5 or 6, though production bottlenecks were actually responsible) which raised the import penetration ratio enormously. High rates of import penetration, once achieved, were then maintained as importers consolidated their hold on their new market shares.

It is the view of the CEPG that increasing import penetration is associated with growing real incomes rather than with supply bottlenecks in particular years. In consequence they have overestimated the income elasticity of demand for imports if the above interpretation of Table 9.6 is broadly correct. If that is the case, the import ratio need not rise as rapidly as the CEPG fears.

## Exaggerated Export Pessimism

The CEPG believes that a competitive gain in labour costs per unit of output of 4 per cent per annum will be needed if the United Kingdom is to hold its share of world export markets of manufactures. Happily the United Kingdom held that share at 9.4 per cent between 1973 and 1977, in which period relative unit labour costs actually rose in the United Kingdom, but the relationship between unit labour costs and export penetration is obviously a lagged one. In 1972–6 the United Kingdom's relative unit labour costs fell at an annual rate of 1.3 per cent, and in 1971–6 they fell at an annual rate of 1.8 per cent. This suggests (if a lag of between one and two years is appropriate) that a fall in relative unit labour costs of about 1.5 per cent may conceivably suffice to maintain a constant United Kingdom share of exports in world markets. After 1974 the United Kingdom had adequate spare capacity to exploit such competitive gains as resulted from effective devaluation. Until 1975 much of the competitive advantage which devaluation offered may well have been lost because there were insufficient margins of spare capacity, and because there was often an inappropriate fiscal stance. The disappointing loss of market shares in this earlier period may explain some of the CEPG's elasticity pessimism. British exports have in fact performed extremely well in recent years in very difficult world market conditions, and it is possible that there has therefore been a favourable change in the underlying relationships in the 1970s.

It may also be that the underlying relationship is mis-specified by the customary proposition that an annual competitive gain is needed to hold an export share. A once-and-for-all real gain may be what is needed, and the 8 per cent gain attained between 1965 and 1970 may have made exporting comparatively more profitable than before 1965, so that there was less world market loss in each year subsequently. Similarly, the further 7 per cent advantage obtained to 1976 may, if it can be held, produce a better future performance from now on without an equivalent need for further continuing real devaluation. By specifying their export equations so that these possibilities are ruled out, the CEPG has been driven to a pessimistic view on export competitiveness which hardly squares with recent export successes.

## An Exaggerated Expectation of Productivity Growth in Manufacturing

The CEPG has derived its equation for productivity growth in manufacturing from data for the period 1955–73 (Moore *et al.*, [4], page 26). In manufacturing the share of profits fell sharply during much of this period, from 20.8 per cent of value-added in 1966 to 6.3 per cent in 1974 and 3.8 per cent in 1976 (see Table 10.13 below). A period where profits are falling like this will be one where some low-productivity firms in manufacturing are being squeezed out, also some low-productivity operations in the firms which survive; thus, productivity will advance exceptionally in a period when some of the comparatively inefficient are ceasing to produce. Since 1976 profits have been rising in manufacturing, and the government's employment protection legislation had added a new low-productivity sector, with the result that productivity has stagnated to produce the underestimate of recent labour requirements which 'New Cambridge' acknowledges. The CEPG's failure to allow systematically for the effect of the profits share in their equations (a falling share being associated with extra productivity growth – a rising share with less immediate productivity growth) may well have led them to anticipate a continuing labour shake-out for another decade. If the effects of falling profitability up to 1974 were to some extent exceptional, fewer jobs will be lost in the 1980s.

## Conclusions for Policy

Orthodox policies, combined with perhaps some slight further relative devaluation of the currency, may suffice to reverse the adverse industrial employment trend if there is force in the above reservations about the specification of basic economic relationships by the CEPG. In that event North Sea oil can provide two valuable bonuses which will increase the chances of success. First, there is surely force in Dr Singh's plea for a 'Japanese' industrial policy. Britain's failures with Concorde and nuclear reactors should not blind policy-makers to the potential benefits from products which will be among the most technically advanced and marketable in the middle to late 1980s, and oil revenues could be extremely helpful here. The impending success of the RB 211 derivatives from Rolls Royce, which stand a chance of capturing up to 35 per cent of the world market for this type of engine, and which would not exist today without previous government development finance, show what can be achieved. Such help will be indispensible if the small international cost advantage which may be needed in the 1980s is not attained, and it will be helpful to exports and employment even if industry remains sufficiently competitive.

Finally North Sea oil can provide the necessary 'fat' in the balance of payments to finance the extra import costs of a Keynesian demand-boosting trigger to get expansion under way. Demand should ideally accelerate more slowly than in the past in the early stages of expansion to minimise bottlenecks, but it will necessarily rise faster than capacity, with extra adverse effects on imports of the kind documented in the tables. The capital-stock adjustment effects of higher demand will subsequently lead to higher investment and to the faster rate of growth of productive capacity which is so patently needed – especially as the labour force will be growing. It is also essential that the United Kingdom balances North Sea oil with extra imports of manufactured producer goods, to avoid a 'Dutch' rise in the exchange rate when a slow continuing fall will be needed. Therefore Britain may be well advised to indulge in the luxury of a once-and-for-all Keynesian demand expansion to provide the conditions in which the rate of growth of industrial capacity will adjust upwards to the higher rate of growth of output which is now attainable. Such demand stimulus as will be needed for this would ideally take the form of tax cuts rather than expenditure increases, for reasons which Robert Bacon and I have argued at length elsewhere. Such policies may make sense in the period of North Sea oil.

*References*

[1] Bacon, R. and Eltis, W. A., 'On measuring import penetration' (mimeo.) (forthcoming).

[2] Cripps, F., Fetherston, M. and Ward, T., 'The effects of different strategies for the UK economy', *Economic Policy Review*, no. 4, 1978.

[3] Fetherston, M., Moore, B. and Rhodes, J., 'Manufacturing export shares and cost competitiveness of advanced industrial countries', *Economic Policy Review*, no. 3, 1977.

[4] Moore, B., Rhodes, J. and Tarling, R., 'A return to full employment?', *Economic Policy Review*, no. 4, 1978.

# 10 De-industrialisation: a background paper*

## by C. J. F. Brown and T. D. Sheriff

## Introduction

The purpose of this background paper is to collect together material which throws light on the conference theme of 'de-industrialisation'. It has long been noted that in advanced industrial countries there is a tendency for the industrial or manufacturing sector to decline relative to the service sector. (Because the manufacturing sector is such a large proportion of the industrial sector, we have not concerned our-selves with differences between the two and most of our data relate to manufacturing. The de-industrialisation argument has been couched in terms of both industry and manufacturing.) There are a number of possible reasons for this. Productivity tends to grow faster in manu-facturing than services, so that, even with no change in the pattern of demand, there will be a change in the pattern of employment. Further, it is argued that the income elasticity of demand is greater for services than for goods, so that as national income rises the composition of demand will change and a greater proportion of national resources will be devoted to the tertiary sector. In the long run these forces lead to the 'service economy' (Fuchs, [14]) and in this sense de-industrialisation is thought to be inevitable (Clark, [10] and Bell, [5]; for a critique of these views, see Gershuny, [15]).

However, the object of this paper, and of the conference, is not to consider these long-run tendencies in advanced economies in general; rather it is concerned with the view that the recent relative decline of UK manufacturing is not the outcome of such general economic forces, but is tied up with the UK's economic 'malaise' in such a way that the

* The full Statistical Appendix prepared to accompany this paper was too big to be included here. It is available as a Discussion Paper from the National Institute of Economic and Social Research, 2 Dean Trench Street, Smith Square, London S.W.1 (£1.50 including postage).

manufacturing sector, in some sense, has become too small.

Examples of concern are not hard to find. Writing in the *Sunday Times* in November 1974, Bacon and Eltis [1] argued that 'Britain's difficulties . . . largely result from a structural shift away from industry since 1962'. The then Secretary of State for Industry wrote of the 'devastating trend to contraction of British industry' and added, 'if this trend is allowed to continue, we will have closed down 15 per cent of our entire manufacturing capacity and nearly 2 million industrial workers will have been made redundant between 1970 and 1980' (Benn, [6]). Mr Healey, in his budget speech in April 1975, said 'we must reverse the process of de-industrialisation – of a steady loss of jobs and factory capacity year after year'.

There are two sets of figures which are relevant to the relative decline of UK manufacturing: the first concerns the proportion of national output and employment accounted for by the manufacturing sector and how this has changed over time; the second concerns the share of UK manufacturing in world output and trade. The next section of this paper analyses the available empirical evidence. Although the main hypotheses which have been put forward differ, there is substantial agreement about the series which are relevant to the discussion. These include the change in the proportion of manufacturing in total employment and GDP (both in the UK and in other countries), the UK share in world output of and trade in manufactures, world trade in services, export shares and import penetration and trends in investment and productivity. Summaries of these series are given in this paper. A fuller version of the relevant background statistics (Brown and Sheriff, [9]) contains historical series for the postwar period for the UK and selected industrialised countries. The following section then surveys the main arguments which have been put forward to explain the relative decline of the UK manufacturing sector and discusses them in the light of the figures.

## Empirical Evidence

### Labour experience in the UK

The share of manufacturing employment in total employment in the UK rose 1950–5 and then fell relatively slowly until the early 1970s; from then onwards there has been a rapid fall. The share was smaller at each successive peak in the period 1955–70, but not by very much, fluctuating in the range 34–6 per cent. The fall from 1970 has been quite dramatic, approximately 4 percentage points, as the recession has affected employment in manufacturing to a greater extent than total employment. Over the period 1950–76, the tertiary sector has increased its share from nearly 47 per cent to over 57 per cent. From 1961 a more detailed breakdown of total UK employment by sector is available on a continuous basis (Table 10.1). Chart 10.1 shows that there has been virtually no growth in total employment between 1961 and 1976. From 1961, the fall in the share of manufacturing employment has been similar to that of industrial production, which fell from 47.5 per cent in 1961 to 40.1 per cent in 1976 (compared with figures of 36.0 per cent and 30.1 per cent respectively for manufacturing).

Table 10.1    United Kingdom total employment by sector[a], 1961–76
(percentages)

| | 1961 | 1965 | 1969 | 1973 | 1975[b] | 1976[b] |
|---|---|---|---|---|---|---|
| Agriculture, forestry, fishing | 4.6 | 3.8 | 3.3 | 2.9 | 2.7 | 2.7 |
| Mining and quarrying | 3.0 | 2.5 | 1.8 | 1.5 | 1.4 | 1.4 |
| Manufacturing | 36.0 | 35.0 | 34.6 | 32.3 | 30.9 | 30.1 |
| Construction | 6.9 | 7.4 | 7.2 | 7.4 | 7.1 | 7.1 |
| Gas, electricity and water | 1.6 | 1.7 | 1.7 | 1.4 | 1.4 | 1.4 |
| *Total industrial production* | *47.5* | *46.6* | *45.3* | *42.6* | *41.0* | *40.1* |
| Transport and communication | 7.2 | 6.8 | 6.6 | 6.5 | 6.5 | 6.3 |
| Distributive trades | 13.8 | 13.7 | 13.0 | 13.0 | 13.0 | 12.9 |
| Insurance, banking, etc. | 3.0 | 3.4 | 3.8 | 4.5 | 4.7 | 4.8 |
| Professional & scientific services | 9.6 | 10.7 | 12.4 | 14.0 | 15.2 | 15.7 |
| Miscellaneous services | 8.8 | 9.5 | 9.6 | 10.1 | 10.3 | 10.7 |
| Public administration & defence | 5.5 | 5.5 | 6.0 | 6.4 | 6.7 | 6.7 |
| *Total services* | *47.8* | *49.6* | *51.4* | *54.5* | *56.4* | *57.2* |
| *Total services excl. transport &* communication | *40.6* | *42.8* | *44.8* | *48.0* | *49.9* | *50.9* |

Sources: *Department of Employment Gazette*; CSO, *Economic Trends*, February 1976, pp.119–27, and *Annual Abstract of Statistics 1976*, table 149.
[a] Forces excluded. Details do not always add because of rounding.
[b] Numbers self-employed in 1975 distributed according to 1974 proportions and numbers self-employed in 1976 assumed the same as in 1975.

The increasing share of service employment appears more marked when it is calculated excluding transport and communications; it then increased from 40.6 per cent in 1961 to 50.9 per cent in 1976. However, not all the groups of industries in the tertiary sector have experi-

Chart 10.1   *United Kingdom total employment by sector, 1961–76*

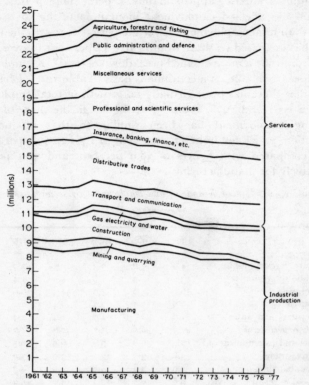

Sources: as Table 10.1.

enced increasing shares of total employment to the same extent. By far
the fastest growing group is professional and scientific services (mainly
in education and the health service), which increased its share of total
employment from 9.6 per cent in 1961 to 15.7 per cent in 1976. There
were about 1.5 million more workers classified as professional and
scientific in 1976 than in 1961, compared with a fall of 1.3 million
in the manufacturing sector over the same period. Public administration and defence, miscellaneous services, and insurance, banking,
finance and business services all had sizeable increases in their percentage shares of the total, but there was a smaller increase in the number
of workers in these groups of services taken together than there was in
professional and scientific services alone. The share of distributive
trades actually fell from 13.8 per cent in 1961 to 12.9 per cent in 1976.

*International comparisons of the share of manufacturing employment*

Writing in 1974, Bacon and Eltis [1] expressed concern at 'the largest shift away from industry in any major Western Economy'. Singh ([31], page 127) wrote, 'the empirical evidence indicates that, since the late 1960s Britain's manufacturing labour force has declined faster, both compared with its own experience over the previous two decades, and relative to that of other countries'. Table 10.2 and Chart 10.2 show the changes in the proportions of manufacturing employment in total employment for selected countries for the period 1950–75. The trends suggest that Japan and Italy (and, to a lesser extent, Germany) experienced considerable 'industrialisation' from 1950 to 1975. The Netherlands, Sweden and the US experienced considerable 'de-industrialisation'. Belgium's share fell slightly, while France's hardly changed. However, the cyclical nature of the share of manufacturing in total employment is immediately apparent. For Japan, Italy and Germany, in all three of which the trend was strongly upwards, the rate of growth declined significantly in the early 1970s. In Germany the proportion fell from 37.4 per cent to 35.9 per cent between 1970 and 1975; in Japan the rapid 'industrialisation' halted in these years and in Italy it slowed down considerably; only in Sweden does it seem to have behaved somewhat perversely.

*Table 10.2*  *Proportions of total employment in manufacturing in various countries[a], 1950–75 (percentages)*

|  | 1950 | 1960 | 1970 | 1973 | 1974 | 1975 |
|---|---|---|---|---|---|---|
| United Kingdom | 34.7 | 35.8 | 34.7 | 32.3 | 32.3 | 30.9 |
| Belgium | 32.7 | 33.5 | 32.7 | 31.8 | 31.5 | 30.1 |
| France | .. | 27.9 | 27.8 | 27.9 | 28.1 | 27.9 |
| Germany | .. | 34.7 | 37.4 | 36.1 | 36.6 | 35.9 |
| Italy | .. | 26.6 | 31.7 | 32.2 | 32.6 | 32.6 |
| Netherlands | 30.2 | 28.6 | 26.2 | 24.7 | 24.5 | 24.0 |
| Japan | .. | 21.3 | 27.0 | 27.4 | 27.2 | 25.8 |
| Sweden | .. | 32.1[b] | 27.6 | 27.5 | 28.3 | 28.0 |
| United States[c] | 34.4 | 33.6 | 32.3 | 31.6 | 31.0 | 29.0 |

Sources: OECD, *Manpower Statistics* and *Labour Force Statistics*.

[a] The series presented is an estimated reference series which makes allowance for discontinuities in official labour statistics due to changes in industrial classification, methods of collection, etc. In some cases, particularly the UK, there are substantial differences between this series and the published inconsistent one.

[b] For 1961; 1960 not available.

[c] Industrial employment.

Chart 10.2   *The proportion of manufacturing employment in total,
various countries, 1950–75*

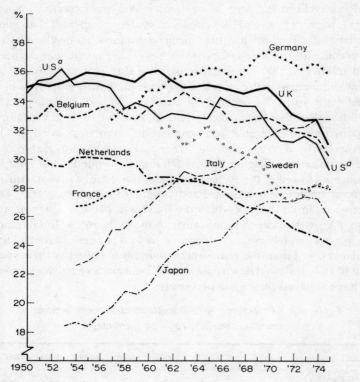

Sources: as Table 10.2.
*a* Industrial employment.

This comparison suggests that the UK's experience is by no means unique. The decisive turning point came around 1970 and it manifested itself in a rapid decline. The turning points in other countries came at about the same time, in some cases appearing as reversals of previous trends. The change in the rate of change of the ratio of manufacturing to total employment appears to have been in the same direction for most advanced industrial countries. The difference in the UK (and the US and the Netherlands) has been in the extent of the decline since 1970.

*International comparisons of the share of manufacturing output*

It is also common to look for evidence of de-industrialisation in the share of manufacturing output in GDP. In the UK the share of manufacturing in net output at constant 1963 prices (Table 10.3) has shown a slightly upward trend from 1950 to about 1970 and a slight downward trend since then. In current prices (Table 10.4) the story is of a continuous decline in the ratio since the war, falling from around 38 per cent in the early 1950s to under 30 per cent in the mid-1970s. The different trends in the two ratios indicate the extent to which relative prices in the UK have moved against manufacturing.

*Table 10.3    Manufacturing output as a proportion of GDP at 1963 prices, various countries[a], 1950–75 (percentages)*

|  | 1950 | 1960 | 1970 | 1973 | 1974 | 1975 |
|---|---|---|---|---|---|---|
| United Kingdom | 29.3 | 31.0 | 31.7 | 31.5 | 30.6 | 29.1 |
| Belgium | .. | 26.0 | 30.3 | 31.7 | 31.5 | 30.0 |
| France | 32.6 | 35.0 | 38.0 | 39.6 | 39.4 | 36.0 |
| Germany | 31.0[b] | 39.9 | 44.5 | 44.6 | 44.5 | 43.2 |
| Italy | 17.9[c] | 25.5 | 31.2 | 32.0 | .. | .. |
| Netherlands[d] | 32.7 | 36.6 | 41.7 | 42.3 | 42.1 | 41.0 |
| Canada | 25.1 | 24.2 | 26.4 | 27.1 | 26.8 | 25.5 |
| Japan | .. | 31.7[e] | 41.9 | 41.8 | 40.9 | 35.5 |
| Sweden | 25.2 | 27.7 | 31.9 | 32.5 | 32.6 | 33.8 |
| United States | 28.2 | 27.4 | 27.9 | 29.2 | 28.1 | 26.0 |

Sources: OECD, *National Accounts of OECD Countries* and *Industrial Production: historical statistics* (for France and Japan).

[a] GDP at market prices, except for Italy and Canada, where at factor cost.
[b] Excludes the Saar and West Berlin, also mining and quarrying.
[c] For 1951.
[d] Manufacturing here refers to manufacturing *plus* construction, mining and quarrying, and gas, electricity and water. In 1970 manufacturing output comprised 74.7 per cent of all four categories. From 1970 production value of crude petroleum and natural gas included in manufacturing output.
[e] This figure not consistent with the series for 1970–5.

The next step is to see whether the UK's experience in terms of the movement in the share of manufacturing output in GDP has been the same as the experience of other advanced industrial nations. For all the countries for which figures are presented in Table 10.3 and 10.4 relative prices have moved against manufacturing and the constant-

*Table 10.4   Manufacturing output as a proportion of GDP at current prices[a],
various countries, 1950–75 (percentages)*

|  | 1950 | 1960 | 1970 | 1973 | 1974 | 1975 |
|---|---|---|---|---|---|---|
| United Kingdom | 36.7 | 36.1 | 32.4 | 31.0 | 29.5 | 28.9 |
| Belgium | .. | 30.5 | 32.1 | 30.5 | 31.0 | 27.9 |
| France[b] | 41.7 | 40.3 | 31.3 | 30.6 | 30.2 | 29.6 |
| Germany | 39.7[c] | 42.2 | 42.7 | 41.1 | 40.6 | 38.6 |
| Italy | 28.8[d] | 27.2 | 28.8 | 28.7 | .. | .. |
| Netherlands | 31.9 | 34.5 | 29.0 | 28.5 | .. | .. |
| Canada | 29.2 | 26.7 | 23.5 | 23.2 | 22.8 | 21.6 |
| Japan | .. | 28.9 | 35.9 | 35.0 | 34.4 | .. |
| Sweden | 27.6 | 26.8 | 26.8 | 26.9 | 30.1 | 28.9 |
| United States | 29.2 | 28.4 | 25.7 | 24.9 | 24.0 | 23.0 |

Sources: as Table 10.3.

[a] GDP at market prices except for United Kingdom, Italy and Canada, where at
factor cost.

[b] Manufacturing here refers to manufacturing *plus* mining and quarrying, and gas,
electricity and water. The ratio of this group of sectors to manufacturing moved quite
closely up to 1969. From 1970 there is a break in the consistency of the series.

[c] Excludes the Saar and West Berlin, also mining and quarrying.

[d] For 1951.

price ratio shows more of an upward or less of a downward trend than
the current-price ratio. At 1963 prices, there is an upward trend to
varying degrees for all the countries except the US, where it seems
constant (Table 10.3), the upward trends being most marked in
Japan, Germany and Italy. However, only in the UK and the US
is the ratio smaller in the most recent postwar peak than in the
previous one; the values are about the same in the last two peak years
for Japan, Germany and Canada, and higher at the last peak than the
previous one for all other countries. Sweden's recession began later
than 1975, which explains why its ratio has not declined.

The continuous postwar decline in the ratio of manufacturing
output to GDP at current prices is also observed in Canada, France
and the US (Table 10.4). The ratio has declined noticeably in
Germany and the Netherlands since 1970 and 1965 respectively,
following periods of stability. For Sweden the ratio has increased more
recently after years of stability. Italy's ratio shows a modest increase
since the mid-1950s and Japan's has an upward trend, although
less markedly over the last fifteen years than previously. The ratio for
Belgium seems to have been approximately constant.

The trend in the share of GDP produced by manufacturing industry, whether measured at current or constant prices, suggests that the UK's experience has not been unique. However, it may be misleading to look for evidence of de-industrialisation in these ratios. As Singh ([31], page 127) has pointed out, '... a lower manufacturing growth rate in the UK probably meant a relatively lower growth rate overall'. Poor performance in manufacturing may cause poor overall performance since manufacturing output is a sizeable proportion of GDP. Manufacturing has been described as the 'engine room' of growth (Kaldor, [20]). In other words, the interrelationship between the numerator and the denominator is such that one would expect the movements in the ratio for any one country to differ from the movements for another only to the extent that there may be different lags between manufacturing growth and GDP growth in different countries.

## UK and world trade in manufactures

We shall now examine some aspects of the export and output performance of UK manufacturing industries relative to the performance of other major countries. The UK's share in world trade in manufactures declined steadily over the period, falling from 19.8 per cent in 1955 to 9.4 per cent in 1973. Since 1973 it has remained around that level (Table 10.5 and Chart 10.3).

*Table 10.5    Shares in the value of 'world'[a] exports of manufactures[b] 1950–77, various countries (percentages)*

|  | 1950 | 1960 | 1965 | 1970 | 1975 | 1977 |
|---|---|---|---|---|---|---|
| United Kingdom[c] | 25.5 | 16.5 | 13.9 | 10.8 | 9.3 | 9.3 |
| France | 9.9 | 9.6 | 8.8 | 8.7 | 10.2 | 9.9 |
| Germany | 7.3 | 19.3 | 19.1 | 19.8 | 20.3 | 20.8 |
| Italy | 26.6 { | 5.1 | 6.7 | 7.2 | 7.5 | 7.4 |
| Others[d] | { | 21.0 | 21.8 | 23.3 | 21.4 | 21.4 |
| Japan | 3.4 | 6.9 | 9.4 | 11.7 | 13.6 | 15.4 |
| United States[e] | 27.3 | 21.6 | 20.3 | 18.5 | 17.7 | 15.9 |

Source: *National Institute Economic Review*, Statistical Appendix Table 22.

[a] 'World' defined as the countries covered by this table.

[b] Arms excluded except in 1950.

[c] Re-exports included from 1960; figures adjusted for under-recording from 1965.

[d] Benelux countries, Canada, Sweden and Switzerland.

[e] Special category exports excluded.

Chart 10.3   *Various countries' shares in the value of*
*'world' exports of manufactures, 1953–77*

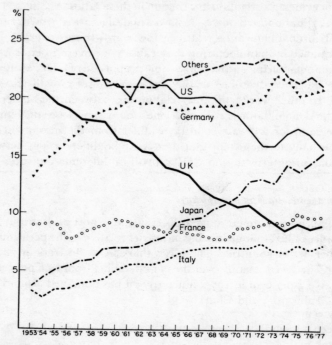

Source: as Table 10.5.

Earlier we argued that it may be misleading to conclude that
de-industrialisation is not a cause for concern because the UK's
experience in terms of the share of manufacturing output in GDP
mirrored that of other advanced industrial countries. It is probably
more meaningful to examine the performance of the UK manufacturing sector by considering the UK's share in OECD manufacturing
output and 'world' GDP, as is done for the period 1960–75 in
Table 10.6.

The UK has fared relatively badly in terms of both manufacturing
output and GDP (although its share stabilised after 1973), so that the
fact that the change in its share of manufacturing ouput in GDP has
followed a path similar to that in other countries cannot be taken to
imply a satisfactory performance by the UK manufacturing sector.

*Table 10.6    The United Kingdom share in OECD manufacturing output
and 'world' GDP, 1960–75 (percentages)*

|      | OECD manufacturing output[a] | 'World' GDP[b] |
|------|------|------|
| 1960 | 9.6  | 8.2  |
| 1963 | 8.4  | 7.9  |
| 1966 | 7.3  | 7.6  |
| 1969 | 6.4  | 6.3  |
| 1972 | 5.9  | 6.4  |
| 1973 | 5.8  | 6.0  |
| 1974 | 5.7  | 5.9  |
| 1975 | 5.8  | 6.3  |

Sources: OECD, *Industrial Production: historical statistics, Industrial Production 1977* and *Main Economic Indicators*, January 1978; United Nations, *Yearbook of National Accounts Statistics 1970*.

[a] At constant prices, based on 1963 weights for 1960 and 1963, and on 1970 weights for 1972 onwards. Figures interpolated for 1966 and 1969.

[b] At current prices and exchange rates; 'world' defined as in Table 10.5.

## Import penetration and the export–sales ratio

Many economists believe that import penetration in manufacturing has been a major factor in de-industrialisation; Table 10.7 shows that in total manufacturing it has in fact been quite rapid. It is not possible to get a consistent series further back than 1970 with exports, sales and imports all calculated on a Standard Industrial Classification (SIC) basis. Although figures are presented for some industries for 1963 and 1968 (as they are for exports–sales ratios), these should be treated as broad guidelines only. In Brown and Sheriff [9] there is a series for import penetration in manufacturing where imports and exports are expressed in the Standard International Trade Classification (SITC). This shows that there was a large increase in import penetration until the end of the 1960s or early 1970s, after which it increased even more rapidly.

On a SIC basis, the export–sales ratio for total manufacturing has tracked the import penetration ratio almost exactly since 1970 (Table 10.7). A longer series, with exports based on the SITC, suggests that exports of manufactures as a proportion of sales have increased since 1955, with the largest increase in the 1970s. Thus, it is clear that the exports–sales ratio and the import penetration ratio are highly cor-

Table 10.7   Import penetration and export–sales ratios for
United Kingdom manufacturing, 1955–76 (percentages)

| | Import penetration[a] | | Export–sales ratio[b] | |
| --- | --- | --- | --- | --- |
| | SIC | SITC | SIC | SITC |
| 1955 | .. | 6 | .. | 15 |
| 1960 | .. | 8 | .. | 15 |
| 1965 | .. | 9 | .. | 15 |
| 1968 | 17.6 | 12 | 17.6 | 17 |
| 1970 | 17.2 | 13 | 18.2 | 18 |
| 1973 | 22.1 | 18 | 19.9 | 20 |
| 1974 | 23.7 | 19 | 21.6 | 22 |
| 1975 | 22.4 | 18 | 22.9 | 23 |
| 1976 | (24)[c] | 21 | (24)[c] | 25 |

Sources; Wells and Imber [34]; CSO, *National Income and Expenditure 1966–76* and
*Annual Abstract of Statistics*; Department of Industry 'Import penetration: trends
in the trade performance of manufacturing industry', *Trade and Industry*,
19 May 1978.
[a] Imports/(sales + imports − exports).
[b] Exports/sales.
[c] Rough estimates.

related over the longer series also. Although experience differs from
industry to industry (Wells and Imber, [34]), the increase in import
penetration has been matched by an almost equivalent increase in
exports as a proportion of manufacturing sales. It is tempting to
interpret these figures, as some commentators have, as implying that
the increases in the ratios are the consequences of increased international specialisation over the period and that the fact that the ratios
have moved to a similar extent is an argument against the 'de-
industrialisation' thesis, since it implies that the UK has matched
its competitors in gaining ground in foreign markets to the extent that
foreign competitors have penetrated the UK market (Westlake, [35];
*Economist*, [11]).

However, this is not necessarily a correct interpretation of the figures
as has been pointed out by Kaldor [21]. It is very plausible that it is
sluggish growth in output which has caused the rise in the exports–
sales ratio. Increasing volumes of imports have not been matched by
an equivalent increase in exports with a deflationary result via the
foreign trade multiplier. This effect has probably been reinforced by
further deflationary action to correct the balance-of-payments diffi-

culties, resulting in low growth of output. Exports, while not matching the growth of imports, have grown faster than output in response to high increases in the volume of world trade. Thus we have had a situation of large increases in both import penetration and the ratio of exports to sales, where the rise in the latter may be the consequence not of increased competitiveness abroad by UK exporters, but rather of our slow growth rate. Kennedy and Thirlwall [22] argue that empirically about three quarters of the rise in the exports–sales ratio is due to an autonomous increase in exports and only about a quarter to the 'Kaldor effect'. This is not to deny that import penetration has become very serious in some sectors.

### Trade in invisibles and services

It has been suggested in recent years that the emphasis in policy discussions on the relative performance of the manufacturing sector may be misplaced, given the apparent relative efficiency of the UK in the export of invisibles. This reflects the belief that the UK's comparative advantage may be in services and not manufactures. It is important, in this context, to distinguish between the balance of trade in *invisibles* and in *private* services. There is an argument for limiting comparisons to trade in services because they make a direct contribution to employment and their contribution to the balance of payments does not require a prior net outflow.

Singh calculates trade ratios – defined as (exports – imports)/ (exports + imports) – for manufacturing and private services for the period 1966–75; he shows that the UK has been doing rather better in private services, which show a 50 per cent improvement in their trade ratio over the period, than in manufactures which show a deterioration of more than 50 per cent. In 1966 the manufacturing trade ratio was almost four times as great as that for private services, whereas in 1975 they were virtually the same. However, despite this apparently growing comparative advantage in services, it still remains true that manufacturing is a much more important export earner than services and the relation between the two has not changed significantly over the past decade. Singh shows that the value of manufacturing exports has been approximately double that of private services in each year from 1966 to 1975. In 1976 the value of manufacturing exports was £21,338 million whereas that of private services exports was £9206 million. Further, although total credits in private services have been growing, so have debits in most categories, so that the net foreign-currency earning potential in this sector has not been great, except for the financial services of the City of London and construction overseas.

*Table 10.8   The United Kingdom share in 'world'[a] trade in manufactures, invisibles and private services (percentages)*

|  | Manufactures[b] | Invisibles[c] | Private services[d] |
|---|---|---|---|
| 1955 | 19.8 | 24.9[e] | 26.3[e] |
| 1960 | 16.5 | 20.9 | 22.3 |
| 1965 | 13.9 | 17.9 | 17.2 |
| 1970 | 10.8 | 15.9 | 17.2 |
| 1973 | 9.4 | 15.3 | 16.0 |
| 1974 | 8.8 | 13.4 | 15.6 |
| 1975 | 9.3 | 13.4 | 15.7 |
| 1976 | 8.7 | 12.5 | 15.0 |
| 1976/1955 | 0.44 | 0.50 | 0.57 |

Sources: *National Institute Economic Review*, Statistical Appendix Table 22; IMF, *Balance of Payments Yearbook*.

[a] 'World' defined as in Table 10.5.

[b] Arms excluded; re-exports included from 1960; figures adjusted for under-recording from 1965.

[c] 'Services' (see note d) *plus* 'investment income' and 'government credits' in IMF 'Standard presentation' (see also IMF, *Balance of Payments Yearbook*).

[d] 'Freight', 'merchandise insurance', 'other transportation' and 'other services' (see also IMF, *Balance of Payments Yearbook*). Negligible amounts of non-monetary gold included for 1955 and 1960.

[e] These figures not strictly comparable with subsequent years, see CSO, *Economic Trends*, March 1961.

Table 10.8 shows the relative performance of UK manufacturing and service exports in world trade and allows us to examine the common notion that, while our share in world trade in manufactures has fallen dramatically, we have not been doing so badly in invisibles or private services. Although the decline in share for services is less than that for manufactures – 57 per cent of its 1955 level rather than 44 per cent – it is still substantial, making the point that the UK has been losing ground here also. It is also questionable how far traded services can provide employment. The services which have become large foreign-currency earners in recent years, such as tourism and overseas construction, are quite labour-intensive, but, on the other hand, the services of the City of London create fewer jobs than manufacturing.

The conclusion is that the shift away from manufacturing has worrying implications for the balance of payments and that services may not be able to earn sufficient foreign currency nor to provide enough jobs in the future if the manufacturing sector continues to decline.

## Investment

One source of concern about the British economy has been its low rate of investment relative to that in other advanced industrial nations. Low investment leads to low gains in labour productivity and so to higher relative unit labour costs, higher prices and a lack of competitiveness. In addition, low levels of investment are associated with a slow rate of adaptation to technological advance and changing demand; that is, industries with low investment tend to not be dynamic and find it difficult to respond to market conditions. Indeed, there is evidence to suggest that the UK's relatively slow growth in output and productivity has as much to do with its relatively low increments of output per unit of investment as to its relatively low investment (Brown and Sheriff, [9], Appendix 11).

*Table 10.9   Gross fixed capital formation per head of employed labour force in manufacturing in various countries, 1960–75 ($)[a]*

|  | 1960 | 1965 | 1970 | 1973 | 1974 | 1975 |
|---|---|---|---|---|---|---|
| United Kingdom | 334 | 460 | 604 | 751 | 920 | 1006 |
| Belgium | 468 | 772 | 1226 | 1740 | 2357 | 2589 |
| France[b] | .. | 905 | 1439 | 2182 | 2288 | 2682 |
| Germany[c] | .. | .. | .. | 1658 | 1707 | .. |
| Italy[b] | 332 | 367 | 751 | 1224 | 1469 | .. |
| Netherlands[b] | .. | 779 | 1633 | 2252 | 2743 | 3108 |
| Japan | 492 | 460 | 1317 | 2147 | 2141 | 1768 |
| Sweden | 669[d] | 767 | 1207 | 2007 | 2443 | 2934 |
| United States[e] | .. | 1675 | 2145 | 2551 | 2785 | 2947 |

Sources: OECD, *Manpower Statistics*, *Labour Force Statistics* and *National Accounts of OECD Countries*, Table 5.

[a] At current prices and exchange rates.
[b] Figures refer to manufacturing *plus* other industrial sectors.
[c] Total investment per employee in production industries excluding quarrying and construction from *Statisches Jahr Buch für die Bundes Republik Deutschland*, p.159.
[d] For 1961.
[e] Manufacturing employment estimated as industry employment multiplied by the proportion of manufacturing wage earners and salaried employees in industry wage earners and salaried employees.

Economists have been particularly concerned with investment in manufacturing. As Table 10.9 shows, although in 1965 the UK invested more per head of the labour force in manufacturing than Italy, and the same as Japan, by 1974 it had a lower rate of investment per head than any of the other countries. (Figures at constant 1970 prices and exchange rates are to be found in Brown and Sheriff [9]. The conclusions which emerge from these are the same as from Table 10.9.) The figures here for the Netherlands, Italy and France are for industry rather than manufacturing and so the conclusions need some qualification, but Moore and Rhodes [24] give figures (Table 10.10) which tend to confirm the UK's relatively poor performance.

*Table 10.10   Gross fixed capital formation per 1000 operatives in manufacturing, United Kingdom, Germany and Japan, 1963–71 (£)*[a]

|  | Average for period | |
|---|---|---|
|  | 1963–7 | 1968–71 |
| United Kingdom | 207 | 262 |
| Germany | 306 | 380 |
| Japan | 301 | 597 |

Source: Moore and Rhodes [24].
[a] At 1963 prices and exchange rates.

### International comparisons of productivity in manufacturing

Jones [19] compared the UK's performance in terms of output, employment and productivity with those of selected European countries usually considered comparable with the UK (Chart 10.4). These comparisons exclude the US, Japan and Canada, but they serve to illustrate the UK's relatively poor performance. The UK has experienced relatively slow growth of labour productivity in manufacturing. Table 10.11 shows that this has been the case for most sub-periods since 1955. For the sub-period 1969–73, the UK's growth rate of output per man–hour in manufacturing equalled that of the five EEC countries together, and the US and Canada, but subsequently it has fallen back in relative terms. Most countries, with the possible exceptions of Germany and Italy, experienced sharp reductions in the rate of growth of productivity in the recession since 1973.

*Table 10.11   Growth rates for output per person employed in manufacturing, various countries, 1955–76 (annual average per cent)*

|  | 1955–60 | 1960–4 | 1964–9 | 1967–73 | 1973–6 |
|---|---|---|---|---|---|
| United Kingdom | 2.19 | 3.15 | 3.40 | 4.46 | 1.64 |
| Belgium | 3.53 | 4.96 | 6.12 | 4.62 | .. |
| France | 4.40 | 4.87 | 6.32 | 4.58 | 3.85 |
| Germany | 4.92 | 5.34 | 5.55 | 4.37 | 4.77 |
| Italy | 5.00 | 3.54 | 6.53 | 4.14 | 4.16 |
| Netherlands | 4.77 | 4.38 | 7.04 | 7.11 | .. |
| *EEC–5* | *4.57* | *4.81* | *5.94* | *4.63* | .. |
| Canada | .. | .. | .. | 4.00 | 2.28 |
| Japan | .. | .. | .. | 10.30 | 3.54 |
| United States | .. | .. | .. | 4.16 | 3.23 |

Sources: Jones [19]; *National Institute Economic Review*, Statistical Appendix Table 18.
*Note:* These figures should be interpreted with caution, since cyclical peaks and troughs do not necessarily coincide for all countries.

*Chart 10.4   Gross value-added per man–hour in manufacturing, 1955–74[a]
(UK 1970 = 100: semi-log scale)*

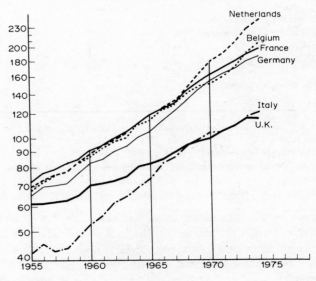

Source: Jones, [19].
[a] At factor cost, converted at purchasing power parity rates for 1970.

*Productivity by sectors in the UK economy*

It is argued that a shift of employment away from manufacturing to other sectors, notably services, will be harmful to the overall growth of the economy. This is not only because manufacturing is assumed to be the growth sector, but because output per person in manufacturing is higher than in services. If this latter condition does not hold, then a shift in employment away from manufacturing will increase productivity overall, even if manufacturing is the sector with higher productivity growth.

*Table 10.12    GDP per head and productivity in the main UK sectors*

| | GDP per head 1976[a] | Average productivity growth 1960–75*[b] |
|---|---|---|
| | (£000) | (% p.a.) |
| Agriculture, forestry and fishing | 4.75 | 6.1 |
| Mining and quarrying | 7.04 | 2.6 |
| Manufacturing | 4.14 | 3.1 |
| Construction | 4.49 | 1.2 |
| Gas, electricity and water | 11.06 | 5.6 |
| Transport and communication | 6.65 | 3.6 |
| Distributive trades | 3.29 | 2.7 |
| Insurance, banking, finance, etc. | 6.53[c] | |
| Professional and scientific services | | |
| Miscellaneous services | 3.32[d] | 0.4 |
| Public administration and defence | 5.20 | |
| *Total services* | 4.17 | .. |
| *Total services excl. transport and communication.* | 3.86 | .. |

Sources: CSO, *National Income and Expenditure* (various issues); Brown and Sheriff [8].
[a] At current prices.
[b] 1975* is an average of figures for 1973, 1974 and 1975.
[c] Includes net interest receipts, which are approximately 50 per cent of value-added in this sector.
[d] For public health and education *plus* other services.

Although the manufacturing sector had one of the lowest levels of productivity in 1976 (Table 10.12), the bulk of the labour that has shifted away from manufacturing since about 1961 has been channelled into professional and scientific services (which have even lower productivity), so that it would appear that value-added per person has been lower as a result.

A problem in evaluating the figures on growth rates of productivity by main sector in Table 10.12 is that some sectors, notably manufacturing and construction, are far more susceptible to cyclical fluctuations than others. Although an allowance for this is made by calculating growth rates from 1960 to an average of 1973, 1974 and 1975 (1975*), doubtless some conjunctural effects remain. For instance, manufacturing output per head grew at 3.7 per cent per annum when the calculation is made from 1960–73, where the terminal years were both peak years. Nevertheless, the manufacturing sector certainly achieved a higher rate of growth of productivity than services, which suggests that the shift of employment has been away from the sector producing faster growth.

### Profits in manufacturing and services

Table 10.13 shows gross profit-shares for manufacturing and services over the last decade. While for services there is no trend, for manufacturing it is downwards; the share for services is consistently higher than for manufacturing. However, such a comparison may be misleading, since there is no allowance for depreciation and these are

*Table 10.13*   *Gross profit-shares$^a$ of United Kingdom manufacturing and services, 1966–76 (percentages)*

|  | Gross profits$^b$ | | Gross profits adjusted$^c$ | |
| --- | --- | --- | --- | --- |
|  | Manufacturing | Services$^d$ | Manufacturing | Services$^d$ |
| 1966 | 26.4 | 35.4 | 20.8 | 33.2 |
| 1968 | 26.7 | 35.3 | 20.9 | 33.0 |
| 1970 | 23.0 | 35.0 | 16.7 | 32.4 |
| 1972 | 24.0 | 37.0 | 17.2 | 35.2 |
| 1973 | 21.8 | 38.8 | 14.9 | 36.2 |
| 1974 | 14.5 | 37.1 | 6.3 | 34.1 |
| 1975 | 13.2 | 33.9 | 4.1 | 30.5 |
| 1976 | 13.6 | 35.2 | 3.8 | 31.6 |

Source: CSO, *National Income and Expenditure 1966–76*, tables 1.11, 3.1 and 11.3.
$^a$ Less stock appreciation; as proportions of net output.
$^b$ Gross profits of manufacturing include trading surpluses of public corporations; gross profits of services include 'other income' *plus* rent.
$^c$ Capital consumption deducted from gross profits.
$^d$ Distributive trades, insurance, banking, etc. and other services.

pre-tax profits which will move differently from post-tax profits (King, [23]). Figures for profit-shares taking account of capital consumption are therefore given as well, but not for post-tax profits. It may be that effective tax rates for manufacturing and services are similar to the extent that a comparison of pre-tax profit-shares will produce the same conclusions as a comparison of post-tax profit-shares, but these figures should be interpreted with caution.

Not only have manufacturing profit-shares taking account of capital consumption been considerably below those for private services, but they have shown an alarming downward trend over the last decade, while there is no such downward trend for private services. In manufacturing the trend appears to have been consistently falling (from 20.8 per cent in 1966 to 3.8 per cent in 1976) with the largest fall coming in the recession after 1973. Thus, the manufacturing sector appears to have been less profitable than private services over the last decade.

## Alternative Explanations of UK De-industrialisation

In this section we survey the main views on the causes of UK de-industrialisation. De-industrialisation is seen by many commentators as a symptom of the underlying problems of the UK economy rather than a problem in its own right and, to this extent, we are concerned with discussing the underlying problems of the UK economy in general and its manufacturing sector in particular.

### The role of the public sector

The growth of service employment in the public sector has been identified by some commentators as an important contributory factor to the relative decline of UK manufacturing. Table 10.14 shows the growth of public sector employment. Central and local government employment grew by 1.2 million over the period and increased their share of total employment from 14.6 to 18.9 per cent. Of this increase, about 1.1 million was in local authority employment. Department of Employment projections to 1981 [12] show the share of public sector service employment rising to 21 per cent, with an annual growth rate of 2.6 per cent between 1971 and 1981, as compared with the projected annual growth rate of total employment of only 0.4 per cent per annum. The projections are based on trends in public expenditure up to 1975. Restrictions on public sector growth since that date suggest that these figures are greater than would be the case if the projections took account of these developments.

Table 10.14    Employment in the public and private sectors[a],
United Kingdom, 1960–75*[b]

| | Public sector | | | | Private sector | Total employed labour force |
|---|---|---|---|---|---|---|
| | Central government | Local authorities | Public corporations | Total | | |
| | (thousands) | | | | | |
| 1960 | 1,639 | 1,821 | 1,865 | 5,325 | 18,335 | 23,660 |
| 1965 | 1,370 | 2,154 | 2,028 | 5,552 | 19,224 | 24,776 |
| 1970 | 1,533 | 2,559 | 2,016 | 6,108 | 18,265 | 24,373 |
| 1975* | 1,757 | 2,909 | 1,949 | 6,615 | 18,037 | 24,652 |
| | (percentages) | | | | | |
| 1960 | 6.9 | 7.7 | 7.9 | 22.5 | 77.5 | 100.0 |
| 1965 | 5.5 | 8.7 | 8.2 | 22.4 | 77.6 | 100.0 |
| 1970 | 6.3 | 10.5 | 8.3 | 25.1 | 74.9 | 100.0 |
| 1975* | 7.1 | 11.8 | 7.9 | 26.8 | 73.2 | 100.0 |

Source: CSO, *Economic Trends*, February 1976 and February 1977.
[a] Excludes forces.
[b] 1975* is an average of figures for 1973, 1974 and 1975; figures for 1975 are in Chapter 2.

Some economists (and politicians) have used these figures to explain the relative decline in manufacturing. But, given the increase in the proportion of the employed labour force in the public sector, there clearly has to be some sector, or sectors, whose share in employment has declined. Thus, there is a correlation between the relative growth of public sector employment and the decline in the manufacturing sector. However, the argument is that the growth of the public sector has 'crowded-out' the private sector; that is, it has deprived the private sector, and particularly the manufacturing sector, of the resources needed for it to grow and make a contribution to real income and the balance of payments. The presumption is that in the absence of public sector growth the private sector, and manufacturing in particular, could and would have grown faster. Woodward [37] writes, 'the single most important factor leading to "de-industrialisation" in the last decade, that is the decline in employment in manufacturing industry, was the excessive growth of public expenditure'. Elsewhere he writes 'simulations with the [CGP] model suggest that if the growth of government employment 1963–73 had been no faster than during the earlier period there would probably have been no decline in manufacturing employment if appropriate tax and exchange rate policies had been pursued. The underlying growth of the economy might have been about 0.4 per cent a year faster – a significant amount' (Barker, [3], page 369). One of the earliest statements of this view is contained in the original article by Bacon and Eltis [1], which gave particular emphasis to the growth of local authority employment. Their argument is conducted in terms of the distinction between the market and non-market sectors of the economy and is particularly concerned with the adverse effects on growth, inflation and the balance of payments of the relative growth of the non-market sector. While they stress that the non-market sector is not identical with the public sector, it is still the case that most of the growth in public sector employment has been in the non-market sector and all of the growth of the non-market sector has been in the public sector. The main point of their thesis is that the 'problem' is the growth of public sector employment. 'The explanation [of the underlying deterioration in Britain's economic performance] is that successive governments have allowed large numbers of workers to move out of industry' (Bacon and Eltis, [2], page 29). It is argued that 'the problem' has resulted from government activity and not merely been correlated with it.

Table 10.15    United Kingdom public expenditure on goods and services[a] as a proportion of GNP at factor cost, 1950–75 (percentages)

| 1950 | 1960 | 1965 | 1970 | 1973 | 1974 | 1975 |
|------|------|------|------|------|------|------|
| 21.5 | 22.3 | 23.8 | 26.3 | 26.3 | 28.0 | 29.6 |

Source: CSO, *National Income and Expenditure* (various issues).
[a] Current and capital expenditure of central and local government, excluding financial transfers between them.

There is no doubt that public expenditure has increased as a proportion of GNP (see Table 10.15), although the figures for 1974 and 1975 exaggerate this because they were recession years. Also, as a recent study by Neild and Ward ([28], page 19) shows, 'in the eleven listed European countries, there was a very large increase in the ratio of public expenditure to GDP between 1964 and 1973, both years of low unemployment in Europe. Canada also shows a large increase but not Japan'. They argue that there is no reason to suppose that in 1973 the UK devoted a particularly high proportion of GDP to public expenditure compared to most of the other countries, even allowing for the low relative GDP per head.

Moore and Rhodes ([24], page 40) consider three respects in which industry might potentially be 'robbed of resources by the rapid expansion of the public sector' – it could be deprived of labour, unable to obtain finance, or over-taxed. In regard to the first possibility they argue that 'there is little evidence to suggest that the labour supply constraint facing the manufacturing sector has been binding or that it has become more marked in recent years than in (say) the 1950s', and they point out that since 1966 many manufacturers have been releasing labour. Unemployment at cyclical peaks has risen continuously since 1955, implying reduced labour-market pressure. In the five postwar 'peak' years, 1955, 1960, 1964, 1969 and 1973, the unemployment rates for Great Britain were 1.0, 1.5, 1.6, 2.3 and 2.6 per cent respectively. To establish that growth in public sector employment has robbed the manufacturing sector of labour which otherwise it would have used, it would be necessary to show that manufacturers have consistently been unable to get the labour they needed. In a period where unemployment is around the $1\frac{1}{2}$ million mark it does not seem plausible that the reason for the slow growth in manufacturing employment is a labour shortage occasioned by the growth of the public sector.

However, has the growth of the public sector created difficulties for manufacturing companies in obtaining finance for expansion, so that they have been 'crowded-out' in this sense? The bulk of companies' investment finance is from profits and, as we showed earlier, there has been a considerable decline in the pre-tax profitability of manufacturing. Arguably, this decline in profitability has made recourse to external funds, from banks and capital markets, more important. Some argue that public sector borrowing has pre-empted funds from capital markets (and helped to push up interest rates) thus crowding-out private manufacturing. In its evidence to the Wilson Committee ([33], pages 52–3), the Treasury disputes this argument, contending that 'there is no evidence that there have been real constraints on the supply of funds to industry – all the signs are that industrial borrowing has been determined by the level of demand ... In the year to mid-February 1977 sterling lending to manufacturing industry increased by about £1350 million, or 24 per cent, while sterling lending to the personal sector increased by only about £200 million, or 5 per cent – a fall in real terms'. As far as interest rates are concerned, they reached a historic peak in 1976–7, with the minimum lending rate rising to 15 per cent for a short time. However, most empirical evidence suggests that it is expectations of demand and profitability rather than interest rates which determine investment decisions (Savage, [30]), though it may be that with historically high levels a 'threshold' was crossed above which interest rates were a significant deterrent to investment. These high rates, however, occurred only at the end of the period and can hardly be an explanation of low investment throughout it.

Finally, has public sector growth resulted in such high levels of taxation that manufacturers have been discouraged from investing? Moore and Rhodes argue that the evidence shows that the effective company tax rate has fallen sharply in postwar years and that 'the slow growth of demand, shortages of liquidity and a declining real rate of return on capital have presented a much greater threat to investment than increases in corporation tax' ([24], page 40). As King [23] shows, the effective rate of tax on companies has fallen continually since the 1950s. Further, he suggests the *post-tax* profit-shares in UK manufacturing over the period 1950–73 indicate that 'there was no long run or secular decline in the share of profits', implying that there may not have been a financial constraint on internally generated funds.

Thirlwall [32] points out that the fundamental question posed by the crowding-out hypothesis is the following: 'Was the growth of the non-marketable output sector a purely autonomous development that absorbed resources that would otherwise have been fully utilised in the marketable output sector for investment and the balance of payments? Or was the growth a response to a much more fundamental bottleneck in the UK economy, without which there would have been growing unemployment?' In the sections which follow we consider some of the views which have been put forward to explain why the manufacturing sector should have been unable to grow fast enough to maintain its share in domestic employment.

### The uncompetitive pound

Earlier we showed that the UK manufacturing sector has declined in terms of its own historical performance, its share of total employment and internationally, as measured by the UK share of 'world' trade in and 'world' output of manufactures. The decline relative to other industrial countries may be attributed to the persistent tendency for UK costs to rise relatively, so rendering UK exports uncompetitive in price terms. Implicit in this view is the assumption that exchange-rate depreciation has never compensated sufficiently for the relative increase in UK costs, but the evidence for the period 1964–76 (Table 10.16) does not substantiate this; if anything, it suggests that there has been a slight tendency for price competitiveness to improve. Nevertheless, neither the UK's share of 'world' trade in manufactures nor the ratio of the volume of exports to imports of manufactures has increased, although both ratios have stabilised since about 1973. Thus, although the exchange rate has fully compensated for the UK's adverse relative price movements, it has not depreciated enough to reverse the decline of the UK manufacturing sector.

Table 10.16    Manufactures: the United Kingdom's export competitiveness and trade performance, 1964–76

|  | Index of competitiveness[a] (1970 = 100) | Share of 'world' trade (%) | Index of relative volume[b] (1970 = 100) |
|---|---|---|---|
| 1964 | 104.1 | 14.4 | 114 |
| 1965 | 105.3 | 13.9 | 119 |
| 1966 | 107.2 | 13.4 | 116 |
| 1967 | 106.2 | 12.3 | 101 |
| 1968 | 98.1 | 11.6 | 99 |
| 1969 | 99.2 | 11.3 | 105 |
| 1970 | 100.0 | 10.8 | 100 |
| 1971 | 103.2 | 10.9 | 100 |
| 1972 | 103.7 | 10.0 | 85 |
| 1973 | 96.0 | 9.4 | 81 |
| 1974 | 93.4 | 8.8 | 81 |
| 1975 | 97.8 | 9.3 | 84 |
| 1976 | 94.3 | 8.7 | 83 |

Sources: Williamson [36]; National Institute Economic Review, Statistical Appendix Table 22; Gould, Mills and Stewart [16].
[a] The average of the four measures discussed in Williamson [36].
[b] From Gould et al. [16], where relative volume equals export volume divided by import volume.

Fetherston et al. [13] provide more striking evidence for these observations. They calculated the UK's share of 'world' trade in manufactures after allowing for changes in relative cost competitiveness and changes in 'world' trade (the latter variable being included for cyclical effects). Even varying assumptions about the elasticity of UK exports to changes in relative costs led to the conclusion that there was a considerable unexplained downward trend in the UK's share in world trade of manufactures and this adjusted trend was similar in size to the actual downward trend. Hence the relative decline of the UK manufacturing sector appears to have occurred despite cost and price competitiveness being maintained; the exchange rate has not fallen to a sufficient extent to reverse this decline. Indeed, it was also estimated that for the UK to have maintained its 1970 share in world trade, costs in 1976 would have had to be reduced a further 14 per cent relative to those of competitors.

## Structural problems in UK manufacturing

Given that there is no evidence to support the view that the UK manufacturing sector has priced itself out of world markets, we look at some further explanations which have been put forward for its relative decline. A wide range of economists have observed that so long as the world income elasticity of demand for UK exports is smaller than the UK's income elasticity of demand for imports it is inevitable that the economy will fail to grow at a rate consistent with its potential because of the balance-of-payments constraint, so that either unemployment or growing public sector employment or some combination of the two must result. A simple example can illustrate this point. If we assume that the UK income elasticity of demand for imports is 1.5, the world income elasticity of demand for UK exports is 1.1 and that both the UK and the rest of the world grow at the rate of $x$ per cent, which is equal to the growth of productive potential in the UK, UK imports would grow by $1.5x$ per cent, but exports would only grow by $1.1x$ per cent. Clearly this position cannot be sustained and eventually the UK economy will incur a balance-of-payments constraint which will force the government to introduce restrictive policies. In this case there is a structural malaise as shown by the income elasticities of imports and exports.

There is a considerable amount of evidence to support this view. Singh [31] quotes a number of studies which point to the high UK income elasticity of demand for imports. For example Panić [29] shows that for manufactured imports it is 3.09, whereas those of Germany and France are 2.14 and 2.19 respectively. Table 10.17 presents some results published by Thirlwall [32]. In a study of 113 manufacturing industries he found that 30 had an income elasticity of demand for imports in excess of two. The export income elasticities of demand for the same industries are also shown and in all cases these are lower than the import elasticities, the (unweighted) averages for

Table 10.17  Money income elasticities of demand: commodities where the
United Kingdom's import elasticity greater than 2.0 and their
export elasticities, 1963–74

| | UK import elasticity | World elasticity for UK exports |
|---|---|---|
| Motor vehicles | 3.7 | 0.9 |
| Linoleum, leather cloth, etc. | 3.5 | 1.2 |
| Men's and Boys' tailored outerwear | 3.2 | 1.7 |
| Radio and other electronic apparatus | 2.9 | 1.8 |
| Cans and metal boxes | 2.8 | 0.6 |
| Motorcycles | 2.7 | 0.9 |
| Plastics mouldings, etc. | 2.6 | 1.7 |
| Domestic electric appliances | 2.6 | 1.1 |
| Insulated wires and cables | 2.6 | 1.0 |
| Iron castings, etc. | 2.6 | 1.3 |
| Furniture and upholstery | 2.5 | 2.2 |
| Tobacco | 2.5 | 1.1 |
| Bedding, etc. | 2.4 | 0.6 |
| Overalls and men's shirts, etc. | 2.4 | 2.0 |
| Other textiles | 2.4 | 1.1 |
| Pharmaceutical and toilet preparations | 2.3 | 1.4 |
| Women's and girls' tailored outerwear | 2.3 | 1.1 |
| Weatherproof outerwear | 2.3 | 0.7 |
| Miscellaneous manufactures | 2.3 | 1.8 |
| Metal products n.e.s. | 2.2 | 1.2 |
| Cardboard boxes, etc. | 2.2 | 1.3 |
| Dresses, lingerie, infants' wear, etc. | 2.2 | 1.3 |
| Telegraph and telephone apparatus | 2.2 | 1.0 |
| Man-made fibres | 2.1 | 1.3 |
| Other drinks | 2.1 | 1.0 |
| Glass | 2.1 | 1.2 |
| Wire and wire manufactures | 2.1 | 0.9 |
| Miscellaneous stationery | 2.1 | 1.1 |
| Biscuits | 2.1 | 1.3 |
| Other electrical goods | 2.1 | 1.3 |

Source: Thirlwall [32].

imports and exports being 2.47 and 1.33 respectively. Thirlwall argues
that the UK income elasticity of demand is not particularly high
relative to other countries; rather it is the lowness of the export elasticity which is the problem. He adds that 'particularly worrying from
the UK point of view is the high income elasticity of demand for
imports of many commodities compared to the low world income

elasticity of demand for our exports of the same commodities' ([32], page 30). In simple terms this implies that not only do foreigners not want our goods, neither do we!

The above analysis suggests that, despite the improvement in the price competitiveness of UK manufactured goods (admittedly via exchange-rate depreciation), non-price characteristics such as low quality, late deliveries and poor design have been such that the demand for them on world markets has remained low (see NEDO [27] and Chapter 7 above). These are consequences of supply difficulties, the more obvious examples of which include lack of mobility in the labour force, poor industrial relations, lack of technological innovation, inability to respond effectively to, or indeed to anticipate, changes in the pattern of consumer demand, and inappropriate skills. It has been argued that many of these factors are a managerial responsibility; that managers in the UK have relatively low status and rewards and that this provides a possible explanation of many such failures (see Blackaby, [7]).

These problems are related to the relatively low rate of growth of the UK economy, since faster-growing, more dynamic countries are in a better position to cope effectively with non-price factors. The issues involved here are those of the 'virtuous' versus the 'vicious' circles of economic development (see Beckerman, [4]; Myrdal [25]). The latter argument suggests that, for the UK, the supply problems causing the adverse elasticities have meant that there is a persistent tendency for the UK economy to go into trade deficit as world incomes rise. This, in turn, forces the government to take measures to restrict the growth of demand. The remaining links in the circle can be illustrated by the following quotation: 'The slow rate of growth of ... demand has in turn been associated with a low rate of investment by the manufacturing sector and a low rate of expansion of productive capacity relative to other industrial countries. Low levels of investment imply a relatively slow rate of adaptation by industry to technical progress, particularly in growth industries, to changing demand and innovation in product ranges and to the need to modernise whole production and marketing processes' (Moore and Rhodes, [24], page 40).

It becomes increasingly difficult over time to break the circle. Beckerman [4] and many economists writing in the mid-1960s argued that it would be sufficient to achieve a once-and-for-all increase in competitiveness, which would increase demand and lead to a take-off into the 'virtuous' circle. Experience since, together with the analysis we have given above and elsewhere [8], suggests that such a stimulus on the demand side may not be sufficient to regenerate the UK manufacturing sector and that policies exclusively oriented towards demand factors are unlikely to succeed because they ignore the large number of supply problems. Although, internationally, there is a high positive correlation between output growth and productivity growth, it is not certain that, in the UK's case, an expansion of demand would be sufficient for a regeneration of the manufacturing sector and entry to a 'virtuous' circle.

## References

[1] Bacon, R. W. and Eltis, W. A., 'A message for Mr Healey: get more people into factories', *Sunday Times*, 10 November 1974.

[2] Bacon, R. W. and Eltis, W. A., *Britain's Economic Problem: too few producers*, London, Macmillan, 1976.

[3] Barker, T. S. (ed.), *Economic Structure and Policy*, London, Chapman and Hall, 1976.

[4] Beckerman, W. and Associates, *The British Economy in 1975*, Cambridge University Press, 1965.

[5] Bell, D., *The Coming of the Post-Industrial Society*, London, Heinemann, 1974.

[6] Benn, A., 'Tony Benn writes about industrial policy', *Trade and Industry*, 4 April 1975.

[7] Blackaby, F. T., 'British economic policy 1960–74: a general appraisal', *National Institute Economic Review*, May 1977.

[8] Brown, C. J. F. and Sheriff, T. D., 'Problems of medium-term assessment: a post-mortem on "The British Economy in 1975"' (NIESR Discussion Paper), 1977.

[9] Brown, C. J. F. and Sheriff, T. D., 'De-industrialisation in the UK: background statistics' (NIESR Discussion Paper), 1978.

[10] Clark, C., *The Conditions of Economic Progress*, London, Macmillan, 1940.

[11] *Economist*, 10 September 1977.

[12] Employment, Department of, 'A view of industrial employment in 1981', *Department of Employment Gazette*, May 1975.

[13] Fetherston, M., Moore, B. and Rhodes, J., 'Manufacturing export shares and cost competitiveness of advanced industrial countries', *Economic Policy Review*, no. 3, 1977.

[14] Fuchs, V. R., *The Service Economy*, New York, Columbia University Press, 1968.

[15] Gershuny, J. I., 'The fallacy of the service economy', *Futures*, April 1977.

[16] Gould, B., Mills, J. and Stewart, S., *A Competitive Pound*, London, Fabian Society, 1977.

[17] Hughes, J. and Thirlwall, A. P., 'Trends and cycles in import penetration in the UK', *Oxford Bulletin of Economics and Statistics*, November 1977.

[18] Industry, Department of, 'Import penetration: trends in the trade performance of manufacturing industry, *Trade and Industry*, 19 May 1978.

[19] Jones, D. T., 'Output, employment and labour productivity in Europe since 1955', *National Institute Economic Review*, August 1976.

[20] Kaldor, N., *Causes of the Slow Rate of Economic Growth of the United Kingdom*, Cambridge University Press, 1966.

[21] Kaldor, N., 'Imports and the growth rate of GDP', letter to *The Times*, 12 September 1977.

[22] Kennedy, C. and Thirlwall, A. P., 'Import penetration, export performance and Harrod's trade multiplier' (mimeo.), 1978.

[23] King, M. A., 'The United Kingdom profits crisis: myth or reality?', *Economic Journal*, March 1975.

[24] Moore, B. and Rhodes, J., 'The relative decline of the UK manufacturing sector', *Economic Policy Review*, no. 2, 1976.

[25] Myrdal, G., *Economic Theory and Underdeveloped Regions*, London, Duckworth, 1957.

[26] NEDO, *The Measurement and Interpretation of Service Output Changes* by A. D. Smith, London, 1972.

[27] NEDO, *International Price Competitiveness, Non-price Factors and Export Performance* by D. K. Stout, London, 1977.

[28] Neild, R. R. and Ward, T., 'The budgetary situation: an appraisal' (mimeo.), 1976.

[29] Panić, M., 'Why the UK propensity to import is high', *Lloyds Bank Review*, January 1975.

[30] Savage, D., 'The channels of monetary influence: a survey of the empirical evidence', *National Institute Economic Review*, February 1978.

[31] Singh, A., 'UK industry and the world economy: a case of de-industrialisation?', *Cambridge Journal of Economics*, June 1977.

[32] Thirlwall, A. P., 'The UK's economic problem: a balance of payments constraint?', *National Westminster Bank Quarterly Review*, February 1978.

[33] Treasury, *Evidence on the Financing of Trade and Industry to the Committee to Review the Functioning of Financial Institutions*, vol. I, London, HMSO, 1977.

[34] Wells, J. D. and Imber, J. C., 'The home and export performance of United Kingdom industries', *Economic Trends*, August 1977.

[35] Westlake, M., 'Exports match rising imports trend', *The Times*, 5 September 1977.

[36] Williamson, J., 'Demand management and the balance of payments in the UK, 1964–81' in M. Posner (ed.), *Demand Management*, London, Heinemann, 1978.

[37] Woodward, V., letter to *The Times*, 5 July 1975.

# 11    Report of the Discussion

## by Frank Blackaby

### The Significance of the Term

Perhaps the main contribution of the conference was to pin down the significance of the term 'de-industrialisation'; on this there was fairly general agreement. The matter for concern was the progressive failure to achieve a sufficient surplus of exports over imports of manufactures to keep the economy in external balance at full employment. Thus, if we had the prospect of an indefinite supply of oil from the North Sea, there might be no reason for concern with some relative decline in the size of the manufacturing sector. The problem was not well measured by the movement of employment in manufacturing; this had been constant for about a hundred years up to world war II, and after the war it rose for a number of years; the recent relative fall would be less marked if movements were measured in man–hours rather than man–years, given the increase in part-time employment in the service sector. There is the further complication that shifts of employment out of manufacturing are to be expected in advanced industrial countries and, in the UK, if such a shift were to be a consequence of a radical change in the productivity trend in manufacturing, it would be welcomed rather than deplored. For all these reasons it was not sensible to have as an objective any particular figure for manufacturing employment; it was sensible to have as an objective a manufacturing sector whose exports of manufactures were adequate to pay for full-employment imports – after allowing for the contribution of services. The points from the papers on services were taken: that there was some evidence that the UK was more competitive in tradeable services than in goods, but that a very large increase in the UK share in world trade in services would be needed to compensate for a small fall in the UK share in world trade in manufactures.

Most participants therefore concluded that this was an 1870 rather than a 1970 problem. It was a problem that had in recent years been leading to an actual fall in manufacturing employment partly because of the depressed state of the world economy and partly because, as imports of manufactures rose, each percentage increase displaced a larger absolute amount of home production. However, there was some disagreement, implicit or explicit, about the present and prospective severity of the problem – this was apparent in the different views expressed about policy. On the one hand, there were those who pointed out that we were already two thirds of the way towards the likely maximum oil output, that we were a long way from full employment and that we still had only a marginal balance-of-payments current surplus. Any projection into the future which assumed that UK exports would continue to move in relation to world trade in manufactures as in the past, and which also assumed that imports of manufactures rose in relation to home demand as in the past, produced either very slow growth rates and rising unemployment or very large and growing balance-of-payments deficits. However, some wondered whether there were signs that things were getting better, at least on the export side – since the UK share in world trade in manufactures had not fallen significantly since 1973. Others were unhappy about using past import propensities to project into the future – the import propensity for competitive finished manufactures was clearly a supply-side problem, which supply-side improvements could alter.

There was fairly general scepticism about the role of public expenditure in the apparent relative decline of the manufacturing sector. First, there was the question whether the manufacturing sector had been unable to get enough labour: the case was put that this had particularly been so in boom periods, when the rate of expansion had been too fast – and it was particularly in these periods that import penetration had risen, with a ratchet effect so that there was no subsequent fall. There were counter-arguments to this thesis: West Germany had had a constant shortage of labour throughout most of the postwar period and had had to make use of a great deal of imported unskilled labour; it might have been expected that 'labour bottleneck' periods would show up in exports as well as imports – but they did not; the 'ratchet effect' on imports was puzzling – was it not that consumers had discovered better products? The car industry was suggested as an example of an industry whose output had not been held back by labour shortages, either of skilled or unskilled labour, but by other factors. There was some greater sympathy – but not universal agreement – for the other arm of the 'public expenditure' argument:

that the rise in public expenditure had led to an increase in personal taxation, which had intensified wage push, which had squeezed profits, and so had reduced investment. It was certainly argued that this had been the Dutch experience in recent years.


## Diagnosis

Given that the conference had taken the view that 'de-industrialisation' was a new label for an old problem, the participants turned to the discussion of the old problem. In the nature of things they were concerned with arguments that were not new.

There was general agreement that the problem, apart from being long-term, was also widespread. There were very few industries which, on the basis of their past export and import figures, could claim to be fully competitive. Consequently the search was for general explanations, rather than for explanations specific to particular industries. Further, there was also general agreement that over the long period, when adjusted for exchange-rate changes, neither UK export prices nor UK unit labour costs had moved much out of line with those of competing countries; to this extent, the problem was clearly one of non-price competitiveness. Beyond that, most doctrines (as in the Church of England) were affirmed by some and questioned by others.

For example, Freeman's propositions that the UK's research and development expenditure had been misdirected and that engineering was a Cinderella profession were supported by some: the high status of Italian engineers was cited as an example, with the special emphasis in their training on design. On the other hand, it was argued that in the United States also the status of engineers was low and that in any case a good deal had been done in this country to improve engineering education. On research and development in general, the French example did not fit Freeman's thesis: France had achieved a rapid growth rate over a long period, although total R and D expenditure was much smaller than in the UK.

The question was broadened to cover management efficiency in general, on the grounds that the effective management of innovation was simply one of the attributes of a generally efficient manager. The class question was brought up – that managers were recruited from a relatively small group in society whose education had been inappropriate. It was questioned whether this was still true; in any case it seemed that City institutions, whose managers tended to be recruited from an even narrower social group, were more successful in meeting world competition than manufacturing industry. British plants abroad, managed by British nationals, seemed efficient enough – possibly because they escaped British industrial relations problems. (It was generally accepted that in Britain many managements had to spend too much of their time on industrial relations.) The issue of education was raised, not only for management but at all levels: British secondary education, it was suggested, did not sufficiently encourage exactitude and rigour.

On foreign manufacture by British firms, the arguments incorporated in the contributions by Mrs Morgan and Holland were not resolved. Some qualifications were suggested to Mrs Morgan's thesis: for example, the total stock of managerial talent in a firm was limited, so that if a firm opened a new plant abroad it might well not be able at the same time to open one in this country. Holland was concerned to argue, not that all foreign investment was bad, but that the government should more explicitly recognise the existence of 'mesoeconomic power' in the hundred largest firms, and should equip itself with leverage to influence their behaviour.

In general, the emphasis was on supply-side limitations. The point, however, was made that factors which explain a low relative *level* of productivity do not explain a widening productivity gap. Here the question of cumulative causation comes in. It was pointed out that, within a country, it was not considered surprising that a region which had begun to decline should continue to do so; cumulative processes were clearly set up which tended to perpetuate the decline (unless strong policies were adopted). There could be much the same sort of decline for individual countries in a relatively free trading world. When it came to policy, however, a number of participants stressed the need for high and rising demand as a necessary (though not sufficient) condition for industrial success.

## Policy

On policy, as on diagnosis, many declared themselves agnostic. There was a certain division between those who felt that existing policies, with some adjustments, were adequate, and those who argued that the situation was serious enough to justify fairly radical policy changes.

On exchange-rate policy, Posner's advocacy of a rather mild use of the exchange rate was generally (but not universally) accepted: that it was worth using the exchange rate in a moderate way – moving it down now by, say, 10 per cent – but that it was not an instrument which could be used fully to compensate for the failure of non-price competitiveness. Some were doubtful about the erosion embodied in the wage equations in current short-term models – on the grounds that there were no good wage equations; the model-makers put them in mainly for convenience in simulation. If money earnings could be held in spite of some rise in import prices, the effects of devaluation could be more powerful than the models showed. The question of the effect of devaluation in stimulating particularly the exports of down-market products, which sold on price, was left open. It was not disputed that it was undesirable to increase the proportion of down-market products in UK exports: the UK ran some danger of being unable to compete with other industrial countries in high-technology products, and also being unable to compete with newly industrialising countries in 'stable-technology' products. It was noted that industries which had been successfully competitive were frequently industries where value per ton had risen faster, and not more slowly, than in competing countries.

The conference was naturally divided on import controls. The critics argued that they could not be kept on for long enough to produce that 'vacuum' in demand which would bring about an industrial response – and that in any case businessmen would not believe that they could be there for very long. It would be very difficult to make them internationally acceptable at a time when the output of North Sea oil was still rising, and they would aggravate the world trend towards protectionism. On the import control side, it was argued that without them demand could not possibly rise fast enough either to prevent rising unemployment or to provide a stimulus to adequate industrial investment. (The need for a significant expansion of demand was supported by many not in favour of import controls.) An import control proposal was put forward which did not violate the Kantian imperative: 'Act only on the maxim whereby thou canst at the same time will that it should become a universal law.' No temporary expedients would do. Unregulated free trade was chaos and a snare for weak countries. Trade had to be of advantage to all participants. All countries should be allowed to limit their imports to their ability to sell their own goods abroad. Trade had to be of advantage to all partners, and countries should not be expected to accept imports which reduced their capacity to produce. Indeed one could consider that the true costs of imports should include the cost of the unemployment created by excessive imports. Free trade, with this import limitation, would thus not be pushed beyond the point where a country's productive capacity was damaged. This limitation of imports to the amount which could be covered by exports could be a universal and permanent system; it could be operated by issuing import licences to exporters to the value of their exports. (There were, of course, doubts about this proposal.) Those in favour of import controls also tended to favour an aggressive industrial strategy.

The comments on Dutch policy had some relevance to the UK case. Although manufacturing industry had become less competitive in recent years, devaluation was not considered a possible policy because the balance of payments was still in current surplus. Import controls were not considered either, because of membership of the Common Market. The policy was to rely on a social contract and incomes policy to keep wage costs down and eventually improve competitiveness in this way. There was also fairly strong support for continued incomes policy in the UK, since the attempt to offset the effects of a faster rate of inflation in the UK by the use of the exchange rate served to exacerbate the inflationary process.

Some wanted less industrial intervention, on the grounds that government intervention in the past had been catastrophic, and a number were in favour of reductions in the high marginal rates of taxation. They conceded that the effects of such a reduction were uncertain, but considered that since the cost was so low it might as well be tried. Some were happy to build on the present system of sector working parties, on the grounds that a cooperative approach was essential, and it would be counter-productive to threaten business-men with vague possibilities of further extensions of intervention. Some none the less considered that there was a great deal of *de facto* planning as things stood now, with the large companies in almost daily negotiation with the government on some matter; the government should not be nervous of finding ways of exerting more leverage on their behaviour.

There were mixed views, too, about a greater degree of industrial democracy. It might help efficiency; on the other hand, it might simply improve job-satisfaction at the cost of efficiency. Workers might feel more satisfied, having been consulted, but the process of decision-making might be slowed down.

In sum, the conference was reasonably agreed that, in 'de-industrialisation', we had a new label for an old problem – the relatively poor competitive performance of British manufacturing industry; but on the appropriate diagnosis and treatment of this problem there was less agreement.

# List of Participants

ECONOMIC POLICY CONFERENCES
CONFERENCE ON DE-INDUSTRIALISATION

Chatham House, London, 27 and 28 June 1978

Lord Balogh
Professor C. A. van den Beld
F. T. Blackaby
C. J. F. Brown
Sir Alec Cairncross
Sir Charles Carter (*Chairman*)
T. F. Cripps
W. A. Eltis
M. Fogarty
Professor C. Freeman
S. Holland
P. M. Jackson
Lord Kaldor
H. Liesner

Sir Donald MacDougall
R. C. O. Matthews
Mrs A. Morgan
J. H. M. Pinder
M. V. Posner
G. F. Ray
T. M. Rybczynski
J. R. Sargent
T. D. Sheriff
A. Singh
D. K. Stout
A. R. Thatcher
Professor A. P. Thirlwall
G. D. N. Worswick

# Index